Fifteen Minutes

Bamboozled in Buffalo

Michael F. Rizzo

Explore Seattle

ISBN: 979-8-218-21284-1 (Paperback)

Library of Congress Control Number: 2023915449

Book Cover by Anis El Idrissi

Back cover photo by Debra Kolodczak

1st edition: May 2024

Explore Seattle

Everett, WA

Contents

My life would not be what it is without my chosen family. Thank you to my best friend and partner and my kids. Without you, nothing is worth doing.

Foreword

Micheal Rizzo's book "Fifteen Minutes" is a cautionary tale and an exposé of what can occur when the interests of politics, commercial development, and art align and mis-align. Within the tale of Billie Lawless III's quest to be a sculptor and to place a significant work *Green Lightning* in his hometown of Buffalo N.Y. maneuvering, inattentiveness, incompetence, and ego from all quarters amalgamate into a social stew neither tasteful nor nutritious-- these pave the way for laughable human folly and authoritarian impulses to seize the day.

A diversity of agendas not immediately contradictory proceed down well-meaning bureaucratic and cultural structures towards a presumed end that surprises and disappoints all involved. The book presents both a visionary and truthful account of how Art and culture can pragmatically lift and re-purpose declining civic terrains but also where differing core objectives between artistic and political motivations unattended to can scuttle this promise—Artist Billie regardless of one's evaluation of the merits of *Green Lightning* attempts to generously share with excitement his unique voice, and his discovery of synergies rooted in history, place and his own humanity—but is silenced and wounded by relationships gone wrong. Through Rizzo's telling we learn his undoing is in part his own—but shared by expedience and myopy within the public bodies that lacked real interest and passively dismissed the artist and artwork in the rush to harness art as a gear in a political-economic contraption. Author Rizzo takes us with great detail through both the artist's formation and the evolution of Lawless's work-- then steers us into the details of the bureaucratic labyrinth of opportunity that results in the removal of the artwork.

The historic events in this Buffalo, N.Y. saga seem to portend the bland contentless public formalism, and wholesome feel-good figurative depictions that can dominate the public sculpture sphere. We learn by 'being Billie' why institutions and civic leadership might favor when supporting art to separate artists and their human complexities from the objects we encounter as art in public places.

Professor Duane McDiarmid, Area Chair, Professor of Sculpture + Expanded Practice, Ohio University, College of Fine Arts

Preface

Fifteen minutes: a quarter of an hour. Fifteen minutes: the time artist Andy Warhol said everyone would be famous for. Fifteen minutes: the time that the sculpture *Green Lightning* by Buffalo artist Billie Lawless was lit. Just 15 minutes. It took more than a year and hundreds of hours to build, and at least a month to assemble and install. But in 15 minutes, its life in Buffalo was officially over.

Who actually got bamboozled in Buffalo? Was it the City when the sculpture was lit and there were dancing neon penises? Or was it Billie Lawless, who had jumped through all the hoops and had every department approve it, only to have the mayor order it demolished?

When I set out to write this book, I really did not know what the story was about. In September 2022, the idea jumped into my head out of nowhere. In November 1984, I was just 20 years old. I vaguely remembered the story and probably read about it over the years, but I never really thought about writing a book.

So as I searched the Internet for people relevant to the story, I saw a bigger picture, about a sculpture the city dismantled. This was a story about truth and honesty. It's about conservatism, obscenity, sleight of hand. It is a story that the more I dug into it, the more I was unsure of where it was going.

I kept changing my mind about what I thought the answer was, but I never was sure what the ending would be. In order to tell the story of *Green Lightning* and Billie Lawless, I'd have to tell the story of Mayor Jimmy Griffin, and of the Buffalo Arts Commission, and the City of Buffalo.

I spoke to so many wonderful people, some who easily gave their time. There were others who either remembered nothing or wanted absolutely nothing to do with it. I contacted dozens of people. But in the end, I believe I've been able to tell a story about my hometown of Buffalo, and how public art can be controversial.

The mayor, the arts commission, and the urban renewal agency all approved it. Everyone up and down the line thought this was a positive idea for an area dead for decades, in a city that was trying to crawl back from depression and job loss. Originally planned for a private lot on the city's East side, a primarily Black area that rarely saw anything new and exciting, the councilperson moved it to a more prominent location right off the expressway where thousands of people could view it.

On the night of the unveiling, the artist thanked everyone, then turned on the power. There were gasps, then laughs as penises danced across the four panels. Billie was going to leave early, possibly to avoid the furor he foresaw or the press, but then the vice squad showed up.

Once the sculpture was up and standing, I don't think Billie Lawless thought Jimmy Griffin would act as swiftly as he did, and that was probably his fatal mistake. Because Jimmy Griffin didn't hesitate. When he made his mind up, that was it.

Several days later, Griffin ordered the statue taken down and sent a tree service to dismantle it.

What led up to this and what happened afterward is what we're going to explore.

Early Years

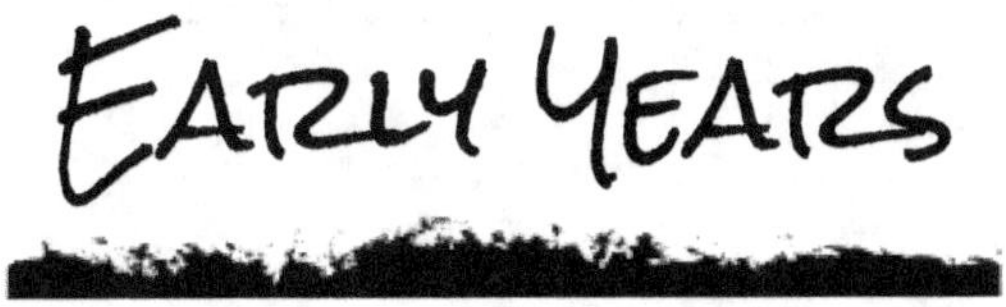

"An artist must evaluate himself realistically.
Many artists wish to excuse themselves from
the 'dues paying.'" Billie Lawless

H E STOOD PERCHED ABOUT thirty feet in the air, feeling the cold steel of his neon artwork under his feet. It was chilly and dark that mid-November day, but at that moment, he refused to back down. "I didn't know what to do. I was extremely frightened and shaken," he would recall.[1]

Who was he and why was he on top of that structure? His name is William Burns Lawless III, but he goes by Billie. He was born July 16, 1950 in Buffalo, New York, the third of 12 children born to Jeanne and William Burns Lawless Jr. His father went to Notre Dame Law School, then Harvard Law School. Lawless Jr. served as youngest corporation counsel in Buffalo and was president of the Common Council in 1956. After serving in that position, they appointed him to the New York State Supreme Court in 1960.

Six of Billie's siblings would practice law, a path they expected him to take, but he took one much different from the rest of his five brothers and six sisters.

He would attend St. Joseph's Collegiate Institute, a highly rated Catholic school in Buffalo. "I was a jock in high school," he recalled in 1980.[2] As a rower at St. Joe's in 1967, he was the stroke of the varsity team. "We were the first high school team to win both the American and Canadian varsity championships in the same year," he said. In his senior year, Billie represented the United States at the World Rowing Championships held in the Netherlands, competing in the straight four.[3] Mark Griffis, son of Buffalo sculptor Larry Griffis Jr., attended high school with Billie. "He was a lot older than I was. He was a great athlete at crew, yet that did not define him."[4]

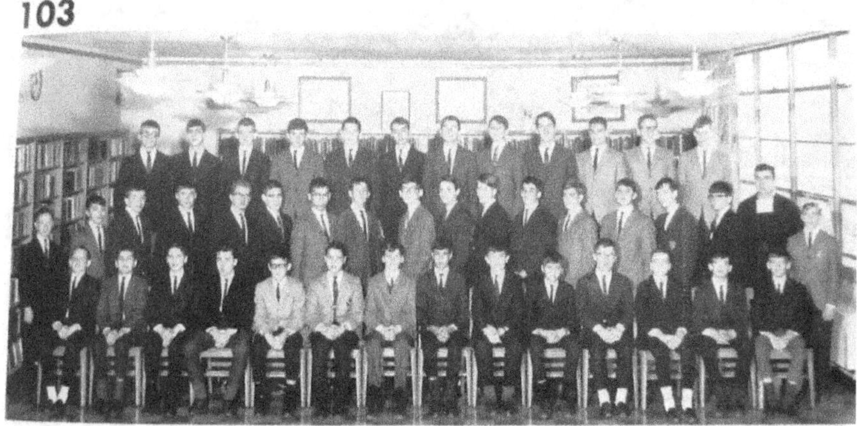

Front Row: J. Schneeberger, M. Miller, W. Mischler, Craig Pawlak, W. Else, E. Calisto, D. White, R. Rizzone, T. Heine, R. Ehni, R. Thill, W. Peters, C. Tarantino, L. Steinkirchner. Row Two: W. Group, T. Rizzo, D. Steinwold, W. Christman, C. Josef, F. Zusi, K. Barone, F. Rodgers, M. Lodick, T. Makin, W. Nowak, M. Becker, C. Hanny, P. Calandra, J. Kenny, M. Szymczak, P. Mundy. Back Row: T. Cesare, R. Reilly, R. Eberle, T. Biersbach, A. Abt, T. Lazarski, R. Cronin, G. Jakiel, L. Schork, N. Targuinio, Z. Malowicki, W. Lawless, R. Standing; Br. Thomas. Missing: R. Mills.

1965 St. Joseph's Collegiate Institute yearbook. Billie Lawless, back row, far right. Courtesy of Craig Pawlak.

Billie was involved in the art club at school and developed an interest in art from Mark's father, who was a family friend. Although he had an interest in art, "artistic inclinations were not encouraged for males at my school," Billie said. "As a matter of fact, we even thought the members of the jazz quartet were a little funny."[5]

His father authored a famous opinion in 1967, after Black Muslims from three prisons sued New York State. His opinion stated the state prison system must recognize their Islamic religion.[6] In 1968, he quit his position as New York State judge to become dean of Notre Dame Law School in South Bend, Indiana and the family moved to nearby Niles, Michigan.

After graduating from St. Joe's in 1968, Lawless attended Rutgers University in New Brunswick, New Jersey, to pursue rowing. He said he took political science courses that he failed. After writing some essays in the fall, an English teacher encouraged him to start art courses in the spring. He took a variety of classes, including performing, but he was shy, "so I stayed in the background," he said. [7]

From 1970 to 1972, Lawless fought against the war in Vietnam. Draft Board officials removed his student deferment, which made him available for the draft, so he left Rutgers.

He then went to the University of Notre Dame in the fall of 1970 and studied with his friend, artist-in-residence Konstantine Milonadis. He invited Billie to work at the studio which had a foundry, but he had to be enrolled in the University. Here was where Lawless learned about steel. "It was fire, probably. It's primal. I love fire and torches and the way steel feels in my hands. I burned the third floor of a house down when I was about nine."[8]

He said that from that day on, "I pretty much knew what I wanted to do with my life. I started working with steel and welding steel. I've always thought of that as being my base material." Lawless said he didn't know how he got into Notre Dame, but in 1989 he said he thought his father used his influence to get him into the school with an exception. "I don't believe I had to submit grades or transcripts from my other university to be allowed to work there," he said.[9]

In April 1971, the Draft Board informed him to report for induction into the armed forces. His Buffalo attorney, Carmin R. Putrino of Lipsitz, Green, Fahringer, Roll, Schuller, James, claimed that they did not reach Billie's lottery number of 120. On May 6, 1971, he applied for classification as a conscientious objector. The draft board then changed his induction date to November 15, then again to December 28.[10]

On November 30, 1971, he sued in federal court in Buffalo to bar the government from inducting him into the armed forces. He said the time was over the 120 days permitted under law and asked for it to be canceled. They asked the court to issue an injunction to prevent any attempts to induct him.[11] Lawless dropped his suit on December 20 when the draft board agreed to cancel his induction order and consider his conscientious objector application.[12]

On December 22, 1971, Billie Lawless married Bonnie Link in Buffalo, then the couple moved to New Jersey, where he returned to Rutgers University to finish his degree. Billie was taking art classes and working with Melvin Edwards, a famous African-American sculptor. He graduated with a Bachelor of Fine Arts degree in 1974 and moved back to Buffalo in June 1974. (The marriage lasted four years, and they divorced in 1975.)

About 1976 Billie was living on Delaware Avenue near Forest Avenue and founded Lawless Studios, creating functional art work, "which was essentially …art furniture, it was steel furniture that combined steel with stained glass." He said, "I came up with the idea of doing functional pieces that people can relate to and, obviously, there's a need for. I was doing tables and chairs and music stands, candelabras, fireplace screens, combining steel with stained glass. When I started doing my functional work, I thought it would be interesting to combine different materials, so I started actually inlaying stained glass into the pieces so that the tables had, I thought, something that no one had ever done before."[13]

By 1977, his art was developing, and he was creating parody art. "During the late '70s there started to become a transition in my work where I …became a viable small business. I was able to support more of my interests in sculpture, which was my first love." By the early 1980s, he was spending about 50 percent of his time on functional work, and 50 percent doing sculpture work.[14] He admitted it wasn't as easy to sell a sculpture as it was a functional piece. He saw corporations and banks as the "new patrons of the arts" in 1979, and started asking for their financial help for his sculptures.

He won a grant from Sculpture Space, Inc. of Utica, New York to build a 19 foot steel sculpture that would be too expensive to create on his own. So Lawless approached Kenneth Lipke of Gibraltar Steel, who agreed to donate $9,000 worth of steel. They displayed the finished sculpture on the front lawn of the Gibraltar plant in the Buffalo suburb of Cheektowaga.[15] The company removed the sculpture after they downsized and moved. (Its current whereabouts are unknown.)

In September 1979, he purchased a home at 324 Highgate Avenue a few blocks from University at Buffalo. He had his office in the house and converted the garage into a studio. "I was pretty much working a lot of the time," he said.[16]

The inside of Billie's home was as conventional as the artist himself. When the Buffalo *News*' Margaret Sullivan visited his home in 1984, she said, "There's a big abstract painting in the bathroom, right where most people have their towel racks. In the living room, there are dozens of colored paper cutouts shaped like rats that scurry up a wall or hang by their tails from the ceiling. Everywhere there are sculptures, including one called *The Politician*, an all-steel structure that looks like a cross between a tricycle and a wheelbarrow."[17] This was an initial design for what would become a popular sculpture later in his career.

He lived in the house with his girlfriend, Kathy Quinn, who had attended fashion school in New York City before arriving in Buffalo. She attended University at Buffalo to study design and embark on a career combining her training in fashion and art.

In a 1980 interview with the *Buffalo Courier-Express,* she discussed bejeweling clothing. She said it was hard to do it on her own, but she had the support of her boyfriend, Billie Lawless. "Economically it's feasible to live (in Buffalo)," she said. "And it's stimulating because there are a lot of artists here. There is more of sharing, it's not as fast and commercial as New York City. I'd like to eventually work with architects to design stuffed walls in new buildings — something reflecting the community, or perhaps an abstract design... It's possible. Banks and businesses are a lot more adventurous today."[18]

Billie's art began progressing into more sculpture work in the late 1970s. "I started doing three-foot pieces," he said, "then that led to six and seven, eight-foot pieces." He received encouragement from George Enos, who owned the Enos and Sanderson steel company, to do a larger piece. "He suggested that ...they would make a donation. I could do a larger piece, which actually meant renovating part of my studio so I could go right to the ceiling, and that was the creation of *Lament* in 1979."[19]

His first neon piece was *Sink Totem #2,* assembled in Summer, 1979. "I decided to do a vortex of neon tubes going down the drain of this old sink."[20] Flexlume sign company had been providing technical help for his work "since the day I lumbered into Flexlume... with a found sink... to the dismay of the employees." He worked with Paddy Rowell, Sr., Paddy Jr., and Pete D'Orsaneo. They expressed reservations about doing the neon because of the high voltage used until Billie assured them he would display it safely.

Lawless added, "And there is even a macabre element here, mixing high voltage with water."[21] And no wonder they were concerned.

Flexlume was a sign innovator and moved to Buffalo in 1911. Paddy Rowell retired and sold the company in 2015.

From 1980 to 1982, Lawless attended State University of New York at Buffalo, studying with poetic modernist artist Duayne Hatchett, (who assembled "junk metal and found objects for sculptures and print plates")[22] and George Smith. He graduated in June 1982 with a Master of Fine Arts.

In 1980, the Gowanda *News and Observer* published two articles about the local art scene. In the second one, they explored the views of artists, with "varying levels of accomplishment, on the subject of who defines art, and their struggle for recognition."

They included comments from Lawless, where he said, "Art is a commodity and as such, its acceptance is proportional to what the market will bear." He said that gallery directors know what their clientele will purchase, and that determines who's exhibited. "Galleries exist to put out an artist's works, mine or anyone's. The immediate benefit is that it allows any artist to exhibit nationally, affording the artist time to work as opposed to marketing. Personally, I'm comfortable with galleries. Flaws exist, but they exist in any system.

"An artist must evaluate himself realistically." He asked why, "many artists wish to excuse themselves from the 'dues paying.' I can tell you a period of hustling, door knocking, and all that goes with it is necessary." He said that Buffalo is a blue collar town, and it can support only a few artists. Because there were not enough galleries to handle all the work, he said that artists should export to "New York, Toronto, wherever ... If the talent is there, the recognition will come." [23]

Mark Griffis said that Billie was intelligent and an interesting person. Rowing would remain a constant in his life through college and beyond. From 1982 to 1985, he was a rowing coach at his old high school St. Joseph's Collegiate Institute, as well as at the West Side Rowing Club.

· · · ● · ● · ● · · ·

In 1966, brothers Larry and Guy Griffis, along with others, founded the Ashford Hollow Foundation. Named for the sculpture park started by Larry in Ashford Hollow in Cattaraugus County, south of Buffalo. In 1968 they purchased brick buildings on Essex Street on Buffalo's West Side that had been an icehouse, firehouse and other properties, and started the Essex Arts Center.

Larry converted part of the property into artists' studios and set up welding and foundry facilities. Guy did some theater in the building. Around 1974, a group of college student artists hung artwork outside their studios inside the Arts Center and started a gallery called Hallwalls. The Artists Committee (a group inside of Essex) said some artists had issues with Albright-Knox Art Gallery, the big gallery in Buffalo.

After a series of back-and-forth debates between the Committee and the Albright-Knox in 1975, the Artists Committee held their own sculpture show, the first "Western New York Invitational Sculpture Exhibit" in Delaware Park, held behind the Albright-Knox.

By 1976, there was a shuffling of people and reorganization at Essex Arts Center. Under the new visual arts side was Hallwalls Gallery, directed by Robert Longo and Charles Clough. Their goal was to search for new and exciting art. In the end, Billie Lawless would find his way there. By 1982, Clough had left Buffalo for the greener grass of New York City. "The city is a disaster," he said. "Everybody seems to leave Buffalo. That is a rule. It's such a wasteland."[24] (Clough didn't really hate Buffalo, as he returned in 2013.)[25]

In 1980 the Artists Committee dissolved, but their gallery and Sculpture Exhibition continued on. The 1981 Exhibition took place from September 5th through 27th. Artists Gallery curator Joy Pepper sent invitations to every known sculptor in the Buffalo area and twenty-eight replied. Artists Gallery Chairperson Kenneth E. Peterson said each artist could choose up to three of their works for the show. This made it a self-juried show that "provides for a richness and diversity" rarely seen.[26]

Billie Lawless, Duayne Hatchet, Marvin Bjurlin, Adele Cohen, Amy Hamouda, Larry Griffis, and Tony DeCorse were among those who exhibited. Several of those artists were well-received in New York City, and although some had considered moving to New York City (like Charles Clough did), they realized it was cheaper to live and work in Buffalo and "bring the finished work to New

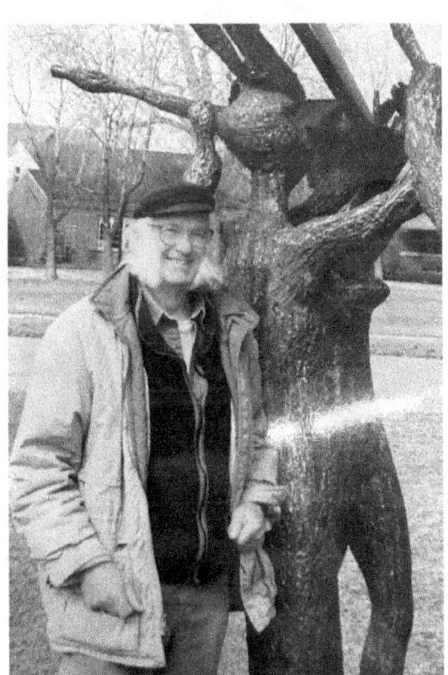

Sculptor Larry Griffis next to his sculpture "Birds Excited Into Flight" in Buffalo. He would encourage and help Lawless over the years. Courtesy of Nila Griffis Lampman.

York."[27]

"A lot of the more prominent local arts patrons here will buy work by a Buffalo artist," Peterson explained, "but only if it's been displayed in a New York gallery, when they could have bought the same work here for much less money."[28]

The Essex Arts Center is still running strong today and hosts community organizations, artists, and events.

Buffalo Arts Commission

"The beauty of Buffalo is that it's a melting pot.
It's not a question of highbrow or lowbrow; it's a
question of quality." Harold L. Cohen

ACCORDING TO THE LATE Alfred Price, Associate Professor Emeritus – Department of Urban and Regional Planning, University at Buffalo (U.B.), Mayor Jim Griffin was not a guy who one would have described as being well educated or sophisticated. "He was a kind of a rough and tumble guy, and a hard scrabble kind of guy," he said.[1] They elected him to the Buffalo City Council to represent the Ellicott District in 1962 and in 1967, then to the New York State Senate, serving until 1977.

It was in 1977 that New York State Deputy Assembly Speaker Arthur O. Eve became the first serious African-American candidate for the office of mayor in Buffalo. Eve was a Civil Rights leader that had helped to negotiate with the Attica prisoners in 1971 and he rallied Black voters. He ran in the Democratic primary against Griffin and Corporation Counsel Leslie Foschio. Al Price said, given the changing demographics of Buffalo, he believed there was a concern with Eve running as a Democrat.

"In the politics of this city," Price said, "there were so few registered Republicans, to win the Democratic Primary was tantamount to election, right?" Almost 80 percent of the Black community voted in that September 1977 primary, and Arthur Eve did the unimaginable, and won the Democratic Primary.

Peter J. Crotty had been Erie County Democratic chairperson from 1954 to 1965. His protégé, Joe Crangle, took over in 1965 and was at odds with many people in the area. It was no surprise that Arthur Eve and Crangle were "really arch enemies," Price said, "and as a consequence of that bad blood... there was an interesting kind of conundrum."[2]

Amid all of that, Jimmy Griffin, after losing the primary, decided he would wage an outsiders race. "He had always been a ...maverick," Price said. He was a registered Democrat, but was conservative, so he made the decision that he would run as an independent against Eve.

"So here's Eve running as a Democrat," Price recalled. "There were only 7,000 registered Republicans in the city ... and Griffin registers as an Independent. Traditionally in the ethnic politics of this city, there had been a Polish-Irish coalition faced off against an Italian and Black coalition."[3]

Price said with Eve winning the Democratic primary, everyone assumed he would be a shoo-in. Then Griffin declared his independent candidacy. Where would his support come from?

Price said, "I can remember going to give a talk to a group of business-men that met at the Hotel Lenox once a month. I was this new young hotshot and the name of the club was the Equity Club. My father had been a part of that group, so I got invited to come and give this talk."[4]

"And I walked into the Hotel Lenox on North Street ... and tucked way back in the back corner of the restaurant, who do I spot but Jim Griffin and a woman named Alfreda Slominski." She was the head of the Conservative Party in Western New York and had served as a Buffalo city councilperson and county comptroller for many years. Price found the meeting to be very interesting. "It was clear that the two of them were involved in a very deep conversation," he said.[5]

Not long after that, the Conservative Party endorsed Griffin, so he ran on both the Conservative and Independent lines. Because Eve and Joe Crangle were arch enemies, "the Democratic Party just slowed down any... monetary support to the Eve campaign and Eve had to go into a substantial personal debt in order to even get signs up on lawns," according to Price.[6]

Griffin ended up defeating Eve in the general election. According to Price, everybody wondered how he was going to govern. [7]

One person who got Griffin's attention was Harold Cohen, the dean of the School of Architecture and Environmental Design at the University of Buffalo. Cohen had established a reputation dating back to about 1974 of being public spirited and interested in being an activist dean. Price said Cohen wanted to get the School of Architecture "pressed into service to help the city in its efforts to rejuvenate and resuscitate itself and get out of the long term structural decline that it had fallen into."[8]

Buffalo was a steel and grain milling city. Part of Griffin's claim to fame was that he had been a grain scooper down on the waterfront. The grain industry was one of the industrial sectors of this region's economy. Grain milling employed about 2,000 people as a single industrial sector in the 1930s, but by 1995 there were less than 200 people. "That's a function of automation and the industrialization," Price said. The economy was restructuring from manufacturing and heavy industry to services in the 1970s, and many people didn't understand what was going on. Price added, "But we were right in the in the heart of darkness in the late '70s when Griffin was elected."[9]

Buffalo had nine council districts that corresponded to the socio-economic geography of the city. Griffin won strongly in South Buffalo and the East Side. But he had not done as well in the Delaware district, which was where Buffalo's old money was, the center core of the city, and in North central, which was toward the University at Buffalo.[10]

Price said that Harold Cohen (and his counterpart David Perry, also from U.B.), in his capacity as Dean, went to the mayor-elect and told him he would need support from the entire city to govern.[11] How would Griffin accomplish that?

Private sector initiatives led the way in northeastern American cities, including Buffalo. Looking back into the late 19th century, the old money in the city called in Frederick Law Olmstead to create the park system, and that was done with private money and given to the city as a gift.

A century later, the downtown interests, the major banks and financial institutions in the city, got together with a few remaining industries in the city and formed an organization called the Greater Buffalo Development Foundation (G.B.D.F.)[12]

The business leaders saw the city had been stagnant for decades because of a lack of planning skills. G.B.D.F. hired the Philadelphia urban planning firm of Wallace McHarg Roberts & Todd and brought them to Buffalo. They wrote a report titled "The regional center: a comprehensive plan for downtown Buffalo, New York," which was published in 1971.

"If you go back and look at that plan," Al Price says, "many of the things that the plan called for, like the subway system and the new airport, a lot of those elements were defined in that plan. So all I did was I went to look at that plan and pulled one element out of that which was the resuscitation of the downtown theater district." [13]

Decades earlier, Buffalo had been a major city, with a vibrant downtown and theater district. Most every famous entertainer made a stop in Buffalo. At one point, even the Canadian city of Toronto wanted to be Buffalo. Restaurants would benefit from a downtown entertainment district.

Based on the Wallace McHarg Roberts & Todd plan, they created the Theater District Association. These were the remaining business people who owned businesses in the 600 block of Main Street, which included the Sheas Buffalo and Paramount theaters. [14]

So Harold Cohen contacted the Theater District Association and met Marty Jacobi, who owned Jacobi Brothers, a men's clothing store. Jacobi told Price that Griffin had been shopping at Jacobi Brothers since he was a councilperson in the 60s. Jacobi said if someone approached the mayor, he might be interested in the Theater District plan.

Cohen approached Jimmy Griffin and said resuscitating the Theater District made sense because even if he built offices and hotels downtown, people would still be there during the workday and then it would be dead as a doorn ail. [15] Cohen told Griffin the new Theater District Association was behind it and "the Inteligencia will buy it." This was something that would endear him to people that didn't vote for him, but may. Cohen was persuasive and the rough and tumble Griffin went for it.

With Al Price's help, they cut a contract with the City of Buffalo to do the plan for the Theater District. "We were the ones that kind of pulled that whole plan together," Price said. "I worked on it as director of technical services under the Dean and played a pivotal role in creating the plan that we gave to the city." [16]

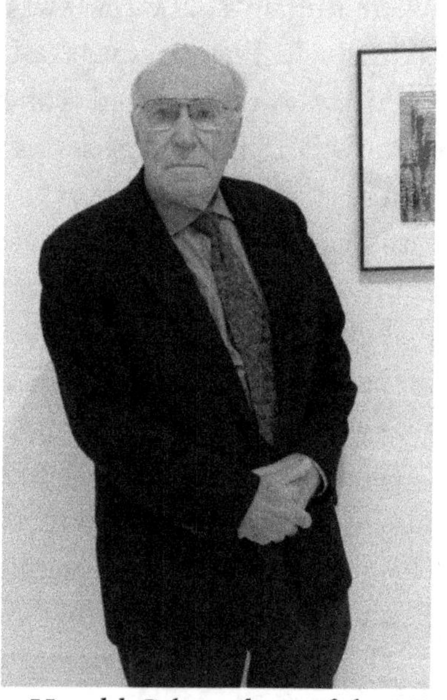

Harold Cohen, dean of the UB School of Architecture. Courtesy of Lore Levin.

Working with Larry Quinn at Community Development, and to a lesser extent David More, Coordinator of Economic Development, Cohen would arrive on the ninth floor of city hall wearing knee high polished black boots and a full-length black cape. "He was a very energetic visionary and I count him as one of my mentors," David More recalled.[17]

The plan laid out what to do and how to do it. "Part of what was appealing to the mayor was that unlike most plans," Price said, "we did a lot of high visibility promotion of the idea of a theater district." To spread the word, they produced a newsprint edition of the plan. Price had the foresight to put a photograph of the mayor on the front page. "So the mayor got a lot of prominent play out of that and because we printed it in newsprint, we printed by the thousands, and that meant everywhere we went, every place we had a public meeting, we were passing those things out like Chicklets."[18]

With Griffin's picture on the cover, it cemented his involvement and support for the Theater District and the idea of the plan. "Everybody in town got very excited about it and Harold really sold it to the community," Price said. "The city got behind it and was prepared to make major investments, public investments in securing the Sheas Buffalo and enlarging that facility."[19]

This led Cohen to approach Griffin to create a committee on arts. There was a lot of art in public places around the city with no formal database. But the impetus was Griffin's hostility towards a sculpture chosen by prior Mayor Stanley Makowski. Griffin claimed *A Coronation,* by artist Kenneth Snelson (which was supposed to stand in front of the new City Court Building in Niagara Square), belonged "on the bottom of Lake Erie."

David More said Dean Cohen's office at U.B. had "a big old barber's chair in the middle that swiveled around. I spent a lot of time in that chair formulating plans for the Mayor's Committee, talking about art, potential development ideas for Buffalo, people we knew in common, etc."[20]

In a surprise public move, Mayor Griffin announced the formation of the Mayor's Committee on the Arts and Cultural Affairs on Friday, July 21, 1978. The new committee would work on "development of a strategy for public policy decisions affecting the arts."[21]

"Cohen convinced the mayor that we should do an inventory of all of Buffalo's public art," Price said. They pitched the project to the mayor, who said he would support it and funded the University of Buffalo. Price directed the study, titled "Buffalo's Public Art," and they inventoried all the art in the public domain in the city.[22]

Price served as an original member appointed by Mayor Griffin and would serve uninterrupted for the first 16 years of its existence.

• • • ● • ● • ● • •

James Militello worked as Griffin's vice chairperson of the Buffalo Urban Renewal Agency (B.U.R.A.), and head of Community Development. Under the Urban Renewal Agency, they would receive block grant funding from the federal government. "It is an authority," Militello explained, "but it was used more or less as an operating shell, a conduit, for the flow of government money." He said the principal organization, the Department of Community Development, had about 160 employees and many sub-corporations. In 1983, there was a lot of free flowing money through President Jimmy Carter. "I was there from '78 to '84," he added, "and the block grant program used to be $5 million a year and it went up to $25 million. I tell my family and friends I sure wasted a lot of taxpayer dollars. I don't know why, but that was our role."[23]

The Department of Community Development hosted the Arts Committee as an administrative home. Militello said all the entities operated separately, but the support and staffing of it came through Community Development. They did everything from putting in streets and sidewalks and trees to financing buildings to economic development. "It was quite a heady period." He said that Jim Griffin was a unique leader and there were many stories about how he operated.[24]

Chairperson of the new arts committee was Harold L. Cohen. He said they would push to make Buffalo "a center of culture" and create a "renaissance in Buffalo. The beauty of Buffalo is that it's a melting pot. It's not a question of highbrow or lowbrow; it's a question of quality."[25]

The other inaugural members of the Committee were Jimmy Griffin's wife, Margaret; Maxine N. Brandenberg, director of Arts Development Services, Inc. (U.B. named her Outstanding Woman of Western New York, in 1978.)[26] Samuel D. Magavern, a well-respected attorney in Buffalo, led his law firm, Magavern, Magavern, Lowe, Beilewech, Dopkins and Fadale, (which dated to 1826), for 50 years. Artist Walter A. Prochownik, born in Buffalo, was a painter and educator recognized for his murals, landscapes, portraits, figurative, and abstract works. He would teach at several local colleges.[27]

Al Price said that Harold Cohen "had a very substantial influence," on Jim Griffin. After they created the Mayor's Committee on the Arts and Cultural Affairs, the question became, who would run it? According to Price, and Cohen's daughter Lore Levin, Harold recommended, quietly behind the scenes, David More.[28]

More had deep ties to Buffalo and the community. He received a Bachelor of Arts degree from Hampshire College in Amherst, Massachusetts with a concentration in the Philosophy of Art and Critical Theory.[29] He would be the coordinator of economic development and secretary of the Arts Committee. His great-great-grandfather was David Gray, a well-known poet and close friend of Mark Twain when he lived in Buffalo. His great-grandfather, Chauncey Hamlin, was president of the Board of Managers of the Society of Natural Sciences (Museum of Science) for over 20 years. More's grandmother, Martha Hamlin Visser't Hooft, was a nationally recognized abstract painter, and his mother, Martje More, was active in the local art scene for almost 30 years, operating three different commercial art galleries.[30]

Jim Militello said, "This gentleman, David More, is a wonderful guy, and he took a path in his life that someone like me can't relate to. He understands the arts and all this and all the symbolism and the importance of creativity and stuff."[31]

The Mayor's Committee on the Arts was unexpected, because of Griffin's hostility towards the arts community over the Snelson sculpture. There was a rumor at the time that Joan Mondale, the vice-president's wife, twisted Griffin's arm to get the sculpture approved. "That's a lot of blankety blank," David More said. "Nobody twists Jimmy Griffin's arm. The real reason the mayor changed his mind was because there had been a misunderstanding about the nature of the work. When we had a scale model of the work, we plopped it in front of his desk and the mayor said, 'I like it.'" [32] Griffin didn't realize where it was going and made a stink about it. By December 1978, he eased his stance on the artwork and they dedicated it in 1980.

The Committee on Arts would be very busy as they were about to have "a very prominent role because the (Light Rail) was coming in," Jim Militello said. "We got a billion, half a billion dollars to do a train to nowhere. And one percent of that money was set aside for art." So the Arts Committee was in their heyday.[33] The original committee studied art commissions in other cities to decide how they would proceed. They would focus on public art.

The creation of a city-run arts organization didn't thrill everyone. On Sunday, June 1, 1980, over 50 representatives from the arts community met to discuss a variety of topics, but the formation of a Buffalo Arts Commission was a top priority. They felt there was too much power already being wielded by the larger organizations in the city.

"That's a little like *1984* (the book by George Orwell)," said Bryna Weiss, a member of the city-appointed Upper Main Street Development Corp, which distributed government funds for property development in the Theater District. Weiss said they needed "safeguards" in the resolution ensuring input from the entire artistic community — otherwise they could come under the stranglehold of the directors of some of Buffalo's biggest cultural guns, such as the Albright-Knox Art Gallery, the University of Buffalo's School of Architecture, the Buffalo Fine Arts Academy, and Arts Development Services (a leading conduit for state and federal arts funding in Buffalo). Maxine Brandenberg of Arts Development Services was on the new arts committee. Those organizations would continue their grip for many years. [34]

"There's a little clique that's been running the arts in this community for 10 years," said playwright Manny Fried. "These people should not be sitting on top of the arts forever."[35]

On July 15, 1980, Buffalo Councilperson Eugene W. Fahey said he would submit a bill for creation of a Buffalo Arts Commission. The final makeup was determined through negotiations, with the mayor appointing ten members and the Common Council president appointing five. The Common Council adopted this legislation on July 23, 1980, and was signed into law by Mayor Griffin.[36]

"That resulted in a number of things," Al Price said. "First of all, was a long-term capital program to preserve and clean and maintain the sculptures in the public domain. But we were able to convince the city council to pass an amendment to the city charter, not only creating the (Buffalo) Arts Commission and giving it jurisdiction over all the public art, but also to pass the 'one for art' resolution so that any construction project that the city council approved, that had a million dollars or more in total construction costs, they had to set aside one percent for art in public places. The Arts Commission was given jurisdiction over the selection process and how to work with the private sector investment community to identify appropriate artists to contribute new art in the public domain."[37]

The Buffalo Fine Arts Academy's president, Samuel Magavern, was the first chairperson of the Buffalo Arts Commission in 1980. [38]

In March 1984, Magavern said, "Whereas before the city haphazardly accepted and placed monuments and sculptures, now considerable time, effort and professional help is invested in considering the location and acceptance of art, as well as helping to find sponsors and helping artists with their problems. We also have been able to take this responsibility off the shoulders of the administration."[39]

Their goal at the time was to be part of a major project, like "the arch in St. Louis. We've done it on no budget," Magavern said. "In fact, we've brought money into the city through grants."[40]

Once the ordinance became part of the city charter, David More assumed he "would continue with my full-time job as Coordinator of Economic Development under Larry Quinn." He had a staff of six and two secretaries. Then Mayor Griffin called and offered More the executive director position. He went behind Ron Anthony's back and met with the mayor privately with "a list of my own recommendations, which he accepted entirely, but Ron later snuck in a few of his cronies."[41]

More admitted to being ambitious and pompous and arrogant. "I'm principally bored with people who, broadly understood, don't have an aesthetic," he declared in 1984. He said he could not excuse painters and sculptors for "not acting businesslike, because they are artists."[42]

"It is interesting to see how worked up people can get about a memorial or a public artwork," More continued. "More letters to the editor were written about Larry Griffis' *Spirit of Womanhood* than for any other subject. This is why these things have to be treated so carefully. It is public, and the public never agrees about art. And memorials deal with peoples' loyalties, deal with peoples' convictions."[43]

Buffalo *News* arts critic Anthony Bannon asked David More what it would take to bring a proposal to the Arts Commission. He said he would ask, "Is it appropriate for the citizens of Buffalo and the viewing public to be exposed to this? You don't have a choice looking at *Birds Excited into Flight* as you drive down Chapin Parkway, for instance."[44] Because Larry

Griffis installed it without the City's permission after being rejected by the Arts Commission.

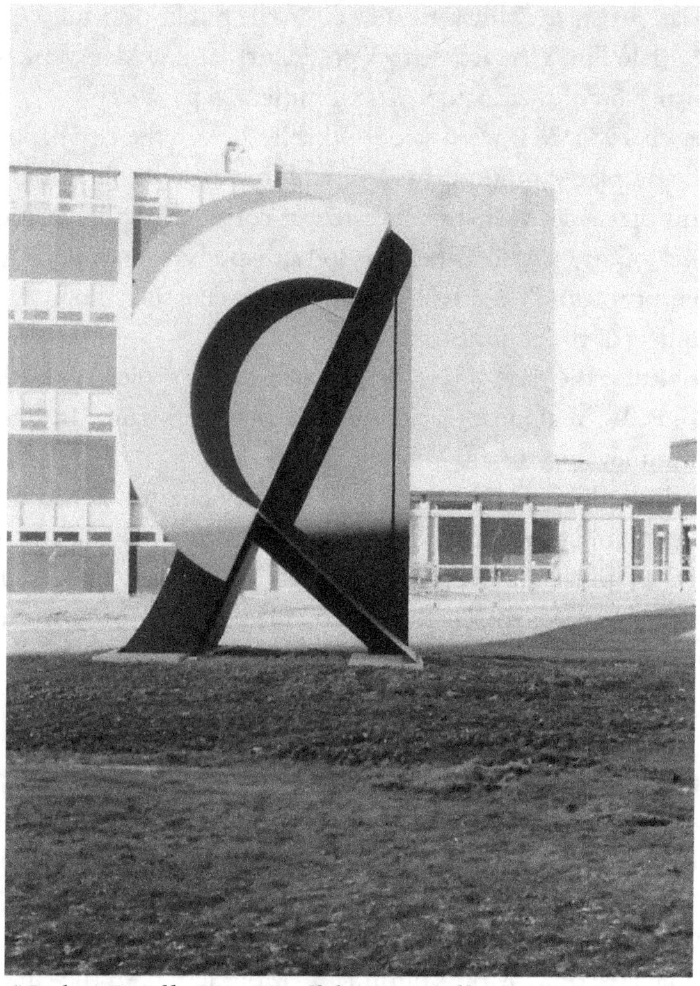

"Cock-a-Doodle-Doo," Buffalo State College, 1981. Courtesy of Lyndie Vantine.

BEFORE THE LIGHTNING

"The visual puns of the piece are enough to swallow
up three-quarters of modern art history." Richard
Huntington

A S AN ARTIST, BILLIE Lawless was always expanding his use of materials. He would exhibit his work whenever and wherever he could. From 1977 to 1981, he exhibited in Boston, Toronto, Buffalo, New York City, Philadelphia, Evanston, Illinois, and others. Some exhibits were invitationals and others juried.

In mid-August 1979, he held an exhibit at East River Savings Bank at Cathedral Park and Main Street in downtown Buffalo. Called "New Outdoor Sculpture," it was an exhibit of recent steel sculptures and ran until August 31.[1]

As he grew as an artist, he began working on larger steel sculptures. "I did a sculpture at The Nichols School entitled *Lament*, which I built in 1979." It was approximately 14 feet in height, three-eighths inch steel plate. He said, "It was really flat pieces that were cut out and then welded and bolted together ... maybe 24 feet in length and it's probably two or three tons... in terms of weight."[2]

He said that creating these large, heavy sculptures was very expensive and often took a toll on his body during construction.

George Enos of Enos and Sanderson steel company gave Billie a lot of encouragement. "He said he would make a certain commitment if I could get the rest of the material." Lawless received a tip that the vice-president at Republic Steel Company was an engineer. So he sent him a cardboard model that he could put together.

"I sent a proposal to Republic," Lawless said, "and they agreed to make the donation. Most of my donation requests, I always make it part of my request that the pieces I'm doing are going to be shown in the public and that this is part of the donation." He often created a bronze plaque to put at the site, naming the people or companies that gave donations.[3]

Nichols School, a private school on Amherst Street in Buffalo, unveiled *Lament* on Friday, October 17, 1980. Republic Steel superintendent of industrial relations Drew D. Egleston, and Gary Stanton, chairperson of the Nichols art department, attended the unveiling.[4]

Billie Lawless did another large outdoor piece in 1981 titled *Cock-A-Doodle-Doo*. "I was working with steel plate, a much larger scale, approximately 30 feet, eight tons." He said that *Cock-A-Doodle-Doo* was *Lament* to the next degree. He needed a fabricator and a local steel company was going to pay for the sculpture. Then, after he had worked on it for a year, they changed their mind. That's when he saw an article in the newspaper where Dr. D. Bruce Johnstone, president of Buffalo State College, said he wanted to beautify the campus. So Lawless approached him to install *Cock-A-Doodle-Doo* on the campus.[5]

"Just like *Lament*, it became more complicated," Billie said, "in that, at that point I needed an engineer to do something that scale, to design the foundation, to design the struts that would support the piece, wind-load tests had to be done. Rustoleum was able to give me the paints for it. I had to get it sandblasted. I had to hire trucking companies, get donations from them to move the piece. So it became *Lament* magnified many, many, many more times."[6]

Other donors of goods of steel were Republic Steel, Bethlehem Steel, and Enos and Sanderson. Pratt & Lambert also donated paint. Computer Task Group and Niagara Frontier Services (the parent company of Tops Friendly Markets), donated. VanWert-Snyder-Sklarsku-Rowley did site planning, and Globe Fabrication did fabrication. [7]

They dedicated *Cock-A-Doodle-Doo*, with an estimated cost of $55,000, on November 30, 1981. They placed it in front of Upton Hall at Buffalo State College on Elmwood Avenue in Buffalo.

Billie exhibited at the Artists' Gallery's "Sculpture '81" in Buffalo. A review of Billie's artwork, *Caged Souls to the Moon*, by art critic Richard Huntington seemed to capture the artist's early artwork. "A work like Billie Lawless' plastic and neon *Caged Souls to the Moon* looks at first very 'aesthetic' because of its use of by now very familiar geometric systems of early Modernism. But this large work is really hedging its bets. It wants to 'look good' in the regular, beautiful art way, but it wants its turn at outrageous parody, too. The visual puns of the piece are enough to swallow up three-quarters of modern art history."[8]

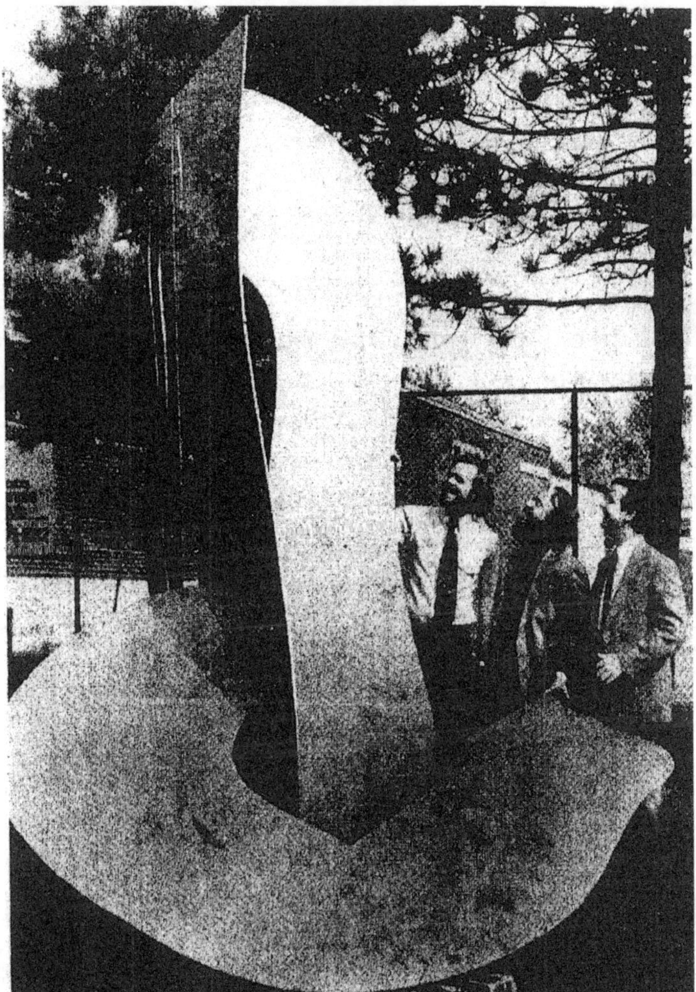

"Lament." Billie Lawless (left) at Nichols School unveiling with Gary Stanton, center, and Drew Egleston. Photo by Richard Roeller.

Billie created a maquette (a French word sculptors use for model) and the finished sculpture *Dancing Fish*, (paint on steel) as well as *Nose Job*, (Plexiglas, neon, steel and wood), in 1981. Dr. and Mrs. Armand J. Castellani, gifted all three to The Buscaglia-Castellani Art Gallery at Niagara University in 1987.

In the fall of 1980, Niagara Falls Aquarium Director Bela Babus sought the help of Kenneth E. Peterson and Billie Lawless to construct a sculpture park on three acres of land outside the Aquarium. "The Aquarium is an educational facility," Babus said, "and as such, it is our responsibility to educate in as many ways as we possibly can."[9]

Babus found Lawless and Peterson through the Artists Gallery in the Essex Arts Center in Buffalo. He told them he had the land and ambition, but no money to commission sculptures. He wanted to create a sculpture park "because human creativity is just as wonderful as nature, but on a different plane."[10]

The artists were interested, so Peterson helped to set up a system and Billie handled the selection of artists willing to donate work. Lawless said there was nothing unusual about a sculpture park at the Aquarium. "They might seem dissimilar at first," he said, "but when you think about it they really aren't. They're both making positive statements about life itself, about the value of life. I think they really are quite supportive of one another."[11]

By April 1981, they displayed six large sculptures on the land with more planned. Alvin Frega, Patrick A. Thibert, Jeff Mase, Tony Patterson, and Glenn Zweygardt were the first to display artwork. The last work was by Billie, a one-and-a-half ton steel-plated sculpture called *Life Savers*, that plays on the idea of colored semi-circular shapes.

The official opening of the Sculpture Park was on Mother's Day, May 10, and coincided with the "I Love New York Spring Flower Festival." Aquarium staff members created a flower bed, spelling out "I Love New York" in the shape of New York State.[12]

Also in 1981, Billie worked on a proposal for a new sculpture. Even though he protested against the Vietnam war and sued the government, he submitted a proposal to the competition for the Vietnam Veterans Memorial to be built in Washington, D.C. "I met an architect at SUNY at Buffalo, and we both thought it would be an interesting project to tackle together. Essentially (he) took one of my sculptures and then dealt with all the design problems around my sculpture." There were 1,432 entries, and Lawless didn't get the commission.[13] For those who fought in the war, they could have seen his winning as a slap in the face.

This experience of working with an architect, though, led to him discovering architectural drafting templates. "Soon, they dominated his drawings," George Howell wrote in 1982.[14]

Billie was constantly searching out galleries to exhibit his work. "In my business, it's very much do or die. If you're not exhibiting ... you have no presence, so it's crucial that your work is constantly on exhibition either in galleries or museum exhibitions."[15]

In 1981, the *Buffalo Courier-Express* discussed the question of censorship in an article about cable TV, a new and untapped medium and was experiencing the growth pains associated with conservative standards. Clyde Pynson, advertising director of the Buffalo *Evening News,* said, "We try to avoid censorship. But we do insist on conservative standards of acceptance. We think this is a fairly conservative community, and we believe our policy reflects the community's standards."[16]

John T. Dugan Jr., Buffalo Police vice squad, said, "In most cities people figure if it's happening then it must be OK. But Buffalo is more conservative, that's why you have the outcry over cable television. I think people should have the right to say what is acceptable in their community."[17]

These so-called standards would eventually boil over and become front and center again and again.

Erie Community College was celebrating the college's opening of a new city campus in February 1982 by hosting an exhibition with about 25 artists. Kenneth E. Peterson from Artists' Gallery, a judge for the juried aspect of the show, was asked to substitute another work for the nude sculpture he had planned to exhibit, because they felt some conservative members of the county-funded college would find it offensive, and potentially controversial.[18] A handful of artists therefore pulled their works from the show.

On Saturday, February 13, 1982, Peopleart/Buffalo, 224 Lexington Avenue, held an exhibition called "Removals" that included the nude sculpture by Peterson that Erie Community College refused to show. Billie Lawless, Larry Griffis, Susan Pollock, Ed Bisone, and Wayne Franklin had also withdrawn their art from the ECC show in support of Peterson and exhibited at this event. Bruce Adams, director of Peopleart/Buffalo said, "Censorship is too important of an issue to let go by. We had to cancel another show ... but we felt it was urgent to have the show be concurrent with the college exhibition. What we are offering is the chance for the public to decide for themselves if the action was a fair one."[19]

This is where the arts community and the public veer off in different directions. Was Buffalo, a rust belt blue-collar city, so socially conservative it was not capable of appreciating art?

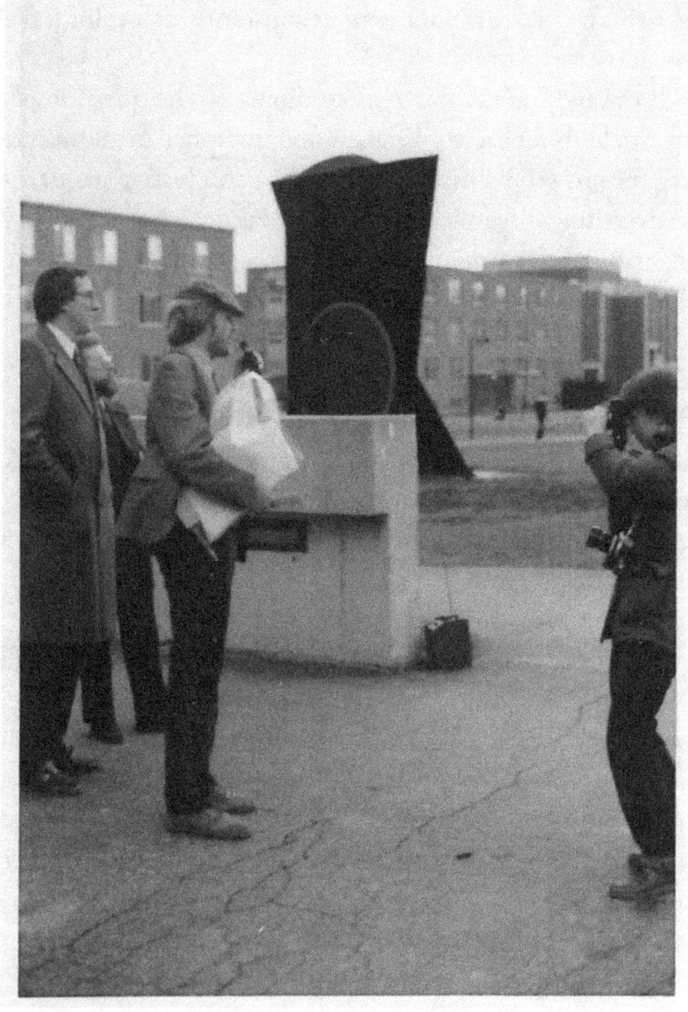

Billie Lawless (hat) at dedication of "Cock-A-Doodle-Doo", November 30, 1981, Buffalo State College. Behind Lawless is State Senator Anthony Masiello. Photo by and courtesy of Lyndie Vantine.

In 1981, the *Buffalo Courier-Express* discussed the question of censorship in an article about cable TV, a new and untapped medium and was experiencing the growth pains associated with conservative standards. Clyde Pynson, advertising director of the Buffalo *Evening News,* said, "We try to avoid censorship. But we do insist on conservative standards of acceptance. We think this is a fairly conservative community, and we believe our policy reflects the community's standards."[16]

John T. Dugan Jr., Buffalo Police vice squad, said, "In most cities people figure if it's happening then it must be OK. But Buffalo is more conservative, that's why you have the outcry over cable television. I think people should have the right to say what is acceptable in their community."[17]

These so-called standards would eventually boil over and become front and center again and again.

Erie Community College was celebrating the college's opening of a new city campus in February 1982 by hosting an exhibition with about 25 artists. Kenneth E. Peterson from Artists' Gallery, a judge for the juried aspect of the show, was asked to substitute another work for the nude sculpture he had planned to exhibit, because they felt some conservative members of the county-funded college would find it offensive, and potentially controversial.[18] A handful of artists therefore pulled their works from the show.

On Saturday, February 13, 1982, Peopleart/Buffalo, 224 Lexington Avenue, held an exhibition called "Removals" that included the nude sculpture by Peterson that Erie Community College refused to show. Billie Lawless, Larry Griffis, Susan Pollock, Ed Bisone, and Wayne Franklin had also withdrawn their art from the ECC show in support of Peterson and exhibited at this event. Bruce Adams, director of Peopleart/Buffalo said, "Censorship is too important of an issue to let go by. We had to cancel another show ... but we felt it was urgent to have the show be concurrent with the college exhibition. What we are offering is the chance for the public to decide for themselves if the action was a fair one."[19]

This is where the arts community and the public veer off in different directions. Was Buffalo, a rust belt blue-collar city, so socially conservative it was not capable of appreciating art?

The Buffalo Arts Commission worked with the Martin Luther King Trust Fund in 1981 to have a sculpture of Dr. King commissioned to put into M. L. King Park in Buffalo. The Trust Fund was collecting private money for scale models, and the Department of Community Development provided funding for the larger project.

By the April 1, 1982 meeting of the Arts Commission, they had chosen the winner, artist John Wilson. "The final statue will be a six foot high head of Martin Luther King," Wilson wrote. "It will be designed to convey some of what I feel are his basic characteristics. The total design should suggest a kind of communal, ritualized area that is similar to the feelings conveyed by the giant Olmec heads."[24]

Almost from the start, the Black community cried foul, saying it did not look like Dr. King, which was Wilson's point from the beginning. But maybe the Arts Commission should have taken that as a sign and paid closer attention to Billie Lawless.

The Buscaglia-Castellani Art Gallery, at Niagara University in Niagara Falls, New York, held "Billie Lawless New Works" from March 5 – April 19, 1982. The Buffalo *News* called Lawless "the popular Buffalo sculptor" and said "these new pieces are wall constructions of neon, plexiglass, plastic and steel rods." A fully illustrated catalogue and essay by Buffalo arts critic and early Hallwalls exhibitor George Howell accompanied the show, which was made possible through private donations and support from Armand Castellani's Tops Friendly Markets.

Howell said he first got to know Billie Lawless in early 1982, when he was asked to write the essay for the show.[25] He wrote, "Following in the tradition of American sculptors like Calder, Di Suvero, and Smith, Lawless is drawn towards monumental scale and massive weight."[26]

Billie would work alone on these large sculptures, often compromising his own health. It was during this time, after he injured his back, that he began photographing images for later use (including on a building on

Bailey Avenue in Buffalo that he would later use in *Green Lightning)* and created these smaller scale artworks. "I was intrigued by the idea of the signs for years. I recognized associations between the complexity of these structures and the sculptural ideas I was drawn to. Late last fall, I spent a couple weeks photographing old, decaying signs with the sense of actually beginning something." [27]

The show was a departure from his early large-scale steel sculpture and explored neon wall relief.

Howell wrote, "Preparing for the essay, I spent a few intense days talking with Lawless about his work and career. I was impressed. A loner who tends to avoid the local art scene, Lawless had managed to accomplish some impressive feats among other things, he had pulled together the financing and engineering expertise to construct a piece like *Cock-a-Doodle-Doo*." [28]

"Here was a go-getter," Howell continued, "a guy who wasn't stopped by size or price tag. But that verve had its own costs: Lawless was forced to spend a year 'resting' because of back problems directly related to his work." [29]

Lawless said, "I was depressed by the injury because it meant a change in the direction and scale of my work that I was unprepared for. That sudden loss of control was traumatic." [30]

Howell said that the rest and photos that Lawless took led to the show at Niagara University. "Here, Lawless joined very formal considerations with playful, cartoonish images, fusing a whole with the help of the cool energy of neon. I think Lawless's openness to the metaphorical power of rocket ships, mice, and swizzle sticks really intrigued me." [31]

Lawless wrote in the show program, "I would like to acknowledge the criticism and enthusiasm shown towards my work by Duayne Hatchett since our meeting a little over two years ago. A wit, exuberance and love in confronting technical problems combined with the unique ability to encourage the sculptural concerns of younger artists, which goes unparalleled." [32]

Sandra Haller Olsen, the Buscaglia-Castellani Art Gallery director, said that Lawless was the first regional artist to have a solo show at the gallery. "This series of new works by an emerging Buffalo artist represents the innovative and independent quality of art produced by accomplished artists in our area. We are most grateful to Billie Lawless for his excellent cooperation, enthusiasm, good humor and tireless efforts toward making this exhibition a success. He has established the highest standards of professionalism and goodwill for what we hope has been the first of many cooperative ventures with artists from Western New York."[33]

The show included eight mixed media wall hangings that incorporated neon, Plexiglas, and iron rods. Apparently steel rods dated back to Lawless' first work done in 1972, a portrait of Sophia Loren composed of steel rods.

"The work I like is often highly expressive," he explained, "but my own work is usually very tight. It has to do with my own inner tensions, keeping things very contained."[34]

While Lawless liked his 1979 work, *Sink Totem #2*, he chose not to pursue that direction. But working on drawings for *Caged Souls to the Moon*, he saw ways to adapt his drawings to a sign format. He said, "There is something about neon signs that really hold people's attention. Maybe it's the electricity, all that power and buzzing, the life-force."[35]

"For Lawless, as for an amazing number of artists in his generation," Howell wrote, "toys have found a place in the creative imagination."[36]

Howell said that *Swizzle Sticks*, 1982, "might well be a summing-up piece" for the series.

"One of my early childhood memories is of cocktail parties my parents used to throw for their friends," Lawless said. "Swizzle sticks always bring back those party images."[37]

He told Howell that he always felt uncomfortable titling his work. "In the mid-Seventies, though, after rethinking this, I felt the titles were an opportunity to provide some clues to the emotional content in the work." The titles of the work in this series refer to "personal things from either his childhood (*Hootchie Skootchie*, 1982, *Surfacing*, 1981) or his adult years (*Dancing All Night at Z's Place*, 1982). "The other pieces in this show were *Caged Souls to the Moon*, 1981; *Nosejob*, 1981; *Lunar Watch*, 1981; *Danger: Do Not Touch! High Voltage!!* 1982; *and Senor Mouse*, 1981.[38]

• • • • • • • • • •

The Philadelphia Art Alliance sponsored the Tricentennial Show from June to August 1982. This juried show, titled "S/300, Outdoor Sculpture in Rittenhouse Square" was held in Philadelphia. Billie Lawless submitted *Life Savers*, the sculpture that had been on display at the Niagara Falls

Aquarium. They accepted the piece for the show.

"I guess he didn't have to think very hard about it," wrote an online blogger about the sculpture, "because he already designed a sculpture one year earlier called *Cock-A-Doodle-Doo* ...that was EXTREMELY similar. He made this 1,200 pound pile of metal dogshit in the shape of 3 half circles, painted them goofy colors, and called it *Life Savers* because they kind of look like the candy of the same name."[39]

Lawless said the title came to him during the creative process and is based on the circle within a circle motif of the design.[40]

Pennsylvania art patrons Phillip and Muriel Berman purchased *Life Savers* from Lawless and donated it and another sculpture to the University of Pennsylvania. Dean Robert R. Marshak said, "We are delighted to have such a lively, colorful piece of art for the entrance of our hospital. We hope it will lift the spirits of our clients, as it adorns the hospital entrance with a distinctive work of contemporary art."[41]

Not everyone felt the same way. That same blogger said, "UPenn put it up right next to the doorway of their veterinary hospital's emergency room, I guess so that when you bring your dying dog in, you can see the sculpture and say to yourself, 'Well, it sucks that my dog's dead, but at least I didn't make that shitty sculpture!'"[42]

The University of Philadelphia honored the Berman's at a luncheon at the Veterinary Hospital with Lawless as a guest. A spokesperson for the Bermans in discussing the choice of the hospital as the site for the sculpture noted, "We want people to feel enlivened. The hospital building is cold, and we feel this sculpture adds fun and color to the area." Another consideration in the Bermans' gift to the school was that they wanted *Life Savers* placed where the public would see it.[43]

According to the previously mentioned blog post, it sat in the same spot for 31 years until, late 2014, when it was moved to the corner of 38th and Spruce streets.[44]

• • • • ● • ● • ● • • •

Billie continued to exhibit across the country, from Roswell, New Mexico, back to Buffalo. In 1983, the Albright-Knox Art Gallery in Buffalo announced the artists selected for its fourth biennial invitational, "In Western

New York 1983." More than 350 artists submitted works for consideration and a couple dozen, including Billie Lawless, were selected for the exhibition, which ran from April 8 to May 8.[45]

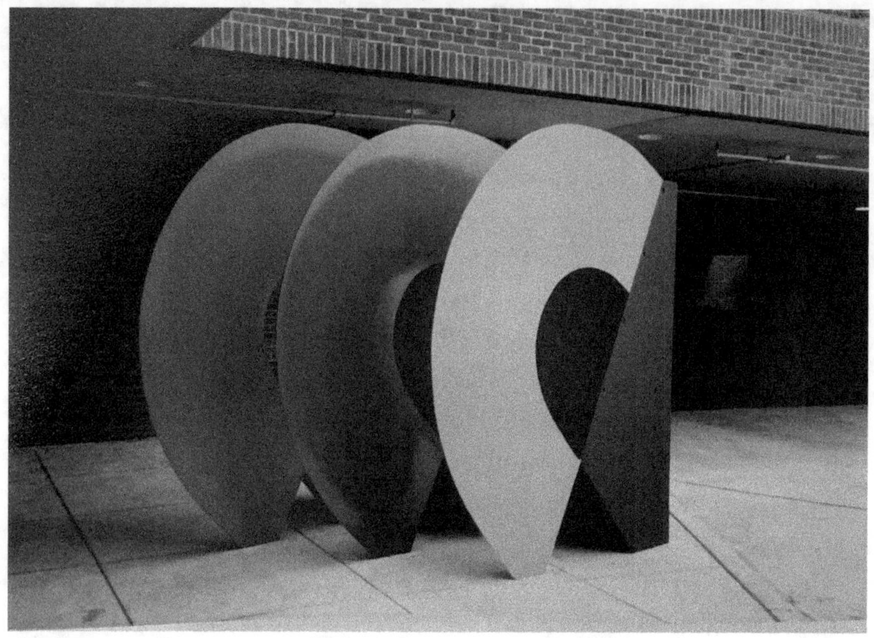

"Life Savers," 1981. Installed at the University of Pennsylvania, Philadelphia. Photo Courtesy of the Philip I. and Muriel M. Berman Papers, Lehigh University Special Collections.

MR. PEANUT

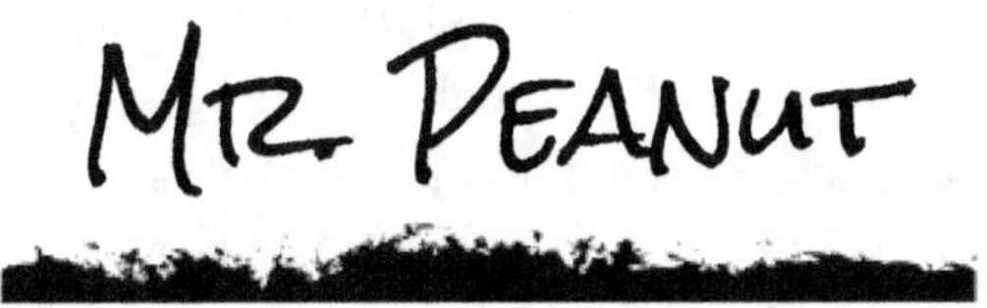

"When it was rejected, I just sort of went on to other
work I had at the moment." Billie Lawless

IN 1989, BILLIE LAWLESS described the origin of *Green Lightning*. He said the "Genesis... is my birth. ...My work is the totality of my being, so if I were to start a piece today and make a new sculpture, *Green Lightning* would be incorporated. *Green Lightning* was an idea that ... was sort of a culmination of my interest in signs and sign imagery. It was an allegorical piece that dealt with a lot of different issues. I had collected a lot of images. I always had an interest or, at some point, developed an interest in decaying sign imagery. I would, I guess, just in my daily travels, whether I was doing errands or whatnot, I always kept photography equipment with me. If I found something interesting, I would document it and then just save it."[1]

Billie was interested in the texture of signs, and how the paint would peel off of an old sign. He also liked graffiti images on sides of buildings. "I spotted an image on Bailey Avenue, probably in the late 70s, early 80s that I photographed and put into my files." He said he would look into his files for inspiration.[2]

The image from Bailey Avenue looked like a play on Planter's Mr. Peanut character. "I think they were playing off, doing some kind of pun on the word of penis and peanuts," Lawless said. "So he had a top hat and cane, and he looked like he was dancing on the side of the building."[3]

When Billie started working on what would become *Green Lightning*, he did a couple of sketches. "I think in the genesis of any idea it's not too dissimilar from doodling. You're playing with a sketch pad, you're coming up with ideas. I had heard about this deadline at Artpark, and I started drawing what looked like big steel structures, and I thought it would be interesting because my work was starting to grow in the ways of combining lots of different materials, that perhaps I could take a big structure like this and integrate lots of different materials into it in some way. I think one of the things I became interested in with signs was this idea that I could start to layer things. When you look at large billboards, and perhaps one billboard is peeling off, there's something else coming through."[4]

Unlike billboards today, in the past they were not large vinyl, but were paper. New ads were often just pasted over the old one, and you could often see the layers if one was peeling.

Artpark is a park and cultural institution in Lewiston, New York, that was established in 1974 by New York State. It was "an experiment in artist-public interaction and site-specificity that balanced a populist mission with the commissioning of some of the most Avant-Garde, investigational art of its day."[5] They had artists creating pieces, and crafts people doing workshops so that people could interact with them.

"I decided to submit a piece to... Artpark for their 1983 season," Billie said. They wanted to have a model of it, but first he did some drawings, and the Mr. Peanut graffiti image appeared on that drawing. From the start, he knew the piece would include neon elements. The first drawing for *Green Lightning* described the blinking that the neon would do on the final piece by use of an electric timer.[6]

After he finished the drawings, around October 10, 1982, he put together a model made of steel. "I used tin for the lightning bolts. (There) are steel welding rods that I cut up, and I welded together, and I used paper for the bunting on the top and magic marker."[7]

There are four boxes that were made of acetate. "I used an overhead projection marker to... at least put markings onto the acetate and Scotch tape to hold them together. This was the idea of again working with layers. I thought that if I did, I could make large boxes, I could integrate them into the structure. So this structure did not have to be uniform per se... these could actually be integrated in. These bars could come through the boxes so that it looked like perhaps they were almost coming out of... the main structure. And then to give an idea of − -I had previously been working with neon with a series of wall pieces that I had done. To give an idea of what the neon would be of the image I had found on the side of the building. I used the overhead projection marker to draw right onto the acetate. And at that point when I submitted it to Artpark, because I wasn't certain about the imagery on the back, I just actually put the bricks in on the back side of the acetate, again, just to give this idea that there was going to be some kind of layering in the boxes."[8]

"The stars are on poles and soldered onto little platforms and screwed into ... a wooden platform board, I guess maybe two feet diameter. I used paper to make the stars, and I just taped them on, using magic marker again to give some color to the stars. And I think I just used paint on the tin that I cut out by hand for the lightning bolts, and everything was sort of glued down. I included two figures so that there would be an idea to scale of how big I was going to build the piece."[9] He also used thread to give the idea of guide wires, but never used that.

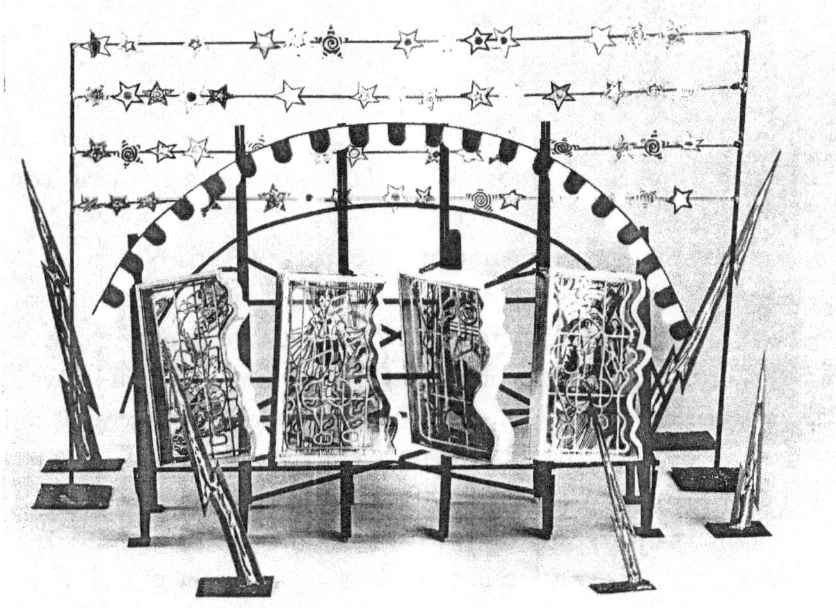

Model of "Green Lightning." Lawless vs. Manhattan Psychiatric Center.

When he completed the model, he delivered it to Artpark on October 15, 1982.[10] Richard Huntington was the visual arts director at Artpark, and had been an arts critic for the *Courier-Express*. He would later be an arts critic for the Buffalo *News*, then after retirement, he would become an artist himself.

Lawless said, "The lightning bolts... were symbolic of fate and the idea of being hit by a bolt of lightning... and the stars, the cosmos." He said the Mr.

Peanut image amused him when he saw it. "I think it's humorous." He said it was playing off the idea of representing male power. When he decided on the images on the backs of the boxes, he said it was a commentary on the state of the world at the time. "I felt very committed to doing a piece ...that was a summation of all my work, the embodiment of my work, and... I always have used some social issues in my work. I was used to satirizing and harpooning different issues in my work, and it was important to me. So I thought this was an opportunity to ... use this image that would play off some of those issues."[11]

When Billie submitted the model to Artpark, he didn't anticipate all the details, but he said he did include the Mr. Peanut graffiti images.

Artpark rejected the piece in a letter dated November 5, 1982, from Huntington. "When it was rejected, I just sort of went on to other work I had at the moment," Lawless said.[12]

After the piece got rejected, he thought more about its future. "When I started thinking more about the decay of signs and there were some around this country that were started in 1947 that are still lighted and there are some that have broken. I - - I don't know. They go through a natural decay process."[13]

He said the graffiti image did not differ from any other parts of the piece. "I didn't give it a lot of thought – - I mean, it's not male genitals. It's just an image. It's a dancing character, it's a dancing figure. Even if you want to look at it that way, some people don't even see it as that, you know. It all depends on your visual sophistication. Some people would see that and not know what it is or have an entirely different interpretation of what it might be."[14]

Around mid-January to early February 1983, Lawless wanted to see if he could overcome the technical problems of enlarging the piece. "That's always one of the major issues in doing a piece like this, whether it was *Cock-A-Doodle-Doo* or *Lament,* was the technical problems one would encounter as you were building a piece. You have to consult with an engineer. You have to start dealing with wind loads, the amount of tensile strength that you might need to keep the piece in place." [15]

The boxes were a problem Billie had to overcome. "When I first started doing the six-foot version of it, I made boxes out of Plexiglas ...it was easy to do them, so that they were totally clear, but when eventually I went to enlarging it to the full scale, that was going to be a technical problem." He said at that size they would need some kind of support.[16]

As he built the six-foot model, he knew he didn't possess the knowledge to do some things, so he read manuals and talked to people who had helped him before. "Some of the boxes were made by Flexlume, so I talked to them. They would give me advice as to perhaps how I could deal with the technical problems. I think I probably had a few boxes put together in that period of time. I actually had the structure, the main structure, put together out of very thin wood so that the boxes could stand. I also recall by that date that I had stars strung and hung up in my studio, and I had a number of roughly like four to six-foot lightning bolts constructed as well."[17]

The primary structure was six feet in height. "As you do these projects, as you bump up like to the next size, you can then really start... to visualize what your technical problems are going to be." [18]

The boxes themselves were about two feet tall. This version also included the Mr. Peanut graffiti image in neon, done by the Flexlume sign company.

Around February 16, the curators from the Albright-Knox arrived to tell Billie that they had chosen him for the Western New York Exhibition. "They were making a studio visit, and I wanted to show her (*Green Lightning*) because I was excited about it. I thought perhaps I could just exhibit the six-foot version. And (curator Charlotta Kotik) was more interested in my wall pieces and showing some of those for the exhibition, but I realized after she left that I really liked the piece, I wanted to go ahead with it on my own."[19]

"At that point I thought that, because of the nature of the piece, that it would be very interesting if I were to do something like on the East Side of Buffalo. It was such an untraditional place to put up a sculpture. It's not somewhere that traditionally an artist would think of doing a piece. You see, a lot of sculptures in the downtown part of Buffalo, and, yet, in an area like that, there isn't any outdoor work. So I thought it ... would be interesting to use an area that had been normally neglected by artists in the past."[20]

So Lawless started driving around the downtown area looking at different locations where he might be able to place it and found one location. "I also went and got tax maps down at City Hall so I could find vacant lots or determine who the owner is on a particular parcel of land." [21]

Now, whether Lawless was looking for a spot that other artists ignored, or a spot he thought wouldn't cause much resistance, is unknown.

The first location Billie found was owned by the YMCA, but they weren't interested. The second location, though, was owned by attorney Carl Paladino, who was partners with Jack Dorn, who was vice-president of the West Side Rowing Club where Billie was a coach. This parcel was on Broadway Avenue. Billie said it "looked to me like an interesting spot for the sculpture."[22]

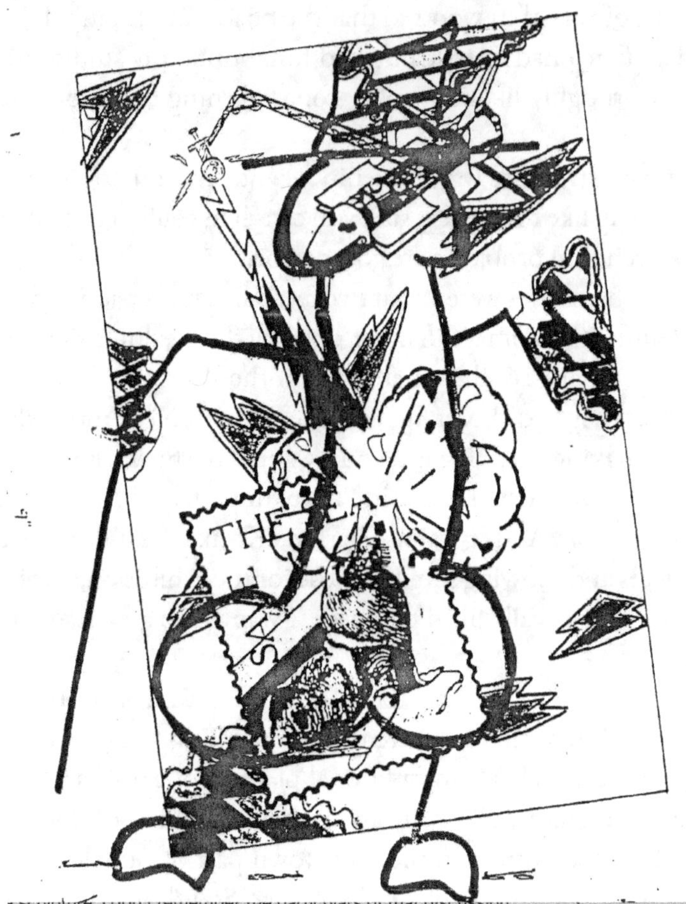

"Space Shuttle Attacks" and Mr. Peanut character drawing.
Lawless vs. Manhattan Psychiatric Center.

In March or April 1983, Billie met with Carl Paladino. "I told him about the project. And I brought slides and my budget and other matters as well." He explained that he found his property on Broadway to be just what he wanted. "He thought it was a great idea," Billie said, but he asked for a million dollar insurance policy and that Billie contact James Pitts, councilperson for the district where the land was located.[23]

The complexity of the project led Billie to double his original estimate of $45,000. He sent out a donation package with a letter about the project, past projects, and its progression. He would ask a potential donor for exactly what he wanted, or needed, from them for the part of the project he was working on.

The letter Lawless included in his donation package said Buffalo is "one of the most enlightened and supportive of the arts that one could find outside of New York City."[24] The early donation packages were not flattering to downtown Buffalo. "Somewhere on the lower east side of Buffalo, not too far from the downtown area. Some possible sites include Michigan and Broadway, Michigan bounded by Sycamore and Cypress streets, preferably an area that is dumpy, overgrown, semi-ghetto-like."[25] Was it the best wording to attract funding or was that a way to tell donors that Buffalo needed to be spruced up?

By this time, Billie had begun working with Hallwalls, Inc. in Buffalo to act as an umbrella for the project, so donors could donate materials to Billie. He explained, "The community gets a work of art, and the corporation gets publicity for themselves and a tax donation, and the artist is able to realize his project."[26]

"I had shown the maquette (at Hallwalls) once and I like the place," he said. "I thought it might be nice for them as well because they've never been affiliated with large outdoor installations. We seemed to fit each other," he continued. "You have to establish credibility for any project you are starting. From a businessman's point of view, your 'track record' is important. Having Hallwalls behind *Green Lightning* helped."[27]

Billie said that Hallwalls handled, "In actual cash, maybe four or five thousand dollars. I have a standard request for two hundred and fifty dollars. I think I got a couple large ones, maybe a thousand dollars from a couple of individuals. As for materials, I don't know. Out of seventy-five companies, maybe seven or eight actually submitted paperwork to Hallwalls. I think GE may be one of them because they gave about four thousand dollars in LEXAN."[28]

One person said that he may have underestimated the actual donations, as Armand Castellani alone donated $5,000.

As Billie built the six-foot model, he said that he always included the

Mr. Peanut graffiti images. The four boxes would later include silkscreen images, and each has a name. The first one is called "The Space Shuttle Attacks," which has a space shuttle attacking a stamp with a seal on it.

The second box was "Jump For Your Life." This one shows the "embodiment of innocence... and amoebas floating in the background and I guess the spikes ...to break up, I guess, the clear fields behind it and likewise... she's jumping rope and... we used like a transparent ink on this so that again it had that effect of a shower of light coming down on you, whereas the image itself of the girl were opaque inks that did not allow light to pass through. I think as well the red spike images were almost like a ruby red type of an ink, so that again they were transparent, that gave it almost like the effect of stained glass on the LEXAN."[29]

The third box was originally called "Homage to the Media," but renamed "Zippity-doo-da." Billie designed it to look like a (1980s) TV set with knobs, "and a figure that looks like he's playing inside the tube itself, and then again I was playing off the theme of using the stars. You can see that I put some stars into the tube itself to sort of bring the stars that were behind the piece actually into the piece itself." [30]

The fourth box is called "The Fleeing Bandito." Lawless said "When I was looking at sights and whatnot in the downtown area of Buffalo, some of the areas, because originally I did want to use the lower East Side, I guess I had the idea of — well, this stereotypical view of being in a downtown area of any city in the country is that it's violent, that it's unsafe and whatnot, and this isn't always true. So I used this image as the fourth box, and... the bandito that I came up with sort of looks like he's running across the field or whatnot and holding a red pistol. You can see the smoke going up behind him. And then what we did was we used the lightning bolts behind him again where I was trying to make the pieces self-referential, in that, the piece — I guess I envisioned some day that the piece, wherever it might be, would be standing and perhaps someone could be running across the field, running from someone, maybe running from the police or chasing somebody, so that the piece was to incorporate elements of our life and our world. And... I guess there's a bit of a vortex behind the lightning bolts. Right here we put like a large vortex behind him and again more of a reference to the cosmos and whatnot, in that, everything — all matter works on the vortex, and that was again — I think I used transparent colors on this, so you got an opaque yellow and it alternated, then you have like a transparent cobalt blue, so those allowed the light to come through, then we just added these large sort of again another, I guess, cosmic reference and just using like amoeba shapes behind the figure. And this box was — obviously was yellow, so that the neon that went into it was also NUVO gold."[31]

Why did he include neon in the piece? "I guess that's a question of almost like an artist's creativity and I'd also add that sometimes you don't know why you pick a material, it just seems to work. It's a visual ... I'm speaking visually. In the way that you pick words verbally as attorneys, I pick things for visual impact and why, I don't know."[32]

The neon sequence on *Green Lightning* went from left to right across as the sequence lit. Each figure was on for five seconds, then a pause, then five seconds, then the last figure came on for five seconds, and then the last figure took a bow. He went down, three positions, then back up. He actually bowed three times and then went back up to the top. Then the entire sequence went on and off, it went totally went dark, and then the sequence would start again.

"So there was like a device that they used that has like little cogs on it, and the device is just constantly turning, and they have circuits on each one of the cogs, and it just turns the circuits on and off, and that's what makes the lights go on and off as well."[33]

The complexity of the sculpture would prove too much for many people in Buffalo.

City Hall

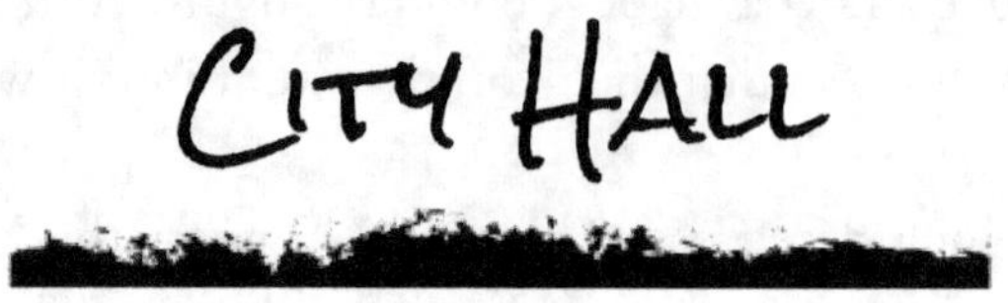

"The Arts Commission was in their heyday." James
Militello

ON FRIDAY, MAY 13, 1983, Nichols School in Buffalo held an art fair
and the chairperson of the art department invited Billie Lawless to
display any work he had in progress. "I showed both the smaller model
and six-foot version of *Green Lightning*," as well as drawings, he said. The
purpose of the event was to have the artist working during the day and
interact with the students. Power was on for the neon on the six-foot
model, "and you can see children playing... in the circle behind the stars,"
Billie said.[1]

By this period in Lawless' career, he was already somewhat respected. On
Sunday, May 15, 1983, he was a guest judge at the first annual student art
show sponsored by his alma mater, (class of 1968), St. Joseph's Collegiate
Institute.[2]

During this time, Billie met with Councilperson Jim Pitts at his office in
City Hall. The purpose of the meeting was to show him the project and if
he okayed it, then Billie could continue on the land that Carl Paladino had
donated. During the hour-long meeting, he showed Pitts "more than the
standard package. I brought a whole notebook of slides to show him my
work and whatnot."[3]

"He said, 'This is nice, this is the kind of thing we should have in the
Elm-Oak Arterial.'" So Billie invited Pitts to his studio, where he had the
six-foot version of the neon figures.[4]

Did Jim Pitts see "the penises" when he visited the studio? According
to Billie, Pitts did indeed see the six-foot panels in late spring of 1983 that

included the neon figures, "though he didn't talk a lot about them. At one point he said, 'Those really look like penises,' and I said, 'well, they could be looked at that way.' That was that."[5]

Pitts seemed to like the project and asked Billie to present a proposal to the Common Council on June 14, 1983.

"Oddly enough," Billie said, "as I got out of the elevator on my way to the Council meeting, I ran into David More in the corridor. He came into the meeting and asked, 'What's going on?' Pitts told him that the Council had approved the piece and David said, 'Nobody told me about this. I'm the director of the Arts Commission.'"

According to Lawless, David More "ensued in a yelling match with Jim Pitts about what I was doing there with the sculpture without anybody informing him."[6]

"At that time," More said, "I informed Mr. Lawless that the Buffalo Arts Commission, as the City agency charged with the responsibility of reviewing and recommending approval of all works of art to be shown on City-owned public property, would be required to review and approve any request by Lawless to exhibit a work on the Elm-Oak Arterial."[7]

Lawless admitted that he never intended to put it on public land. "Up to that point in my career, I had always avoided public land," because his father was a politician.

Billie said he had met David once before at a cocktail party at the home of Buffalo State College President, D. Bruce Johnstone.

David wasn't happy he was out of the loop. "So I had to convince him," Billie said, "that Pitts suggested putting the piece on the arterial and that I wasn't aware of the City Hall protocol."[8]

Present at the Council meeting were - Delmar L. Mitchell, President of the Common Council and Council members Arthur, Bakos, Buczkowski, Collins, Fahey, Giambra, Gospodarski, Keane, LoTempio, LoVallo, Marcy, Murphy, Pitts, and Whalen.

The resolution said that Billie Lawless was a well-known artist in the Buffalo area with several progressive sculptures in the City. He had self-financed all of his projects, and he proposed a sculpture named *Green Lightning,* described "as a colorful, light-hearted sculpture which utilizes different aspects of sign construction and imagery." Lawless wanted to construct it in the Elm/Oak Arterial for high visibility. It would stand for one year and then he would remove it. It would be an interesting art form which would complement the present revitalization efforts in the Downtown area.

Mayor Jimmy Griffin signed the non-binding resolution on June 23, 1983.

Jim Pitts invited Billie to another meeting at City Hall on August 3, 1983 with David More. "He said the piece had to be approved by the Buffalo Arts Commission," Billie recalled. "I said 'fine, no problem with me.' At that point, it seemed kind of humorous to me because this was exactly what I didn't want to get caught in."[9]

"There were a number of people there from City Hall, a fire marshal, Department of Transportation person, I think a buildings inspector, someone from the Buildings Department, perhaps someone to do with electrical, and we were to discuss at this meeting problems that we might encounter with the sculpture in the Elm-Oak Arterial." [10]

"There was a discussion about the effect of the flashing neon on traffic," Billie said, "if it was on the block it eventually ended up on. There was talk about cars entering the ramp there. It seemed there was a lot of discussion about matters that didn't really seem pertinent. I never understood why the fire marshal was there. There was some discussion about electrical. I remember that quite vividly, as to how I would be able to tap into power. I think there was discussion about tapping into the street lighting circuits that were there on the street so that then I could trench out and draw power into the piece. There might have been talk about engineers' drawings for the main structure and would they meet the wind loads and those kinds of essentially practical matters of installing the sculpture."[11]

After the meeting, they invited Billie to present before the Buffalo Arts Commission.

On August 14, 1983, Billie sent a letter to David More. He told him he had applied for a building permit. He also said that he would allow the "City Engineers the opportunity to double check my engineer's computations at no cost to myself." Lawless enclosed two maps of the areas that he thought would be "interesting" locations for the sculpture.

Lastly, he said, "Your tip on Armand (Castellani) was well taken. He has made a sizeable contribution and is also arranging for some of the construction work to be provided. He is very excited about the project."[12]

The Friday before meeting the Arts Commission, Billie spoke to David More on the phone, and Billie said David told him to bring parts of the model, but not the whole thing.[13]

• • • ● ● ● ● ● • •

Artist Joanne Posluszny attended U.B. with Kathie Simonds and said, "she was a wonderful artist."[14] In some ways, being a woman in art in Buffalo was fantastic. "Opportunities to exhibit at galleries came about and in group shows at the Albright and Hallwalls happened," Joanne said. She began to exhibit in New York City, too. Like other artists, she felt Buffalo was, in some ways, limiting.

While attending U.B., Posluszny became director of the Bethune Gallery at the university. They presented all kinds of events there, including poetry readings. She would invite everyone she could think of in Buffalo to openings and events, and sometimes wondered whether her invites were making it to the intended recipients.

It was through these events she met David More, the executive director of the Buffalo Arts Commission. After she graduated, More offered her a job as gallery director for the Arts Commission at Art Space which was located in the Tralfamadore building on Main Street in Buffalo.

More called Posluszny and insisted she attend the meeting with Billie Lawless.

Billie arrived at the meeting on August 22, 1983 in shorts and t-shirt, not what you would expect from someone trying to get the City's approval for a massive art project. He was charming, playing the part of the artist.

In attendance were David More, Sam Magavern, and artists Ann Nowak, Walter Prochownik, Jim Pappas, Ed Karnofsky, George Palmer, and Joanne Posluszny.

At the meeting, David More introduced Lawless as "the Judge's son," and the old boy's club seemed to eat it up. More summarized the project, then Billie "did my spiel" and showed the maquette of *Green Lightning*. "I brought several of the lightning bolts from the six-foot version," Lawless said. "They were maybe four to five feet in height. I think I brought two of those, and I brought a number of the stars from the six-foot version ...that I had made while doing my presentation at the Nichols School."[15]

At the meeting, David More said, "Mr. Lawless presented a maquette, which he identified as the *Green Lightning* sculpture. At no time did Lawless show or distribute any slides of *Green Lightning* or of the maquette to any Buffalo Arts Commission member at the Buffalo Arts Commission meeting, nor did he to me."[16]

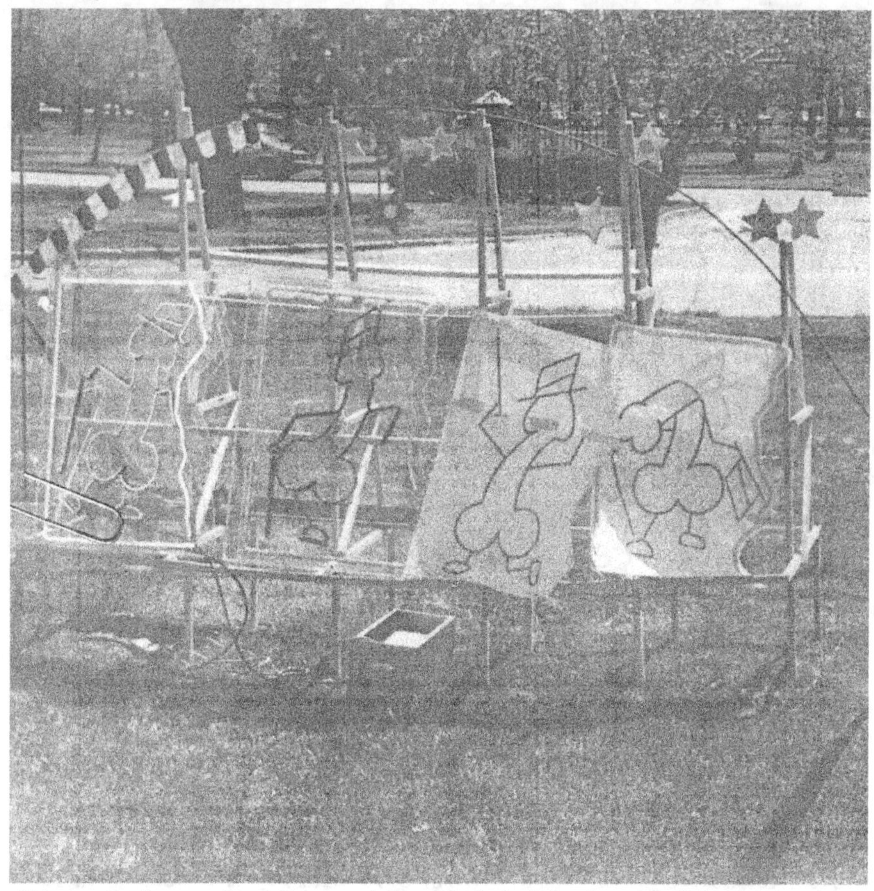

"Green Lightning" six-foot model at Nichols School in Buffalo, May 1983. Photo origin unknown. Courtesy of David More from Lawless vs. City of Buffalo.

"In fact," More said, "I never personally saw, nor was I ever given any slides of *Green Lightning*, either by Mr. Lawless or by anyone else prior to November 15, 1984, when the sculpture was first dedicated and illuminated. I never saw, nor was I ever informed, about any other small model of the plastic panels containing the neon imagery prior to the sculpture's dedication." [17]

The members of the Commission questioned him on several issues related to the sculpture, but "they didn't ask anything about the imagery,"

Lawless recalled. [18]

Most of the members just glanced at the model, but Posluszny said she inspected it. The neon images Billie created were there. They were small, and you couldn't exactly tell what they were. She said they looked more like Mr Peanut, but they were there.

The committee then asked Lawless to leave the meeting while they voted.

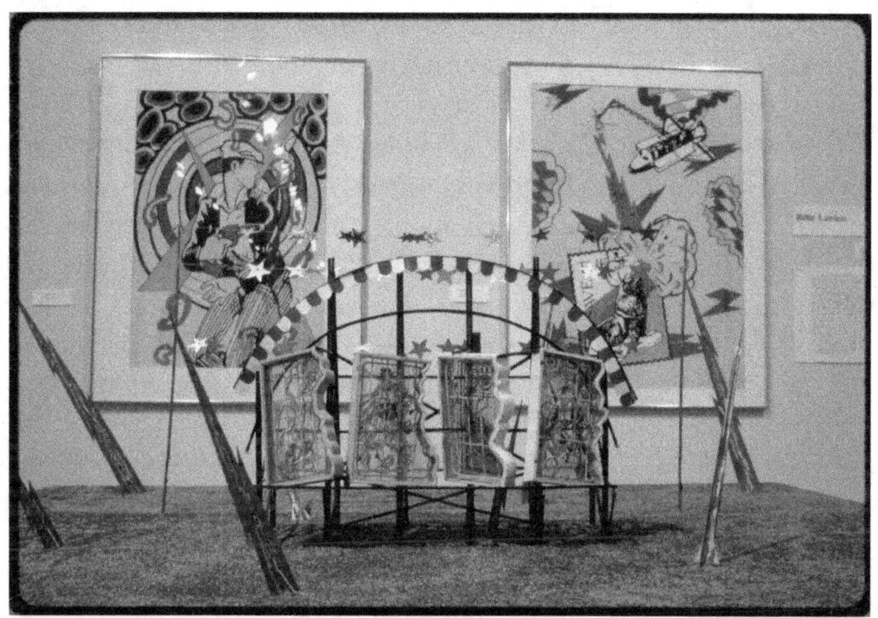

Model of "Green Lightning" when shown at SPACES gallery in Cleveland, 1985. Two prints behind it are from the neon boxes. Courtesy SPACES Archive Collection, Kelvin Smith Library Special Collections.

According to the meeting minutes, Billie satisfied the various concerns of the Commission. "A motion was made and unanimously adopted that approval of the installation be given subject to the following conditions: First, that the site be returned to its original condition. Second, that an insurance policy be taken out naming the City and Urban Renewal Agency as an additional insured. David More will work with Legal Counsel to the Urban Renewal Agency to prepare a lease reflecting these conditions. The Commission congratulated the artist on his efforts to raise the entire funding for the project privately and wished him luck."[19]

Al Price recalled, "I was there when the Billie Lawless sculpture was authorized." He felt that because Billie's father had been a part of the community, he was attempting to make his career as an artist.[20]

"There was no clear indication of what he was talking about other than that this was gonna be an animated electronic, night lighted thing that would be interesting and playful and so everybody thought, 'oh well this is fun, we'll have this big electronic sculpture.' Now, let me also say in the same era, late seventies, this was the disco era, right? There actually was an electronic sculpture that was installed down on Elmwood Avenue at the intersection of Bidwell Parkway called the *Tango Dancers,* and everybody in town loved that. They thought that was fantastic," Price recalled.[21]

Designed by Laura Rankin, Daniel Sack and Andy Ferullo, in 1982, they installed the art déco *Tango Dancers* sign as part of an economic revitalization effort. The design was a moving neon sign with two dancers.

"When Lawless made his presentation," Price continued, "that was the impression that people had in mind. That's what they thought he was talking about, something like that." Price (and others) said that Lawless used his words exceptionally carefully. "He said it was gonna be whimsical and things like that to make it sound like it was gonna be something ...that everybody would like to see."[22]

Ed Karnofsky said Billie described the sculpture at the meeting as "light-hearted, whimsical, bright."[23]

On September 22, 1983, Billie signed a contract with Larry Wood of Neon Graphics in Clarence, New York, to do the neon elements for *Green Lightning.* According to Wood, "He almost got me into doing it. He showed me a scale model of the whole thing, without any neon in it. I like to get involved in neon arts and sculpture; it's good for my business." Wood agreed to do the work and drew up a contract. Then "one of the guys from another shop came in one day and said, 'Gee, do you know what that looks like to me?' And I said, 'Gee, whiz.'"[24]

Billie said that Wood "went through a long dilatory about how he was a born again christian and I was doing the devil's work."[25]

Wood told Billie what he thought, and Billie "got a little funny. He told me it was dancing dog bones. He came in with a dog bone and showed me, making like he was a little put out by my suggestion." Wood then refused to do the work. "There was no doubt in my mind," Wood continued, "what it was, and I don't think there was a doubt in his mind either."[26]

But Lawless said that Larry Wood would do the neon, if he made some changes. Billie agreed to consider it and Wood sent him new drawings. "I turned them down, because I wanted to remain true to the graffiti image on Bailey Avenue." [27]

Billie later denied ever calling them dog bones to Wood and continued his search for a firm to do the neon work that was essential to his design.

· · · ● · ● · ● · · ·

On October 1, 1983, the Buffalo Arts Commission dedicated the new Martin Luther King Jr. Memorial in Martin Luther King Jr. Park. There was almost immediate outrage over the design because a few citizens said it was not an exact likeness of Dr. King. But there had been plenty of community input for this statue.

"You probably cannot and I would almost say should not have the selection of public art be a referendum," Al Price said. "Not because I'm anti-democratic, but you get a whole lot of people coming in and saying, 'I like this' and 'I like that' and 'I like the other' and it's a lot of uninformed opinions."[28]

He said you want a representative democracy of people who are thoughtful, teachers, public servants, and people who are knowledgeable about the arts. He mentioned artist Jim Pappas took part in making the selection. There was a well-credentialed committee of people from the African-American community who took part in the selection process. "All the Arts Commission did was concur with what the community wanted," Price added.[29]

Next up to approve *Green Lightning* was the Buffalo Urban Renewal Agency (B.U.R.A.) Billie discussed bringing the two 24 inch boxes from the six-foot model he had shown at Nichols School, but David More suggested they were too cumbersome. "There was a decision made not to bring them down," Billie said. David More "objected to the transformers, to the high voltage. We had a discussion over the phone ... bringing the model down, and bringing the boxes down and actually bringing the lightning bolts down because I had brought them down to the Buffalo Arts Commission ... and David had concerns about the B.U.R.A. meeting and so many people making presentations and presenting anything whatsoever. David didn't even want to present the model."[30]

According to Billie, B.U.R.A. was "the heavy hitter" in this story. They met in Room 210 in Buffalo City Hall on October 13, 1983. In attendance were Mayor James Griffin, Vice-Chairperson James Militello, Corporation Counsel John Naples, Councilperson Katharine (Kitty) Marcy, Councilperson-at-Large George K. Arthur, Ronald Anthony, Florence Patano, and Gregory J. Dudek, B.U.R.A. legal counsel. An additional 20 people were also present, including Billie.[31]

"The Arts Commission was in their heyday," Jim Militello claimed. "They got to bring in new artists and do things. This is how Billie came in." One of Militello's jobs was to develop the industrial park between Elm and Oak Street as an urban renewal action. [32]

The meeting began at 9:30 AM. They were discussing the waterfront, so there were a few developers there. "Big heavy action was going on," Billie said.

Griffin had already signed the Common Council's proposal on June 23, "but I guess it didn't mean anything," Lawless said. "The council approved it and it became legislation, but the Urban Renewal Agency owned the land, so the approval was meaningless without their OK."[33]

Green Lightning was Agenda item "S." Mayor Griffin told several jokes. He said, "'S' – Got to watch this one. (Laughter) Green Lighting (sic) – Sculpture proposal. As long as it's not red lighting. (Laughter) Why do you call it that?" he asked Lawless.

Billie Lawless: 'Tis the Irish in me, your honor.

Jim Militello: David (More) has been working very hard with the artists and the Common Council.

Griffin: Murray Light will get mad at you. (Laughter)

Militello: It's a very, very interesting proposal.

Griffin: He's going to get the person of the year award. (Laughter)

Militello explained that Billie would post insurance and bond. "I trust Dave More's judgement and the Council and everyone else – we're recommending its approval."

George Arthur: Let me, could I ask, do we have a model or better picture or something?

David More: This is Billie Lawless, who is the artist and he can describe...

Arthur: No, do we have a model?

More: We do have a maquette, which is in the other room, and we can bring it in if you would like to see it now.

At that point, Mayor Griffin said, "Ok, George, would you excuse me please because I have to go out to a Riverwalk (laughter) in Tonawanda." He mentioned that he had attended the ground-breaking for the Martin Luther King Jr. monument but wanted to see the model again. "...it is beautiful. But there are people in the community that have some questions and I just want to see if the end product looks like the model."

Arthur: I'd like to see it too. It is quite a controversy.

Griffin excused himself from the meeting. He and Billie passed each other. Griffin shook his hand and made a comment about Billie's father before leaving.[34]

"My oral presentation was totally spontaneous," Lawless later recounted, "because we had no idea, first, if the model was going to be asked for and secondly, when it was asked for it was too late. David said to me, 'Make it quick.' You know, the whole thing at Urban Renewal was like I was extraneous. I was not a business deal; in fact, the Mayor left before I made my presentation, that's how important it was."[35]

As the other members were discussing the likeness of the King monument to the human, David More asked Billie to bring the model in. "Maybe while Billie is bringing it in, I'd just like to add, President Arthur, on the same subject. This was never intended to fully represent Martin Luther King. There has been some lack of clarity on that subject from the very beginning, and the work is a work of art, it's not simply a photographic image."[36]

After Billie came in, More mentioned *Green Lightning* had private financing, then said, "Billie, do your thing."

He would later say, "I put the maquette on a table, and in a quick three or four-minute spiel, I explained the whole thing. At that stage, the images on the back of the panels weren't defined yet, but the abstracted penises were drawn on the front of the panels, on acetate. I described them as abstracted dancing figures celebrating life. They were there. People could see them. People could have asked me what the figures were. The media was there and so was the (Buffalo) *News*, but no one did anything on it."[37]

He described *Green Lighting* to the members. "The stars up here – these will be wires on poles that will be spinning, hopefully, we still have to work out the wind effect. It will be very colorful. Down here is sort of a sign structure. It will be supporting these large boxes which will have plexiglass on both sides and will be neon elements – sort of an abstracted, dancing figure sort of celebrating life and, of course, the pieces of green lightning from which the piece draws its title. But, I think the piece essentially the reason I thought of this area is that this area as being revitalized and it sort of fits into the whole theme of Renaissance of Downtown and the City of Lights."[38]

Green Lightning was presented as a temporary art exhibit, Jim Militello said. He said he found it interesting because one of his hobbies was model making. He was a woodworker and built his own kitchen cabinets. "It's a fun thing for me to do."[39]

He said he thinks he sat to the left-hand side of Mayor Griffin. Right next to him on the table was this "really neat" model of *Green Lightning*. Militello said it had a little topography, and it wasn't great, but it was nicely done. He said he didn't really focus on the art, but on how it was assembled. Jim Militello viewed "nice little girl scouts" on the cellophane and, in hindsight, there was something behind them. But at the time, it didn't seem important.

While Billie Lawless was saying, "Hey, I showed them everything, that was the real model," Militello said because of the scale of the model, and it didn't light up, it was deceitful. "What you saw were these panels and innocent things. He said it lights up and ...the little girls dance. He didn't say anything about the dog biscuits or anything like that, and I was right there."[40]

David More explained, "Mr. Lawless presented to those present the maquette of the *Green Lightning* sculpture, which the Buffalo Arts Commission had recommended for approval. I personally observed the maquette at that time and can categorically state I saw no figures on the plastic panels on the maquette. I recall that the plastic panels on the maquette were a plain white opaque material."[41]

Did Billie Lawless purposely avoid showing the Mr. Peanut neon penis positions because it might have confused the Urban Renewal Agency? He would later say yes.

There were a few questions about the size of the sculpture and Florence Pantano asked how safe it was.

Billie Lawless: Very safe – it's vandal proof. Because you're talking very heavy steel plate.

Jim Militello: You shouldn't announce that – it's like a challenge. (Laughter)

Lawless: The Material that this is made of is called Toughex. It is manufactured by General Electric Corporation, they are donating it, and it is a vandal resistant plastic, it will be on the face and the neon elements will be inside and everything else is steel and probably indestructible.

George Arthur: How long will it take you to construct it?

Lawless: The piece is almost constructed. I've been working on it for almost ten months now.

Arthur: Ten months?

Lawless: Yes.

There was discussion about installation time and if there would be any impact on traffic getting on the expressway, where the sculpture would be located.

Katharine Marcy: It's an eye catcher.

George Arthur: I move to approve.

Marcy seconded it.

Ronald Anthony: "I think it is an attraction, and I think we're looking at the City of Light, the lighting of City Hall, the new light displays for the Main Line Mall and all the rest. I really think it really adds to it also."

Militello: All in favor?

Unanimous: I.[42]

Ronald Anthony later said the outlined figures in red on the acetate panels as presented by Mr. Lawless were "absolutely not" on the model that was shown that day.[43] Anthony was a City Hall insider who had his own office in the mayor's office. He was Griffin's right-hand person, who attended meetings, recommended political appointments, and even opened the mayor's mail.

• • • • ● • ● • • • •

On November 1, 1983, David More sent a letter to Billie congratulating him, and thanking him for his "fine presentation. We feel this is an exciting project and will result in an enhancement, albeit temporary, of downtown Buffalo. You are to be commended for your fundraising efforts."[44]

Even though *Green Lightning* wasn't finished, and Billie hadn't even signed an agreement with B.U.R.A., he was prematurely excited to get the site prepped for installation. Attorney Jack Dorn, Billie's friend from the

West Side Rowing Club, was going to handle the legal matters related to the project.

218

BY: MR. PITTS

RE: GREEN LIGHTNING SCULPTURE

WHEREAS: Mr. Billy Lawless a well known artist in the Buffalo area has contributed a number of progressive sculptures at various locations within the City; namely Cock-a-doodle-doo at Buffalo State College, Lament at Nichols Campus School, and

WHEREAS: Mr. Lawless has developed and financed all of his projects on his own. His sculptures have been recognized nationally, and

WHEREAS: Mr. Lawless has a proposal for a sculpture named Green Lightning which can be described as a colorful, light-hearted sculpture which utilizes different aspects of sign construction and imagery, and

WHEREAS: Mr. Lawless would like to construct a sculpture in the Elm/Oak Arterial to give it a high degree of visibility. The sculpture will be constructed and stand for a period of 1 year and then removed, and

WHEREAS: Mr. Lawless has developed a budget of $45,000 for the sculpture. These monies would be raised privately, and

WHEREAS: Mr. Lawless's project would be an interesting art form which would compliment the present revitalization efforts in the Downtown area.

NOW THEREFORE BE IT RESOLVED THAT:

The Common Council request Mr. Lawless to come before it to make a presentation about his "Green Lightning Sculpture".

FURTHER BE IT RESOLVED THAT:

The Common Council support Mr. Lawless's proposal to develop the "Green Lightning Sculpture".

FINALLY BE IT RESOLVED THAT:

The Common Council give its' permission to establish the "Green Lightning Sculpture" in the Elm/Oak Arterial.

JAMES W. PITTS

Passed.

APPROVED

JUN 2 2 1983

MAYOR

146A

Resolution by Councilmember James Pitts signed by Mayor Jimmy Griffin.

"At that point," Billie said, "I started to proceed to put *Green Lightning* into the Elm-Oak Arterial. I actually started digging foundations within a few weeks. I started digging foundations on a site south of Genesee Street. I started constructing the sculpture in the wrong spot after I was approved by B.U.R.A. Instead of going on the north side of Genesee between Elm and Oak, I started digging on the south side of Genesee Street. When we had discussed the site, it was in the afternoon of a very busy afternoon, and I rushed down, I met David, and we decided on the north side, and just because in the confusion I marked it on the south side.[45]

"I do almost all my own work. I mean, I didn't excavate. Someone, I think, gave me a donation for excavating the foundations, but I put all the steel work in and supervised the pouring of the concrete, doing all the finishing work as well. I started actually building foundations. I excavated and — and I built some of my foundations, so I'd probably been working there into — I remember one day I was pouring foundations and it was snowing, and then I got a series of frantic phone calls from David More."[46]

Lawless had been working there for several weeks already before someone realized he was working at the wrong site. "It created quite a flap in City Hall," he said. "They felt that I was conspiring with Jim Pitts to block further development in the Elm-Oak Arterial." [47]

Buffalo has been the mainstay of a practice known as redlining dating back to the 1930s when white people in power made it virtually impossible for Black and Brown people to purchase houses. Even though the public knows about it, the practice continues to this day. The people in power created the Elm-Oak Arterial to separate the downtown area from the predominantly Black East side. Could African-American Jim Pitts have suggested this public land to display *Green Lightning* and its neon penises as a "gotcha" to the white folks in Buffalo? Anything is possible.

Billie sent a letter to Patrick M. Marren, Director of Economic Development, on November 14, 1983, apologizing for the mistake. He explained it wasn't David More's fault. "What with the work and effort which I have spent on this project over the last year. If anything, perhaps it is too much for one person to try and accomplish.

"In all due respect to David More, he has done an excellent job not only with this particular project but in his capacity as Director of the Buffalo Arts Commission and in no way is he responsible for this error. Unless I had been led down to the site by hand and told where to dig I, in my excitement, would have executed the same error."

He added he understood that a lot of hard work had gone into the development of downtown, and "did not want to introduce any more complications."[48]

Billie also sent a quick apology note to David on the 14th.[49]

On November 15, 1983, Patrick Marren sent a letter to David More, letting him know Billie had dug at the wrong location. Marren said the event disappointed him. He looked to More to notify Lawless to backfill the electrical conduit trench and remove the concrete foundations. "I would strongly urge you and the artist to give serious consideration to other available locations for his art piece."[50]

The apologies were flying wild as David More sent an apology letter to Patrick Warren on November 17, 1983.

As Executive Director of the Arts Commission, More wanted *Green Lightning* to be a success. He was upset that Billie jumped the gun and started digging on the wrong site, so he sent him a letter on November 23 reminding him they didn't yet have an agreement. This time, the tone was much more businesslike, addressing "Mr. Lawless," and instructing Billie to "cease all work on this site. If the project still proves feasible, I will be in contact with you regarding a necessary agreement."[51]

Billie and David discussed the issues over a phone call in late November 1983, followed by a meeting on December 1 and a quick letter on December 2. In this letter, Billie sent a copy of his electrical permit.

On December 21, 1983 David More sent Gregory Dudek, legal counsel for B.U.R.A., a letter in which he said he "drafted a copy of an agreement between the Sculptor and Buffalo Urban Renewal Agency for temporary use of a plot of land in the Elm-Oak Arterial."[52]

Billie then sent More a letter dated December 30 to outline the progress he had made to that point, including: a parcel of land was donated for the sculpture; Councilman James Pitts suggested the Elm-Oak Arterial for erection; Lawless began construction in the early part of November in the wrong area; and Developer Carl Montante said his heavy equipment would remove the foundations for Billie.

"If everything moves ahead on schedule and meets with approval," Lawless wrote, "I envision completing the sculpture in the early spring of 1984. Estimating a totally installed sculpture by May 1st, 1984." He mentioned that over 30 businesses had donated to the endeavor.[53]

The New Year came and went, and David responded to Billie in a mistakenly dated letter of January 6, 1983, which should have been 1984.

His greeting was more friendly, although the tone of the letter was not. He hoped the letter "will assist you in putting into proper perspective the current situation and help lead towards successful completion of the project."

He clarified that "No land has been donated, per se. A Common Council Resolution was passed which, in my opinion, gave only a dubious endorsement to the general concept."

He admonished Lawless for not filling in the trench. He also seemed taken aback that Lawless had spoken to developer Carl Montante and chose another location. "I take this to be your final choice," he added.

"I trust you can appreciate the indulgence of the many officials now counting one.... two.... three.... Billie, many people want to see this project move forward, myself not the least among them, but it will only happen if all parties involved are clear about their respective assumptions, intentions, responsibilities. I will assist you in any way I possibly can and have written this letter for the sole purpose of clarifying the present situation in the interest in of leading the project to its successful conclusion."[54]

Billie, apparently, did not like the tone of More's letter and responded on January 7, 1984. (He corrected the year also.)

"I appreciated hearing your suggestions in your letter dated January 6th, 1984, though I think a simple phone call would have resolved the misreading you gave the letter. It's unfortunate, from my perspective, that so much paranoia is generated by what could be an uplifting experience for everyone involved. I am delighted to hear that 'many people want to see this project move forward' and I can assure you that the building of the sculpture itself is progressing wonderfully. This is, of course, what it's all about to me; the sculpture."

Lawless explained that a private individual (Carl Paladino) had originally donated land, "and this is how I came to be in Council(person) Pitts' office in the first place. This would be an excellent spot for a little Shakespeare, something like, 'Oh, ye, tangled web...' but let's not. So, we have an individual who wants to donate a piece of land to me to use on a temporary basis (one year; a consistent part of this whole affair) and just like the city, he wanted a one million dollar policy (sounds like he has done business with the city or vice versa). I am sure that you are familiar that a common courtesy within City Hall is to let a councilperson know of an impending project which might occur in his/her district. I believe that this private individual was exercising precisely this option; nothing more than a courtesy to Council(person) Pitts. In a rather interesting way, it seems that the more 'blessings' the project receives, the less secure I feel. Somewhere, there must be a story in all of this; if not a story, perhaps a moral.

COMMUNITY
DEVELOPMENT

City of Buffalo
920 City Hall
Buffalo, New York 14202   855-5035

The Buffalo Urban Renewal Agency
Room 920 City Hall
Buffalo, New York   14202

RE: "Green Lightning" Sculpture Proposal

FUNDING AMOUNT: No Cost to BURA   FUNDING SOURCE:

Dear Agency Members:

The Department of Community Development has reviewed the item described below, and finds it consistent with its policies and practices.

I, therefore, recommend its passage, contingent upon certification of funds by Financial Control of Agencies and approval by the Agency Counsel.

BRIEF DESCRIPTION: Buffalo artist William Lawless has proposed a temporary sculpture installation on the northeast corner of Elm and Genesee Sts. His proposal has been reviewed and approved by the Buffalo Arts Commission and Common Council. "Green Lightning" is proposed for a period of one year at which time it will be disassembled and offered to other cities. Since the site selected falls within the Oak/Michigan Industrial Corridor it is recommended that approval be given contingent on BURA's authority to order its removal at any time. The project will be financed entirely by the artist and contributions he has secured.

Very truly yours,

JAMES R. MILITELLO, Commissioner

JRM/ /
Attachments:
___X___ Project History
___X___ Map
_______ Budget
_______ Scope of Services
_______ Agreement
_______ Salary Review Committee Approval

Project Manager

Item No.

PLAINTIFF'S
EXHIBIT
6

Deputy Commissioner

James D. Griffin, Mayor / James R. Militello, Commissioner /

Letter to the Buffalo Urban Renewal Agency from Jim Militello recommending they approve "Green Lightning."

"If officials are counting 'one... two... three...,' David, then they should be, for all the tomfoolishness which has gone into this matter. If they want communication and to be 'clear about... respective assumptions, intentions, responsibilities,' then why no response to my letter of November 14th, 1983 to Patrick Marren requesting a meeting? Further, why did you convey to me via phone on December 28th, 1983 that Mr. Marren was terribly upset over my meeting with Carl Montante? Where does the 'public's interest' lie in all of this? Ad infinium.

"Look, David, I am a very reasonable person. A mistake was made on the site location. If a mistake had not been made on the site location, there would have still been a problem because of the subsequent development in Carl Montante's plans. Meeting with Carl was one of the most logical choices in this dilemma. Yes, this is my final choice as to the site location of 'Green Lightning' and yes, I will provide 'written evidence' of Carl Montante's intentions to take care of the trench and foundations.

"I am happy to hear that you will 'assist' me, David, and I only hope that when you speak of a 'successul (sic) conclusion' to the project, we are holding the same vision of what is meant by 'conclusion.' As an artist, I keep getting this strange compulsion to begin writing those letters on red tape."[55]

Billie was rather perceptive, as he notes that the courtesy to Councilperson Pitts was turning into something he didn't expect, or want.

Because of the "flap" over the wrong location, Billie's new attorney, former Corporation Counsel Leslie Foschio, began working on the agreement between Billie and the Buffalo Urban Renewal Agency. Foschio was a friend of Billie's and his father's.

At the Buffalo Arts Commission meeting on January 26, 1984, there was an update on *Green Lightning* that included approval of a site between Elm and Oak streets north of Genesee Street.[56]

Leslie Foschio sent a letter to Lawless dated February 10th, 1984. Billie said, "I provided him with the boilerplate that was provided to me, the initial contract to negotiate." Either via telephone or correspondence with Foschio, he expressed concerns that he wanted to have addressed in the contract.[57]

On February 28, 1984, Billie sent another letter to David More. They certainly kept the postal service busy.

Lawless said, per the telephone conversation held on Friday, February 24th, 1984, he was under the impression B.U.R.A. wanted the permit agreement resolved as quickly as possible. "To this end, I have worked diligently in regards to meeting those requirements set by the Agency and trust, will see this business handled as expeditiously as possible."[58]

Billie spoke with David More by phone on Tuesday, March 8, 1984. In that call, they discussed that April 1st, 1984 would be satisfactory to begin the Permit Agreement. That date came and went as they continued negotiations.

At the Buffalo Arts Commission meeting on April 9, 1984, a status on the construction of *Green Lightning* was noted. "After a protracted discussion period" the two sides came to an agreement on all the aspects of installation, term of installation, and various responsibilities. [59]

April 18, 1984, David More sent a memo to Greg Dudek:

> I have reviewed the permit specifying the terms agreed upon with Messers. Marren, the artist, and myself for Mr. Lawless's temporary installation of a sculpture between Elm and Oak Streets, north of Genesee. Additionally, I have discussed a few minor changes with Mr. Foschio, the artist's attorney, which are reflected in the attached revised Pemit Agreement.
>
> In view of the fact that circumstances contributing to the delay in execution of said agreement have been satisfactorily resolved and the artist is ready to commence work, your approval as to form is respectfully requested.[60]

Billie received a letter on May 16, 1984 with the copy of the permit agreement enabling him to begin installation of *Green Lightning*.[61]

It finally looked like things were moving along.

Permit Me To Introduce Myself

"If a piece isn't noticed, it isn't worth putting up."
Marsha Moss

To construct *Green Lightning*, Billie would need a very large studio. Buffalo artist Mark Griffis said, "We've been on (Essex Street) since 1969. So we have one large bay that just happened to be free for those few months that he needed to use it because we have several things to make sculpture. So we just gave it to Billie. I don't think Billie paid any rent or anything. I think (the studio space) was donated by my dad."[1]

Mark said, "I hung out in the studio while he was making it. I was doing my own sculpture in the next bay." [2]

Mark and others noted Billie would ask, "Where is your mind?" when anyone commented on the neon designs at Essex Street studio. "You're the first person who said that."

"So, of course, he makes the whole thing this huge, monumental sculpture," Griffis said.[3]

For the inside of the boxes, Billie chose LEXAN (made by General Electric) because he said it was resistant to vandalism. "It also enabled me to silkscreen or paint on the material at the same time," he added.[4]

The Ferguson Electric Company designed and installed all the electrical components on *Green Lightning* in the summer and early fall of 1984. They regulated the components by a timer that activated the neon about one hour before twilight, then turned it off about 4 AM the next day.[5]

According to art restorer Steve Wisenbaugh, *Green Lightning* "would fall into two categories of art which have developed rapidly in the later half of the twentieth century. They are kinetic and light art. Kinetic art, that which is powered so that it can move, would include such illustrious sculptors of the twentieth century as Alexander Calder, George Rickey, Jean Tinguely and Marcel Duchamp and Naum Gabo. Light artists of the twentieth century include Dan Flavin, Chryssa, Billy Apple, Stephen Antonakos and Robert Irwin."[6]

• • • ● • • ● • • ● • • •

The permit agreement took a while, so Billie worked to get *Green Lightning* ready for an exhibition in Pennsylvania. Penn's Landing in Philadelphia is the historical site where the city of Philadelphia was founded. In 1984 independent curator Marsha Moss oversaw "Sculpture/Penn's Landing/84," which ran from August 3 – September 14. It was "an outdoor exhibition of massive site-determined installations and monumental free standing sculpture on the exterior walls and surrounding the Port of History Museum."[7]

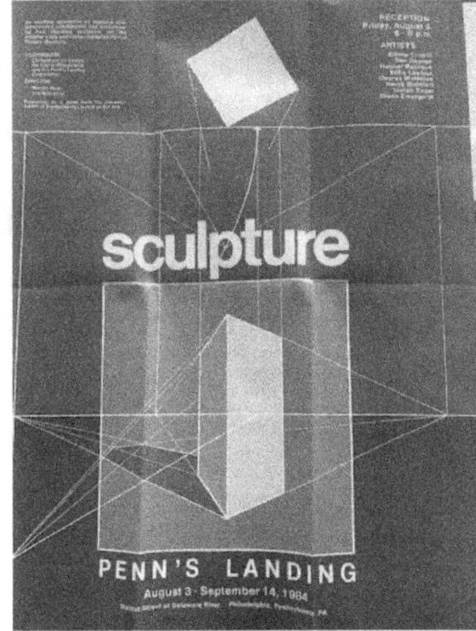

Poster from Penn's Landing Sculpture Exhibition, 1984. Courtesy of Marsha Moss.

Billie was one of eight artists chosen to display their artwork during this show. They commissioned the artists to let the citizens of Philadelphia interact with abstract art for free. It's unclear how Lawless thought he could prepare the piece for Buffalo and display in Philadelphia, but he tried.

Ms. Moss said a city official who was involved with the arts brought the Mr. Peanut figures to her attention when they noticed them on Lawless's documentation. She said that Billie's maquette was so clear that "you couldn't pass it off after a second look."[8]

Billie said, "The woman putting that show together called me and asked if the figures were penises. She said the official in charge of cultural events had asked her and so she wanted to clarify it. Then she said, 'OK, fine.'"[9]

When asked if she was concerned about negative reactions, she said, "Yes, it occurred to me. I talked to city officials about it. They agreed that it shouldn't be rejected because of its imagery. The city was not involved in its selection. I showed them the slides because I needed their support and encouragement. There was no hesitancy. Nobody thought it was offensive."[10]

"I considered its artistic merit," Moss said, "and I didn't make an issue of possible public response. If a piece isn't noticed, it isn't worth putting up. I would not have expected the kind of public response it got in Buffalo."[11]

Interestingly, Moss did not feel that Billie had to be explicit in identifying the figures as penises. "They are semi-abstracted. If he calls them 'abstract figures celebrating life,' that's his prerogative."[12]

According to Lawless, they accepted *Green Lightning* for showing in Philadelphia, in March or April 1984.

Why did he still seek to have the piece shown in Philadelphia? He said he didn't have a signed contract with B.U.R.A. and he needed to continue to exhibit. It was what he did.

On May 14, 1984, B.U.R.A. and Lawless finally executed the Permit agreement.

The key points were that Billie would design, fabricate, construct and install a unique, contemporary sculpture for the Elm/Oak Arterial in an area midway between Elm and Oak streets. The completed sculpture was to "fully resemble" the model approved by the Buffalo Arts Commission, Buffalo Common Council, and approved by the Buffalo Urban Renewal Agency at its meeting on October 13th, 1983.

This was a clause that Billie and Les Foschio had specifically negotiated. He said he was happy with the agreement and intended to adhere to that clause.[13]

By this time, he had already built a lot of the sculpture. "I believe the main structure was probably almost completed, most of the lightning bolts were probably close to completion and likewise with stars, the poles, but, obviously, because of the complexity of the project ...many things were going on at many different places at the same time."[14]

As part of the agreement, he had to begin and complete construction and installation of the sculpture within ninety days of the start of the signed agreement. He must vacate the land within one year or 14 days of written notice. "Such notice, if any, shall be directed to the Artist at his studio by registered United States mail."[15] This would prove to be a sticking point down the road.

By July 1, 1984, progress was being made on the construction of *Green Lightning* and David More was planning a September 15 "gala champagne reception."[16]

Billie was still trying to get stone for the foundation. He finally received the donation and poured the foundation in late July 1984. But he was also trying to secure two trucks to move the sculpture to Philadelphia for the show there. It would be a tight schedule: transport the sculpture on July 30 and 31 and install by August 5. The show would run until September 10, then disassemble and transport back to Buffalo.

An article on opening day in the Philadelphia *Daily News* mentioned Lawless as creator of *Green Lightning*, "the one with the fuchsia-striped bolts."[17] But the sculpture wasn't complete, and it hadn't even left Buffalo. Despite being named on the posters and Marsha Moss thinking he actually exhibited, Billie admitted he did not exhibit. He said he couldn't finish *Green Lightning* in time for that show. "No, I couldn't complete it and I couldn't get the money to move it there."[18] Lawless also did not get the sculpture up in Buffalo within 90 days, like he agreed to. "It just was so complicated," he conceded. He didn't expect it to be ready until late September 1984. He needed to amend the completion date again.[19]

After the foundations, he expected elements of the sculpture to arrive in mid-August.

"Dedication, which, if all goes as scheduled, should be in the latter part of October," he explained to David More. That would be a month after the previous letter stated. So he sent a letter to David More on August 22, 1984.

Lawless mentioned he was over the 90 days allowed for construction and installation and requested an extension.

"A dedication would be appropriate, and right now the last Thursday or Friday of September looks good, September 28th or 29th. Let me know if that would be agreeable for those city officials who would like to attend."[20]

Why did Lawless, in one letter, say he expected to be done in September and in another letter he said it would not be until October?

"It was just too much work for one person," he later admitted, even though he wasn't working on anything else. "No, I was just working on *Green Lightning*."[21]

During a meeting of the Buffalo Arts Commission on October 22, 1984, they said the sculpture was on schedule to be dedicated the following month. "It was further acknowledged that the conspicuous setting of the piece was likely to lead to some degree of controversy." [22] They expected potential controversy over the location, but at this time none of them were apparently aware of the Mr. Peanut neon design.

Amy Sparks wrote *Green Lightning* was "a massive structure made of steel, LEXAN, tin, concrete, silkscreen, neon, paint and wire. *Green Lightning* was a wealth of cultural iconography, layered and staged in a billboard-like setting. Sharp bolts of lightning shot down into the ground, surrounding a structure containing four silkscreen icons- cartoons of our society: a girl skipping rope, a space shuttle, television, a burglar and wildlife stamp. Superimposed on these figures, visible only at night, were neon penises decked out in top hat and cane. Strung above this were flashy stars and a vivid arch. Meant to be carnivalesque and garish, the piece was wildly humorous and deadly serious, a grave burlesque of our culture."[23]

Lawless said, "The imagery resulted from collaborating with (Buffalo artist) Kathie Simonds."[24]

On November 7, 1984, Billie Lawless met George Howell at his Days Park apartment, one week before the public dedication of *Green Lightning*. "Lawless was in a cheerful mood, eager to talk about the ideas behind the sculpture and the problems he faced in bringing the piece into the public forum," Howell would write. "While he was uncertain about the likelihood of a controversy, he thought that the local art world would appreciate his project." [25]

Although Billie had been working on the installation for months, he did not install the neon until a week before the unveiling. One person close to the event said it was mere days. He had Central Neon Supply in Albany, New York, build nine NUVO neon units, for $450. He had some neon repairs made by Robert L. Powers of West Henrietta, New York, a week before the unveiling.[26]

Howell asked, "Enough people have seen the maquette that no one could accuse you of deceiving them, but it sounds like the mayor is key to this happening and he didn't actually see it. After you talked with the guys in the neon shop, did you design the neon yourself?"

"They were the middlemen," Billie replied. "So I went to the guy who actually does the neon work. I took the large drawings of the figures to him and left them there. He went bananas." That person was Larry Wood from Neon Graphics in Clarence, New York.

"He realized what the figures were," Lawless continued, and "called me up (and) said I was doing Satan's work. It really upset me. I consulted one of my lawyers who thought the piece was great, humorous and lighthearted. I talked with Bill Currie (from Hallwalls) and a lot of others after that. I gave it serious reflection."[27]

"That makes me wonder about the site," Howell asked, "because there is a large church on the other side of the expressway. Will they think you are being insensitive to them?"

Billie said, "A Boy Scout leader from that church came over to talk to me and he was really excited about the piece. He wanted to bring his Boy Scouts out to my studio." This was before the sculpture was lit.

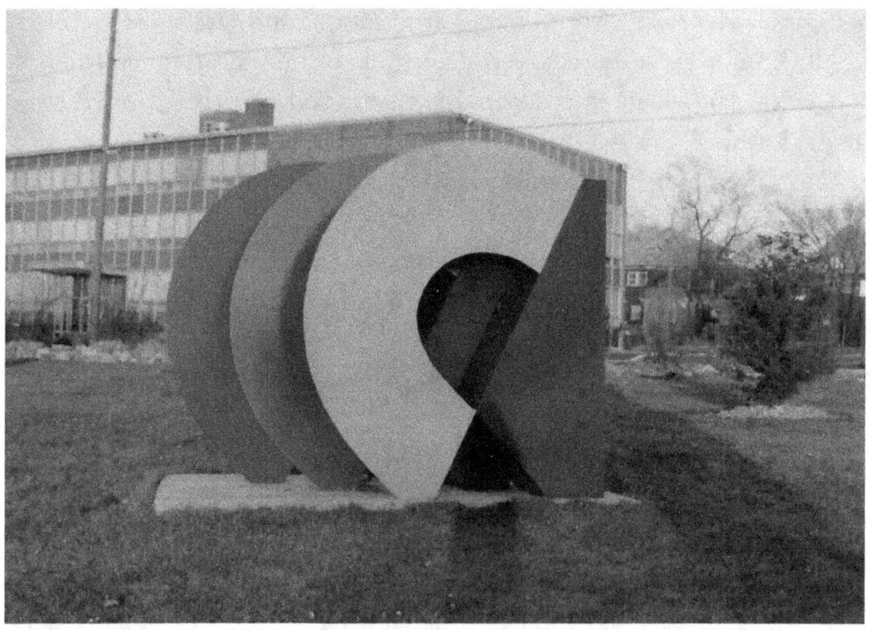

"Lifesavers" at Niagara Falls Aquarium, 1981. Photo by Lyndie Vantine.

"The whole piece is allegorical. The girl skipping rope is like the embodiment of innocence. Kathie added things to make it look even more threatening, like the girl's dancing or skipping on top of spikes or jaws; I took the abstract penis figure and put it on top of the panels as a symbol of power, perhaps men and power and what that has brought us to. I was also burlesquing the idea. When I first saw that image on the side of a deli on Bailey Avenue, I thought, 'wow, that is a powerful image.' I think the response people have to it is always powerful."[28]

"When you did the Buscaglia-Castellani show (in 1982)," Howell said, "you seemed to respond to cartoon images on a lot of different levels. Out of all the people who passed that image on Bailey, you are the only one who saw monumental possibilities in it."[29]

"That's my job; that's what I'm here for," Billie laughed. "I remember years ago when they made that woman remove her male nudes from the County Hall show. Have you ever seen female nudes removed from a show? People have this silly reaction to genitalia. When one of the guys at the Ashford Hollow complex found out what my images were, he asked me, 'What if I'm taking my kid home from the Aud and he sees this?' And I said, 'What can I say? It's a penis.' It's like adults have to protect their kids from their own genitals."[30]

Howell said it wasn't the real thing, it was symbolic, but he had mixed feelings about it. "It is important to take a significant image that isn't looked at and put it some place where people have to deal with it. But there's also the problem of what a community finds offensive-where does informing the public end and offending them begin? This is something you'll have to deal with, especially if people are really offended by it."

Interestingly, Billie had thought of the possibility of it being damaged and was concerned about a controversy. "I can see the thing being destroyed. But what is the role of the artist? I'm not looking forward to this. To be honest, I hope there isn't any controversy, that maybe the art world can appreciate it for what it is. But what is public sculpture supposed to be? Why is everyone so content with it now? I thought there were areas it had ignored - being narrative, perhaps, and confronting people with important issues which are even more important now, the day after the elections. I feel disenchanted with monumental sculpture and where it has gone. It has got to go some other way besides these huge abstractions. They are so cold and don't say anything about our existence. They are like jewelry hung on buildings."[31]

Howell asked Lawless if he had a lawyer, if there was a controversy. He believed he had prepared with a one-year contract that stated the only reason they would force him to move is if they approved development on the site. "Of course, they could hastily approve something," he added.

"I'm not interested in hurting anybody," Billie said. "A lot of people have given me things. In my packages, I've included slides of the model. Obviously on the slides, you can't see the details all that clearly. I don't know, did I dupe people into giving me things? That is a loaded question; I don't think I have and also, with something like this, you have to give the artist a certain amount of leeway. Artists have to have a certain amount of integrity."[32]

As it grew closer to the planned unveiling, David More sent a memo to Jimmy Griffin on November 1, 1984, outlining the upcoming dedication. In it, he mentions that all the relevant city departments approved the sculpture, and reminds Griffin that he left before seeing it. More saw possible "public dissatisfaction, which inevitably seems to accompany these things." He said the City had no actual financial interest and no participation, so they should be in the clear.

"Basically, the sculpture is intended to be a humorous statement," More said. "Making use of vacant land mainly surrounded by automobile traffi c."[33]

So, what could go wrong?

1980s and Collaborating

"To put comedy into my painting is not really a conscious decision; it's more like an attitude ingrained." Kathie Simonds

THE 1980S USHERED IN a new era of art and music. MTV (Music Television) could make or break bands. Michael Jackson would become known as the "King of Pop." New wave and its synthesizers and hair metal were also welcoming a new generation and differentiating them from their parents.

Artsy.net said, "Departing from the visually sparse and intellectual Minimalism and Conceptualism of the previous decade, the 1980s saw a proliferation of artistic approaches that included painting, photography, graffiti, and sculpture. Conservatism surged during the decade, a backlash to the radical countercultural efforts of the 1960s and 1970s." [1]

Keith Haring, Annette Lemieux, Jean-Michel Basquiat, Ross Bleckner, Eric Fischl, Jack Goldstein, Jeff Koons, Sherrie Levine, Robert Longo and other artists left a lasting impact on the art world.

Tiernan Morgan asked in a "Hyperallergic" article in 2018: "Where were the boundaries between advertising, art, and entertainment? Could artists simultaneously commodify themselves and critique consumer culture?" [2]

And Liam Otten wrote in 2003, "The art world of the 1980s was a place of artistic diversity and aesthetic contention. Neo-expressionists jostled for theoretical (and commercial) position with abstract painters, installation and performance artists, appropriationists and others. And little, upon reflection, was as it seemed." [3]

Billie Lawless and Kathie Simonds mixed media with cartoons, layering their artwork with steel, cellophane, and neon. Using sign imagery, graffiti and telling a story about our culture.

Depending on whose view you took, the art community in Buffalo was vibrant in the early 1980s or a total failure. Hallwalls had unique exhibits, drawing a different group of people than Albright-Knox.

Lawless saw himself above other artists. He talked about working artists versus "Sunday" artists and said he felt they had to pay their dues. Yet he himself preferred not to be part of the art scene and was a loner.

Katharine B. Simonds was born in 1949 in Buffalo. She is a painter and mixed-media artist. Her career included shows at Hallwalls in Buffalo in the 1980s through the 2000s. She also was part of three major exhibitions at Burchfield-Penney Art Center in Buffalo, in 2018, 2012, and 1982. In 2021, she took part in Buffalo Arts Studio's "Live on Five 2021," as well as many small shows over the years. She exhibited at AC Gallery in July 1979, and Long Island University in 1985.

In April 1982, she took part in an exhibit of rubber stamp art at Peopleart/Bflo. One review said it showed rubber stamps as instruments of wit, satire, decoration, grace, and sentiment. "Kathie Simond's 'Pig*Mint' series consists of six lithographs whose original impressions appear to have been at least partly made with rubber stamps."[4]

The Duns Scotus Gallery of Daemen College also presented a solo installation of her multiples in 1982.

They often focus the story of *Green Lightning* on the orange neon penises in the four panels. Simonds collaborated with Lawless on the painted panels behind the neon. But whose idea was it for the panels? What did Simonds do? And how much credit does she deserve for the result?

It's been a challenge to find out these answers. When first contacted, Kathie was surprised I found her, and "intrigued and maybe interested in helping." We corresponded several times, and she said she found a bone she "should have picked with Billie." She wanted to speak with some other people and see what they recollected, but must have decided she still wasn't ready to tell the story. One person who knows her said that Simonds is still afraid to tell her story.

Her work at the time seemed to be exactly what Billie was looking for. In 1980, she took part in the Artists Gallery show "Directives." This show involved community input into what the artist was to create. Kate ignored the format and, according to Diane Bertolo in the Buffalo *News*, she "approached her directions with the sense of humor and whimsy associated with her work outside this show."[5]

In May 1981, Simonds was one of seven U.B. art students who exhibited at the H.H. Richardson building of the Buffalo Psychiatric Center, in a show for their master of fine arts. Buffalo *News* arts critic Jack Foran said, "Sometimes she hangs layers of clear plastic, each one decorated with paint or cut paper collage, on top of one another to make huge three-dimensional imaginary maps. And in one room she presents large paper sheet works on an angled display stand and under clear plastic. One sheet analyzes with dictionary definitions, graphs and legends to interpret the graphs."[6]

For the "Sculpture '83" show at Artists Gallery, George Howell described her work in the *Buffalo News* as "virtuoso painting with odd pun s."[7]

She considered life itself a comedy. "We must acknowledge the existence of the mundane in art," she said in 1987. "My subject is the whole human condition, things that I do in daily life. Much of the human emotional gamut has been ignored. You can talk about humor, about satire, as a surface thing, but it is not just part of art, it's part of the human personality. To say that it is trendy is like saying that personality is a fad," she said.[8]

"To put comedy into my painting is not really a conscious decision; it's more like an attitude ingrained," Simonds continued. "When you get to that point where all the parts are jelling, that's my point of satisfaction. ... I used to get down on myself because comedy was interpreted as very light, without much depth to it. But now I realize that some people do it well, some don't."[9]

Simonds doesn't remember exactly when or how she met Billie Lawless. She thinks it was because she was friends with his girlfriend at the time, Kathy Quinn. "I think I first met Billie because she and I were friends," she recalled. "She lived with Billie on Highgate for a while, but it may be because of that I got involved in *Green Lightning*." Billie was also a grad student at U.B. at the same time she was there. "We didn't have contact cause he was rarely at U.B."[10]

The two definitely knew each other before *Green Lightning*. In his 1982 show at Buscaglia-Castellani Art Gallery, he thanked her "For helpful suggestions in the design and layout of this catalogue."[11]

It would appear that Simonds had the whimsical, fun style that Billie wanted to incorporate into *Green Lightning*. The layered designs she did in 1981 certainly sound like aspects of the four boxes contained as part of *Green Lightning*. Throughout 1983 and 1984, she worked with Billie to produce the ten-foot boxes. Together, they knew what the final sculpture would look like. Were they just thumbing their nose at the establishment?

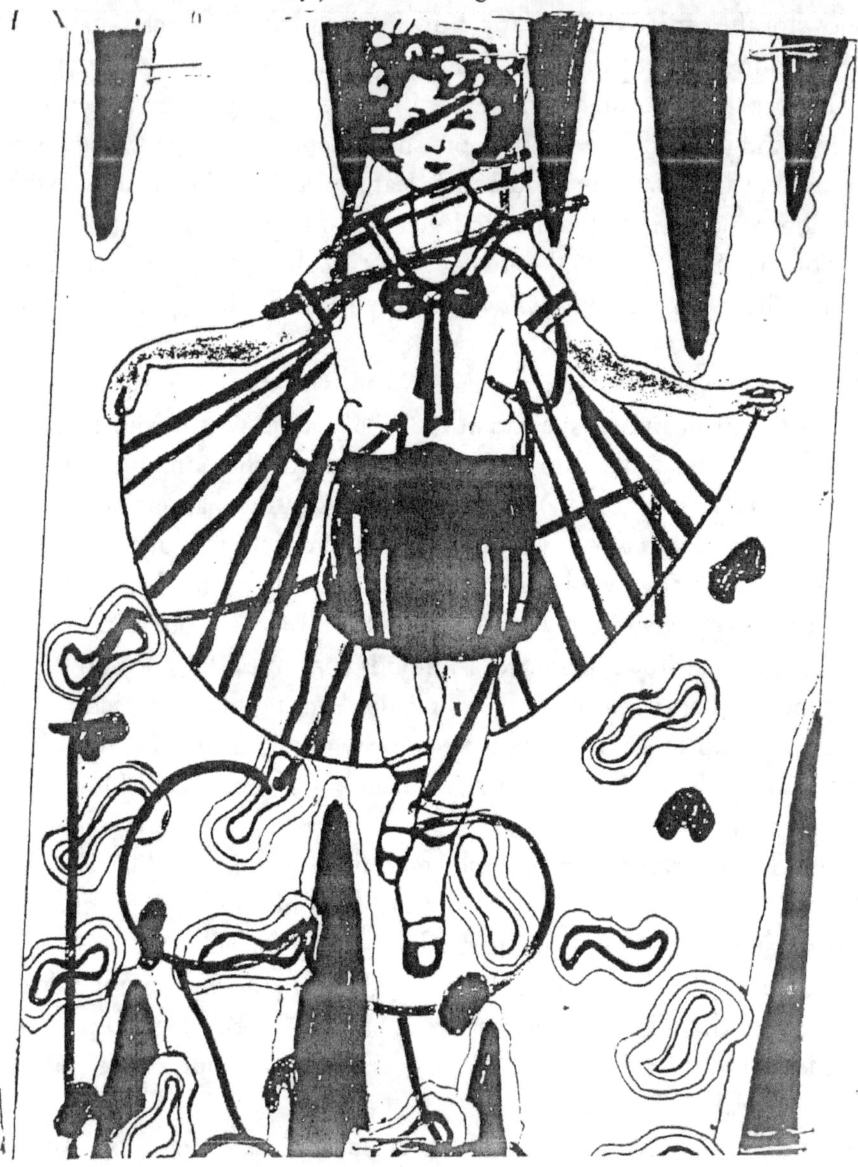

One of the four panels that Kathie Simonds collaborated with Billie Lawless, titled "Jump For Your Life." Lawless vs. Manhattan Psychiatric Center.

UNVEILING

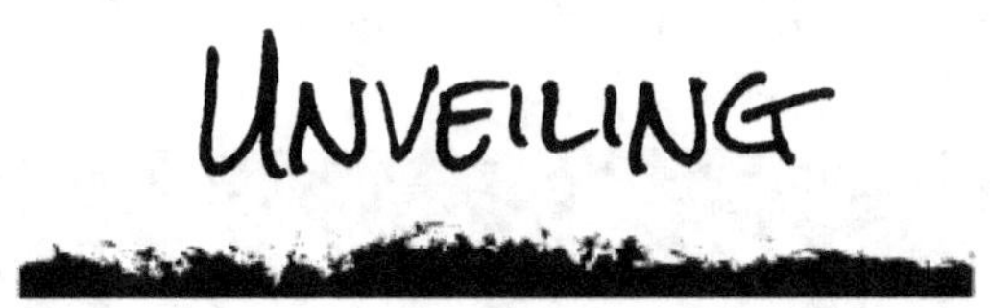

T HE NIGHT BEFORE BILLIE was to unveil his latest work of art, he held a private party to celebrate. Close friends, family, professors, and art patrons received invitations to mingle with the artist. One very important person, however, was conspicuously missing from that party. In fact, David More, who said he was one of Billie's biggest cheerleaders for this project, didn't find out until much later that there was even a pre-party.

More said, "the controversial image had been displayed on invitations Mr. Lawless sent to certain select individuals the day before the dedication of *Green Lightning*. Needless to say, I neither saw nor personally received such an invitation before November 15, 1984."[1]

Mayor Jimmy Griffin said he didn't attend the unveiling because he went to a retirement party for a friend. [2]

The weather in Buffalo the week of November 11, 1984, was getting cold. From a peak of low 50s on Sunday, the week progressively got colder, with lows in the 20s and highs in the 30s. The Dedication and Lighting ceremony took place on Thursday, November 15, 1984. By the time the program started around 5:00 PM, it was drizzling and 46 degrees, but probably felt much colder.

David More was excited to see the sculpture finally unveiled. He still hadn't seen the finished artwork. He dragged Jimmy Griffin's podium to the event to make it look official. More called the Buffalo Police at 4:45 PM to have some officers on hand. "I was concerned about people crossing the street because it was in the middle of the arterial, which was, you know, a busy transit way, whether you're going to the airport or heading downtown." So he called the police to monitor traffic and pedestrians crossing the street.[3]

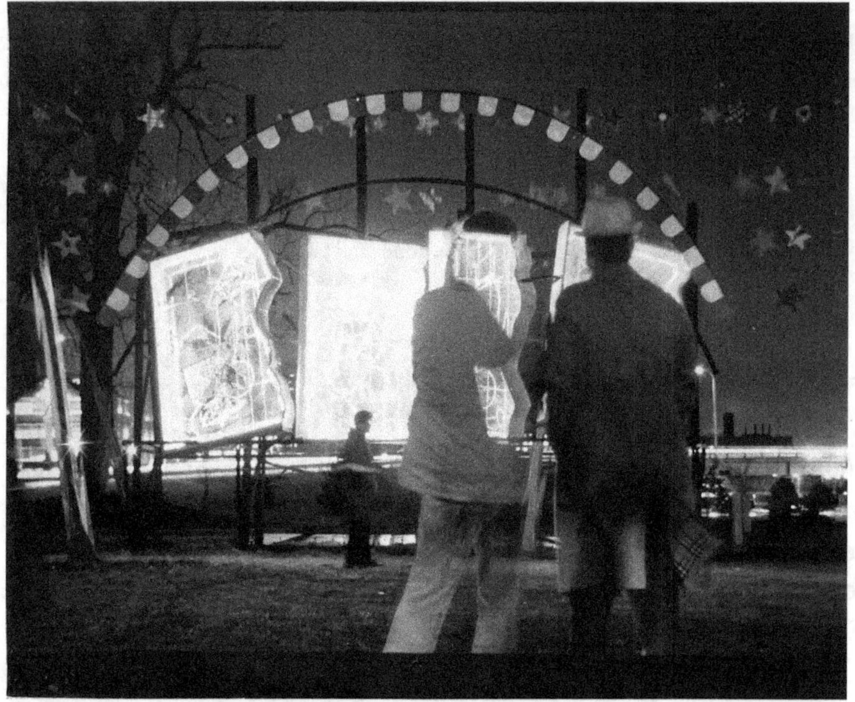

The unveiling of "Green Lightning" in Buffalo, November 15, 1984. It would be lit for about 15 minutes before Billie Lawless turned it off. Photo courtesy of Debra Kolodczak.

Billie Lawless wore a trucker cap that said "West Side Rowing Club" (where he was a coach), jeans, a sweater, and a heavy winter coat. He was unshaven and looked anxious as he milled about. The local television news stations were setting up, their lights shining across his heavy metal sculpture. People were waiting, trying to stay warm.

George Howell was there recording the event and doing interviews.

Channel 7 asked Billie about the unveiling. "I've been just, really essentially, just working on this piece day and night for the last year and a half. I would like to say though that... it will probably be going to Philadelphia next summer" and onward out west to Chicago, take it to LA, maybe do the whole route. ...It's going to be here for another nine months."[4]

The cameraperson couldn't think of anything else to ask.

Lawless: Maybe George can give you some questions here.

Howell: Oh no. Well, I ... I think he should just wait for the, ah... thing to go up... and you know...

Lawless: Take it from there.

David More served as emcee for the event. "Why doesn't everyone come in a little closer?" he asked.

Billie told George he had Molson's beer and offered him one. George got one and handed it to Billie, then started narrating as the unveiling began.

Howell: David More is calling us to the podium.

"To the podium," Lawless repeats.

Samuel D. Magavern, chairperson of the Buffalo Arts Commission, gave the welcoming remarks in front of the giant sculpture. His love of art was well known and in 1990, Magavern would receive the Buffalonian of the Year award from Mayor Griffin.

Magavern started, "You know, some great man, in talking about art, said that art is disturbing, science is reassuring. Billie Lawless' great sculpture here tonight, it's ah, particularly (unknown). Billie is a Buffalo boy that we are proud of and who has been recognized throughout the country and the world. And we have a couple of his pieces of art already in Buffalo. So he is a familiar figure. I think it's very appropriate ...that this is where it is. Because most of the people coming into Buffalo from the airport pass this spot. I am sure that they are going to know Buffalo is up and doing and not asleep when they go by and see Billie's work of art. Katharine Simonds, he collaborated with in preparing the panels with the figures and the work is going to be here for one year. It's a temporary stay.

"We are fortunate having with us tonight some speakers. I'll call on the first of these, which is Mr. William Currie, Director of Hallwalls. Bill, you step up and take over."[5]

Bill Currie was the Director of Hallwalls, Inc., the organization that was Billie's pass through so he could receive donations and they would receive a tax deduction.

"Thank you, Mr. Magavern. Ah...how nice it is to see the weather cooperating with the spirit and...ah.. theme of Billie Lawless' *Green Lightning*," Currie deadpanned. "On behalf of Hallwalls, I am honored to have played a rather minor role in the major part that Billie did in his efforts to create the sculpture. Billie should be praised, not only for his work on *Green*

Lightning, for the citizens of Buffalo as well as visitors who will come through the City, but more importantly for his efforts to show through hard work and persistence he could garner and get together people from the private sector to donate and support his efforts as well as getting the permits and the government to cooperate for this sculpture. I am happy to be a part of it and I hope many artists in our community will take Billie's work as an example of what can be done in the future. Thank you."

Sam Magavern continued, "Hallwalls were very helpful to the artist. It served as a sponsor and helped him in many ways."

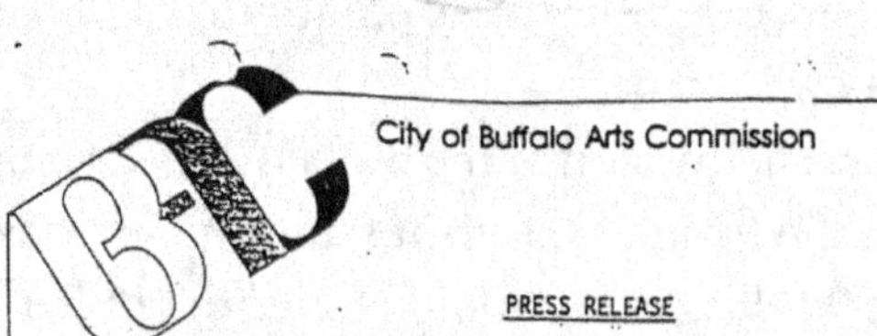

City of Buffalo Arts Commission

PRESS RELEASE

Buffalo Artist, Billie Lawless, will dedicate his public sculpture "Green Lightning" on Friday, November 16th at 5:00 p.m. The sculpture is a whimsical installation combining a variety of media in a colorful and humorous fashion encompassing an area 7,500 sq. ft. large. Mr. Lawless collaborated with artist Kathy Simonds on images within large plastic panels located at the center of the installation. It is a temporary structure located within the Elm/Oak Arterial north of Genesee St. scheduled to remain for a period of one year. Soon afterwards it will be installed at the Port of History Museum in Philadelphia, PA.

This $80,000 project was financed entirely by donations the artist was able to secure from a multitude of private sources ranging from several of the areas largest corporations to individuals. Contributors number over seventy-five. The dedication is a tribute to the artist's persistent efforts on several different levels and the broad base of community support the project has enjoyed since it began over two years ago.

Mr. Lawless's proposal was reviewed and unanimously approved by the City of Buffalo Arts Commission, Common Council, and Urban Renewal Agency which has provided the land on a temporary basis. HALLWALLS gallery has served as a sponsor assisting the artist in many of the necessary arrangements.

Mr. Lawless was graduated from Rutgers College in 1974 and received an M.F.A. from the State University of New York at Buffalo. He has exhibited extensively throughout the United States. Other outdoor installations in Buffalo can be seen at Buffalo State College and the Nichols School campus.

For further information
contact: Billie Lawless
          837-3818

920 City Hall   Buffalo, New York 14202

Press release from the Buffalo Arts Commission announcing
the unveiling of "Green Lightning" on November 16, 1984.

In the late 1960s, D. Bruce Johnstone had been Senator Walter Mondale's Administrative Assistant and wrote "his first anti-Vietnam War speech along with him." When he became president of Buffalo State College, he got involved with the local arts community, including Studio Arena Theater, and worked with the Black and Hispanic communities to bring minority students to the college.[6]

Magavern continued, "Our next speaker is known to us as the president of the University College of Buffalo, who has done so much in the community and brought the community and the college together and a good example of this is tonight coming out here tonight to tell us about some of his thoughts. Bruce."

"Thank you Sam," Johnstone started. "I like Bill Currie's introduction. I think the weather tonight, with its whimsical, warm, wet, mercurial atmosphere, is right in keeping with this *Green Lightning*. It is a privilege for me to be here. I think I'm here in part because Sam thought I would come out on a night like this. (laughs) But, also because I was one of the first, I think, in Buffalo to grasp this extraordinary combination of artistic talent and what I can only call great citizenship of Billie Lawless. I was in the city only three months, I think, made a speech, a very wise speech, Billie read. And I talked about beautifying Buffalo State College campus. And Billie wrote to me a letter within a few weeks of that and said 'I want to help' and extraordinarily it wasn't just talk. He included in his letter a marvelous series of slides of models and maquettes, prints of sculpture he was prepared to do and secondly he said, 'I'll make it possible to build it and I'll raise the funds for you.' That was a deal I couldn't refuse. He worked at it with us, we have a marvelous piece of Billie's at the College and, I'll invite you to go there and see that one as well, but I think what it represents is not only the talent... ah, and I think in this wonderful, playful, whimsical piece here we see more of that talent but also Billie Lawless the citizen who makes it possible to put this public art in this city. So Billie, on behalf of an awful lot of people who have become your admirers, I also want to thank you for continuing this brand; your artistic citizenship to our city. Thank you."

Sam Magavern, "Thank you Bruce. Our next speaker we are fortunate to have, I understand, is very close to Billie. He's a teacher at the school at the University, and he knows Billie's work and ...is known nationally and internationally, Duayne Hatchett."

Hatchett was a prolific sculptor, painter, and State University at Buffalo professor that Billie had studied under. He arrived in Buffalo in 1968 and for 24 years headed the sculpture program at U.B.

"We choose graduate students from the level of their ability," Hatchett started. "Almost always to be artists and we hope that they will develop into (indistinguishable). I certainly think that Billie Lawless fits that category. It's a pleasure to work with Billie Lawless and I must say that I have never met another person in the community, another artist especially in the University, who had the ability to go out in the community and develop conceptually the financing and the acceptance of placing works and developing artistic ideas. This has been revealing to me especially interesting because I think it's difficult enough for artists to fit into society, which always seems hostile to the artist. And Billie Lawless has proven that he can do it and do it with a lot of class. I think that Bill Lawless has certainly proved with each piece that he puts up that he has an inventive, humorous attitude towards his concepts of art and, oh, always comes through with flying colors. And I hope that the public appreciates this as much as I'm sure his endeavors should pay off. It's a very difficult thing to build this kind of thing. I went down to his studio a few times while this thing was going up and you can't believe the kind of involvement which goes into this. And I congratulate the City to continually to be helpful to experimentation in art and to the ideas of further developing artists and ideas."

Sam Magavern continued, "Thank you Duayne, and that's very good, from a known great artist to a becoming artist. Bill has some great faculties. Anybody that can come into Buffalo and raise 80,000 bucks to put this up has to be, oh, quite a man. So he has lots going for him and it's wonderful. I know he appreciates and we all appreciate your coming tonight. The work has been approved by the Buffalo Arts Commission and by the Urban League (he meant Urban Renewal) and the Buffalo Council and I don't think they could have picked as better place than they have here. And I'm sure it will be a trademark for us for the next year."

David More stepped up and said, "I think Billie might want to say something."

"Oh, that would be great," Magavern said. "Bill, if you would. I'm sorry. Over here."

It was finally Billie's turn to speak. He stood next to Sam Magavern and glanced around the crowd of about 30 cold and excited people. He thanked some of his sponsors, and "Pamela Mays, my loved one, who has put up with this whole *Green Lightning* for a year and a half, (she) has, oh great patience and understanding and been very supportive. People, throughout the city, the City government, the Mayor, who was wonderful when it came to installing this piece here in the Elm-Oak Arterial. The Griffis' with the Ashford-Hollow complex, giving me the space to construct it with the overhead cranes, were just very supportive. And, oh, I think this is a great town for the arts and we should all really push forward and I think there's really much more potential here to be tapped. And I see other great great projects possibly for other artists here in this town. I would like to thank you all for coming out in this very bad weather tonight, and I think, without any other to-do, I'm gonna turn the switch and throw *Green Lightning* on for its first showing here in Buffalo."

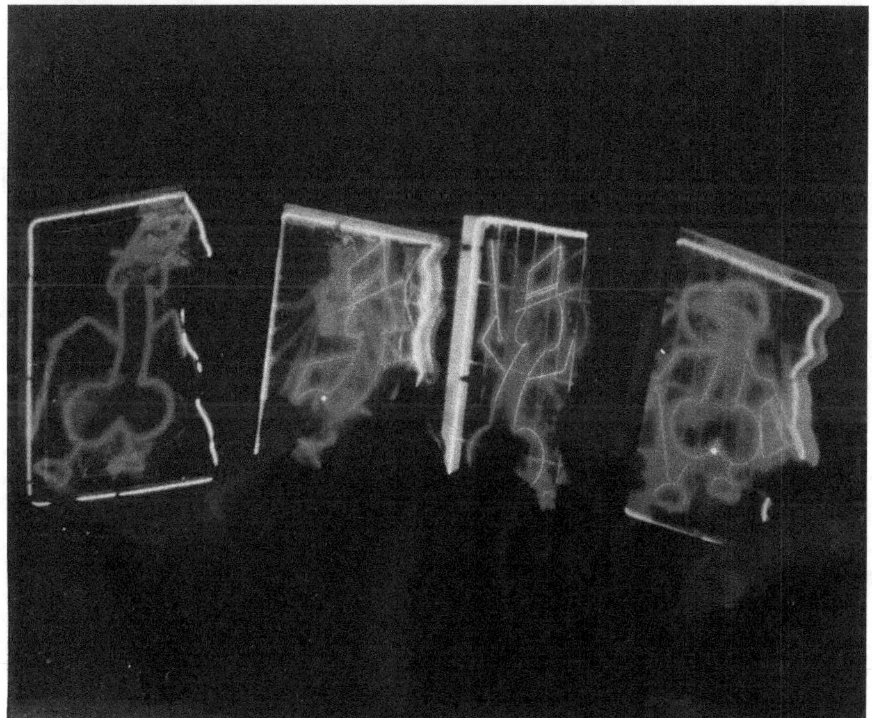

The four neon panels of "Green Lightning" lit simultaneously for effect.
Photo by Debra Kolodczak.

The crowd gave him a roar of approval and applauded as he grinned and raised his fists. He turned away and walked back about fifteen feet to the power box, crouched down, opened the box, flipped the switch, and the crowd roared its approval as the sculpture powered on. But the applause died within seconds as the bright NUVO colored neon panels were lit, and the blinking Mr. Peanut figures danced across the panels.[7]

Sam Magavern admired the sculpture. "It really is very attractive, it's, it looks like, very interesting," George Howell recorded. Magavern, an elderly man, may have been too close to get the full effect.

George Howell asked him about his insights into the piece. He said, "Oh, I think it's wonderful, that we can have this, be the first place, that he shows this in, first showing of this as he is a local boy, and oh, its well situated to impress people coming into Buffalo that we are really moving out, and it's, an unusual piece and people are going to be surprised how it grows on them, in my opinion."

Howell asked if he thought the piece would be controversial. Magavern said, "As I said in my opening, as one great man put it, 'art is disturbing while science is reassuring.' I think it will be disturbing to many people, but I think it's like anything else that's new, it should disturb and art itself is meant to disturb, not to be complacent. Art is something that moves and moves you and moves along. It is interesting that art over the years, you know, becomes a historical record of our society because you have to look at and you must interpret it in the times it was created."[8]

"So you, you aren't concerned if people are, ah, you know, upset, are disturbed by this piece?" Howell pressed.

"Oh, no," Magavern continued, "Nothing in this world is great unless it does disturb."

David More recalled, "There were a lot of ironic things that Sam said in the speech."[9] More was at the ceremony with his girlfriend, Debbie Kolodczak. While she was taking photos of the sculpture, David was trying to get a better view. He said he was up close, next to the corporation counsel, when the lights went on. "When you're up close, it looked like scrambled eggs because the lights were so bright." You couldn't make out the figures, so he started walking back. "I'm walking away from the crowd, literally walking backwards."[10]

More said he was angry and asked Billie why he didn't tell him about the neon. Billie said he had just installed it within the previous day.

Billie was within earshot of Debbie when she commented to him she liked it until she saw the neon. "Oh, another example of male dominance," she said.

Billie said, "No no no, it's a double-edged sword." He would continue to use those words to describe the sculpture.

Mark Griffis was in attendance with his mother because she wanted to support Billie. "I went to the opening with my mom... because my mother knew the Lawless family very well, just like our family had eight kids, they must have had seven or eight or nine something like that and the families knew each other, so my mom wanted to go to the dedication." When the power was turned on, Mark's mother said two words, "Oh my."[11]

His father, Larry, was also there. He said that Mark was running the Essex Street complex and made it affordable for Billie to do the sculpture. "We have a skylight there, and structure went right straight up into the skylight. In the foundry, the thing's absolutely massive. As it was being constructed, the amount of absolute raw energy it took to build it. I mean, we're used to building big projects over there, but I was really amazed by the effort that Bill put into it. There's so many different media involved too. It's a multi-media piece, and it took a tremendous amount of skill."[12]

When George Howell asked Griffis if he thought it would be easier for other artists to do public work after this, he said, "Definitely," because everybody did their homework, and Billie became a textbook case on how to get art in the public domain. "I think Billie has done it properly with all the proper authority, now whatever controversy there may be that's up to each one of us, individually, our responses to it. But there isn't going to be any question about does he have the authority, the right, the privilege to put it here. That sort of thing should be behind us."[13]

Billie's attorney, Leslie Foschio, was also in attendance. "I think it's just great; it's exciting; it's colorful, inventive; it's refreshing. I think it helps to put Buffalo on the national culture (map?)"[14]

When Howell asked if he thought there would be controversy, Foschio said, "I don't think that it's controversial at all. I think it's delightful and I think that people will think that it adds some needed color and variety to the landscape here. This is a development area: and obviously this is not a permanent facility, so I think people will appreciate that and it's kind of an experimental form of culture and I think it's in the correct place to do that kind of artistic experimentation."[15]

Howell thanked him. "Anything to help my friend Billie Lawless," Foschio said.

Joanne Posluszny had been invited to the unveiling but was out of town and didn't think she'd make it. As she drove from the airport, she realized it was the time of the unveiling and had a little trouble finding it. When she did, it was still lit. She was alone in her car and said it had a very carnival-like look to it. She then saw there were a lot of police in the area and thought it seemed strange for an art opening, and being alone, she left.[16]

By now, David More was back even further away from the glowing neon sculpture. There were four or five police cards and the cops were "laughing their asses off." By this time, he could make out the images. As he's walking back, he was saying to himself, "Oh no, oh my god, holy shit!" He was upset that he went to bat for this sculpture. "As soon as I saw the neon figures, I realized that Billie had been seriously deceptive throughout his official presentations. I took it as a personal and professional insult that I was never informed of nature of the imagery."[17]

More turned to the cops and asked, "'What's so funny?' One cop said, 'Oh Mr. More, the mayor went for this?'"[18]

It is possible that Sam Magavern was also too close to get the full effect of the sculpture when he commented on it. David More said, "Magavern could be a very cagey gentleman, having an uncanny ability to turn situations around." He remembers showing Sam the pictures Deb Kolodczak took, and he said, "I really don't see anything offensive in these."[19]

George Howell approached David. "I'm playing roving reporter here. You care to add a couple of comments here?"

More sarcastically replied, "I'm not going to work tomorrow," then laughed. He said he was responsible for presenting Billie to the city. "All of them approved it."

Howell asked, "Was there any question about it, you know, like the piece creating controversy or there being objections to anything of that sort?"

"I think most of the objections stemmed from a misunderstanding of the piece," More said. "It's really lyrical and more kind of whimsical and humorous."

Howell said, "I can see that these rows of police cars behind us are having a lot of chuckles over this, you know, so you think that the piece is whimsical and, you know, that once people get used to it there won't be any reason for controversy about it then?"

"No-o," More answered. "I think that they're going to basically enjoy it. They're laughing I think (laughs)."

"Within a half-hour of talking with me," Howell wrote in *Buffalo Arts*

Review, "More would be telling newsman Dan Hausle of Channel 7s 'Eyewitness News' that Lawless had misrepresented his work."[20] More denied this accusation.

Howell approached the officers. He said he heard them chuckling and asked if they had any comment. One answered they couldn't comment on the record. A second said, "The only thing I can say is that those are dancing cocks if I've ever seen one."[21]

Lt. William Conwall of the 4th Precinct was not laughing when he submitted his report. He said that he and officer M. Sadlocha were there for five minutes and at approximately 5:20 PM *Green Lightning* was lit up. This Buffalo police officer said he was shocked when the multi-colored panels were replaced by four orange neon "testicles along with the penis." He went into detail and noted that they had feet, hands, and a top hat and cane. "While one went from a flaccid state to a turgid state in several moves of the lights."[22]

After several minutes, he knew this was a job for Detective John Dugan, the city's one-man vice squad. So he contacted Dugan to see if he thought it was obscene. Conwall said that "several" cars stopped them to voice their displeasure, including a family with two children, who, gasp!, saw neon penises. He claimed that traffic entering the Kensington Expressway was "coming to a crawl" and created a hazard and his station house took several telephone complaints from citizens who thought it everything from "dirty, filthy to pornographic."[23]

Conwall said he, his partner, and "most of the men in my platoon" who saw it (even though they claimed to be open-minded) found this sculpture to be "blatantly outrageous and obscene."[24]

Maybe they weren't so open-minded after all.

After about fifteen minutes, Billie turned the lights off. The crowd dispersed pretty rapidly after that. Detective Dugan arrived at the scene to inspect the art. As Billie was preparing to leave, Dugan confronted him and explained who he was.

The Buffalo *News* reported that "shortly after the dignitaries and most of the crowd left, the vice-squad showed up, scouring over the now un-plugged sculpture with their flashlights, looking for what officer John Dugan described as the 'male anatomy.'"[25] They asked Billie to re-illumi-nate the sculpture, but he suspiciously said he couldn't find the key to the electrical box.[26] An officer told him to move his car off the grass or he would be arrested, so Lawless went home about 8:30 PM.

Lawless said he was so unnerved by talking to Dugan that later that evening he called Sam Magavern of the Arts Commission, to complain about alleged threats from Dugan. Magavern stood by the artist who "felt relieved" by assurances of support. [27]

As for David More? He went home. First, he called Jim Militello and told him about the unveiling. Militello suggested More wait for the 11 o'clock news to see if they ran the story. [28]

Jimmy Griffin said he received a call. "I believe it was from a TV station. I got home, and they said that their switchboard was well lit that night with calls."[29]

Channel 7 news anchor Irv Weinstein led his newscast by saying, "You've got to see this one to believe it. Eyewitness News man Dan Hausle is ready to give us an eyeful. But first send the kids out of the room." They then showed the lit-up *Green Lightning* sculpture for about 5 seconds. They ran an additional 15 seconds in total.[30]

On the next day's 6 PM newscast, Weinstein no longer warned to get the kids out of the room. They showed the sculpture five times for about a total of 30 seconds. News director Jim Kirik said, "We showed it whenever it was appropriate to the story."[31]

David More said the TV stations covering the event devastated him. He knew this was bad, so he called Jim Militello back and Militello said, "Uh, I think you better call the mayor." David said he knew the mayor well enough to call him that late at night. He poured himself a stiff drink and called Jimmy Griffin at home.[32] Griffin assumed More knew all along about the suggestive images and yelled at him.[33]

Channel 2 underestimated the seriousness of the incident. On Thursday, they only showed about 10 seconds of footage at the end of the newscast. The next day at 5 PM anchor Rich Kellman "jazzed up" a story with clips from the movie "The Producers," making light of the artwork. Buffalo *News* TV critic Alan Pergament said it was a good way to look at the situation. When the police and city got involved, they took it seriously, but they did not show the artwork again.[34]

Lastly, Channel 4 didn't even run the story on opening night. The next day it was in the middle of the newscast. They ran an "Art or Porn" story and two of the three reporters were leaning toward porn. Channel 4 never showed the sculpture lit up. News director Jim Peppard said, "We didn't show it because it was unsuitable for viewing on this station."[35]

David More said the decision to take down the offending panels "was in the process of being made" that night. "The mayor... wanted it down since he learned the suggestive nature of the piece."[36]

Dan Herbeck was a young reporter for the Buffalo *News* in 1984. Herbeck was astonished that leaders of the city of Buffalo would have agreed up front to something like that. He said that Buffalo is a pretty conservative city and if Billie Lawless told city officials, "I'm going to produce an artwork that shows giant penises with semen spurting out of them into the air in downtown Buffalo," then he would totally side with him and say that he was in the right because he was completely honest with them. But, if that's not what he told him, "then I would have real questions about what he did, right? Because I did see the artwork, and it clearly depicted the giant penis with stuff spurting out of it.

"I was flabbergasted when I saw this thing," Herbeck added. "I mean, I'm not a real conservative guy. But I had little kids at that time. I wouldn't have wanted to explain that statue to my two young sons."[37]

Al Price was sitting in his office at the School of Architecture at U.B. when he received a call from David More asking him to go downtown. Price said they invited him to the unveiling, but he didn't attend. "I hadn't made a point of putting it on my calendar to go downtown for this thing because we were doing enough stuff that I just didn't think it was that critical or important. It was all over but the shouting by the time that I got there," Price said. "David pulled the plug on this trash. So what was to have been a wonderful public unveiling turned out to be a disaster. All the media were there and, of course, they thought it was a big hoot. Poor David More was terribly embarrassed because he had lead the city down the Primrose path with this guy Billie Lawless, and not keeping track of what Lawless was doing only to discover that he had this outrageous piece of work that was coming into the public domain." Price said that David More "was very much chastened after this."[38]

But the dancing neon penises didn't offend everyone. Prolific Buffalo portrait painter George Palmer, still painting at 97 years old in 2022, said that he saw the artwork, but it didn't offend him. He said that fellow artist Lawless "was working on the edge. I mean, we never saw anything quite like that. The artists accepted it for the most part... they were kind of neutral about it... artists don't feel that they should be censored.[39]

"But, there are people who see a nude and they get really upset." Palmer said that he had his share of complaints over the years from people offended by nude portraits he did. But as for *Green Lightning*, "a lot of people were, I mean, just the local man on the street, was really offended by it."[40]

Almost immediately after the fallout from the unveiling started, Larry Griffis lent an experienced hand. "My father went on a bit of a TV circuit with him," Mark Griffis said, "because he had already done the (*Birds in*) *Flight* controversy, (*Sprit of*) *Woman* controversy, which became iconic sculptures in Buffalo. He really went to bat for him and (they did) a few (TV) shows together."[41]

Within the first couple days, Arts Commission Chairperson Sam Magavern said he saw nothing pornographic or questionable about the piece, but said, "If people see something in it that's wrong, we have to change it."[42]

Alan Pergament, the television critic for the Buffalo *News,* graded the coverage by the local news stations, after viewing "private screenings" at each station. "While doing the best reporting job and blanketing the story, Channel 7 is guilty of its usual crime - unnecessary bad taste. For a change, Channel 2 is not guilty of missing a big story and actually handled the case judiciously. Channel 4 got caught with its pants down, completely missing the story on opening night. But it was not guilty of any exploitation and certainly is the station that Morality in Media would support."

He said that other than overusing the video, Channel 7 did the best early coverage of the incident. [43]

But that was far from the end of the controversy.

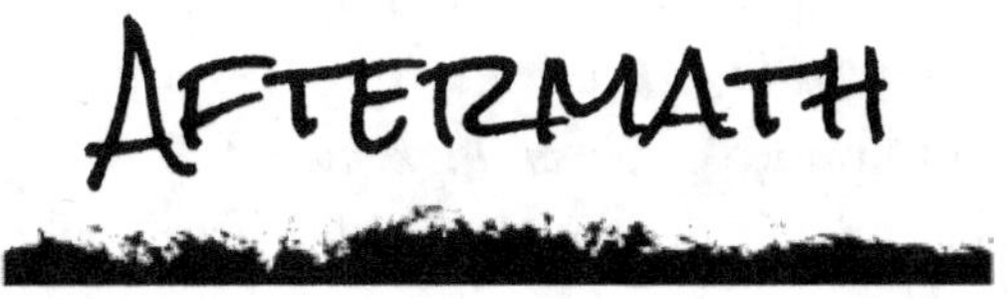

AFTERMATH

"We'll take it down if he's not going to take it
down." Jimmy Griffin

THE NEW YORK *TIMES* wrote, "According to police reports, passers-by began to complain that the neon figures were obscene immediately upon the unveiling of the sculpture."[1]

The day after the unveiling, a lot of things happened. Mayor Griffin claimed many complaints poured into the City Hall switchboard. That morning, Friday November 16, the mayor's office was buzzing. Jim Militello, David More, Griffin, and Gregory Dudek huddled, trying to decide what to do. One can imagine that the mayor's assistant, Ron Anthony, was also present. Dudek and Militello assured the mayor that David More didn't know what Billie had planned.

Jim Militello recalled they were in Griffin's office going over the agreement. They were deciding what the details of the agreement said. "While I'm talking to the corporation counsel about it, Griffin's on the phone with somebody. He says, 'Yeah, you think you can get that front-end loader down there? You think you can get it down right now? Yeah, just run right over the damn thing. Bye.'"[2]

Militello knew that was bad. "Griffin, he was something unique and special. He didn't operate by the normal constraints of society. So all our jaws dropped, we all turned to him, he hangs up the phone and I don't know who said it, if it was me or somebody else. 'Hey mayor, instead of compounding the problem with somebody's suing somebody, can't you just disconnect the power?'"[3]

Billie Lawless also seemed to operate outside of the normal constraints of society. But depending on who you speak to, his decisions seemed unorthodox and Griffin's didn't.

"Good idea," Griffin said. So he called the guy back and ordered them to shut the power to *Green Lightning* off. Militello thought it was hysterical. He said he still had a photo of *Green Lightning*.[4]

"During that period," Griffin later said, "I believe I talked to Dave More ... and I believe that morning I tried to reach Mr. Lawless by phone, couldn't get in touch with him."[5]

Militello said, "Well, the only thing I recollect is a dialogue with Wally Przepasniak. Asked him to make arrangements. I'm sure there was some back and forth, and basically hired a contractor to take it down. I don't remember the specific conversation, but I know I would have had a discussion with Wally about removing the statue, the sculpture. I don't remember the particulars of that discussion."[6]

Meanwhile, Billie says he met with Ellicott council member Jim Pitts, who recommended that he contact attorneys to get ready for a legal battle with the city. Billie then headed to the site to complete some work on the sculpture.

"It's art, it's a sculpture," Lawless told reporters as he continued to put some final touches on the project, expecting to turn it back on. He had a one-year contract with the city and said he would not take it down. "People's interpretation is up to them. Perhaps it has something to do with their minds."[7]

Meanwhile, Mayor Griffin ordered the artwork dismantled. "We'll take it down if he's not going to take it down," Griffin said. "I wondered what the hell was going up there. Now I know." [8]

Advisors told Griffin not to label *Green Lightning* as pornographic or obscene or he'd be wading into murky waters.[9]

There was a letter dated November 16, 1984, addressed to Billie Lawless from James Militello.

Dear Mr. Lawless,

You are herein advised that the Permit Agreement authorizing your installation and display of the referenced sculpture is terminated effective immediately.

Please be further advised that I have ordered said sculpture dismantled and the components thereof stored.

Arrangements for return of those components to you may be made by contacting Mr. Walter Przepasniak, Department of Community Development, telephone number 855-5046.

James R. Militello, Vice-Chairperson City of Buffalo Urban Renewal Agency.

David More said he sent the cease and desist letter, but "I didn't tell the secretary to send it return receipt requested, to send it to me, and then he denied that he ever got it. Of course he got it, but because there was no return receipt requested, there was no proof that he got it."[10]

Lawless said he never received it and no one in City Hall could ever prove they sent it.

While Billie was at the site working on the sculpture, he looked up and spotted a bulldozer heading toward the sculpture. He ran alongside it for 20 or 30 yards, while being "ignored" by the bulldozer driver. Several Buffalo police cars soon arrived at the scene and "they ignored me, as well," Lawless said. "I was dismayed, scared, and frightened."[11]

Things were happening quickly when another person, not yet involved, received a phone call. It was attorney Michael J. Brown, the managing attorney for Diebold, Bermingham, Gorman, Brown and Cook located at 1500 Statler Towers. On the other end of the line was Billie's attorney, Les Foschio. He asked Brown if he could head down to the Elm-Oak Arterial, where *Green Lightning* was located. According to his former partner Mark J. Mahoney, Brown "would have been the First Amendment thinker," which could be why they selected him.[12]

Mike Brown left his office in the Statler Towers shortly after. He arrived at the scene just a few minutes later and was alarmed by what was unfolding in front of him. There were "police officers. I saw workers, I saw a bull-dozer, and I saw various people standing around, and I saw Mr. Lawless on top of the sculpture." At least three police cars had been called to the scene, along with many officers. The bulldozer was "near the base of the sculpture."[13]

James D. Griffin, Chairman

November 16, 1984

William Lawless
324 Highgate Avenue
Buffalo, New York 14215

Re: Permit Agreement - "Green Lighting" Sculpture

Dear Mr. Lawless:

You are hereby advised that the Permit Agreement authorizing your installation and display of the referenced sculpture is terminated effective immediately.

Please be further advised that I have ordered said sculpture dismantled and the components thereof stored.

Arrangements for return of those components to you may be made by contacting Mr. Walter Przepasniak, Department of Community Development, telephone number 855-5046.

JAMES R. MILITELLO
Vice-Chairman
CITY OF BUFFALO
URBAN RENEWAL AGENCY

The letter BURA says they sent to Lawless, which he claims he never received. Courtesy David More.

Billie and his six-foot-one frame had scrambled to the top of *Green Lightning* to stop the bulldozer from knocking his sculpture over. "I was freezing cold and scared.[14] I didn't know what to do," Lawless said. "I was extremely frightened and shaken."[15]

There were also acetylene tanks to the right of the sculpture. "Some of the workers were standing around," Brown said. "One in particular that I was concerned about was getting ready to cut ...the base of the sculpture with an acetylene torch. He was approaching. I was very concerned. He had gotten close to it or was about to. I was trying to get the police officer who appeared to be in charge to get things calmed down so that we could arrange for some – some negotiations."[16]

Brown introduced himself to Billie, still perched on top of *Green Lightning*. "I told him who I was, and that I had been called by Les Foschio and asked to represent him." Brown then spoke to Captain Frank W. Lustan from the Buffalo Police Department. "I asked him if we couldn't back the workers off from the base of the sculpture and if we couldn't get some time so that I could get to City Hall and perhaps talk to someone in the Corporation Counsel's office, someone at City Hall to see if we couldn't reach an accommodation here before someone got hurt."[17]

Lustan was an officer that had worked the night shift with the vice squad on Chippewa Street (known as a red-light district at the time), arresting sex workers and others. In 1978, he was accused of harassment by a man Lustan was investigating on vice charges. They accused him of threatening to break the man's legs and shove an iron rod in his head. The judge dropped the charges. [18]

While Brown was trying to restore calm, Billie was yelling at the workers, "Please don't destroy it, just get away from it." If Billie Lawless had thought he would pull a quick one on the city of Buffalo, he underestimated Jimmy Griffin's swift hammer.[19]

While standing on top of *Green Lightning*, he said he watched as employees "cut open the power pedestal. They cut the lock off the box, they opened it up." This was after the Niagara Mohawk Power company had already disconnected the power to the street.[20]

Lawless said *Green Lightning* was now powerless, so there was no reason to cut the wires on the sculpture. "After he finished cutting the lock off the box," Lawless said, "he started to cut one of the legs of the sculpture... with a cutting torch, a welding torch." All while Billie was standing on top of the sculpture. "I thought I was going to get killed," he said.[21]

Captain Lustan told Brown that he was going to arrest Billie for "the exhibition or promoting an obscene exhibition," which a flabbergasted Brown then explained to Billie.[22]

The Buffalo *News* reported that Sam Magavern arrived to mediate and Billie shouted to him, "The idea of ripping this down without any thought is a knee-jerk reaction, which I oppose. If they go about knocking this down, they'll break a valid contract."[23]

Brown then talked to reporter Wadi Sawabini from television station Channel 4 and asked if he could use the telephone in his news car to call

City Hall.

"I got in the cruiser," Brown said, and dialed City Hall. "I first spoke to Bill Carey in the Corporation Counsel's office. He had been there a long time… and I knew him. I spoke with him and asked him whether he could intercede with the mayor or whoever was in charge… and he directed me to Greg Dudek."[24]

Brown then contacted Dudek, who was with Jim Militello in or near the mayor's office. He asked if it was possible to call people off down at the scene. He also wanted "to arrange a meeting with the mayor or whoever was in charge to discuss how to resolve this thing." He was put on hold while Dudek, Griffin, and Militello conferred. Captain Lustan stood near the cruiser listening in on the conversation. After Brown got off the phone with Dudek, he explained what had taken place to Billie, who then came down off the sculpture.

With Lustan and Billie present, Mike Brown explained that "the status quo was going to be maintained, that was the agreement, and we could all go home." He told Billie, "there would be no further effort to dismantle *Green Lightning*," but the lights would not be turned on "and that there would be no further attempt on his part to display the piece." He also wouldn't be arrested as part of the deal.[25]

Lawless had spent about two hours on top of his sculpture in freezing weather, watching a Niagara Mohawk Power Corp. crew cut off power to the sculpture and a city crew pull apart electrical connections at its base, just as Mayor Griffin had ordered.[26] "It's crazy to send out all these bulldozers and stuff," Lawless said, "but Jimmy Griffin - that's his style."[27]

"His attorney has agreed that his client will not turn it back on," Captain Lustan reported. "In turn, we'll discuss it next week."[28]

They all left the sculpture site and Mike Brown called Greg Dudek when he got back to his office to see when they could set up the meetings that they had discussed. He was told to call Dudek back later that afternoon, but Dudek said they would talk again on Monday, and "I received his assurances that nothing would happen over the weekend."[29]

"In agreeing to leave the neon elements off when first notified that the mayor objected and, in seeking to negotiate its removal, I acted reasonably," Billie said.[30]

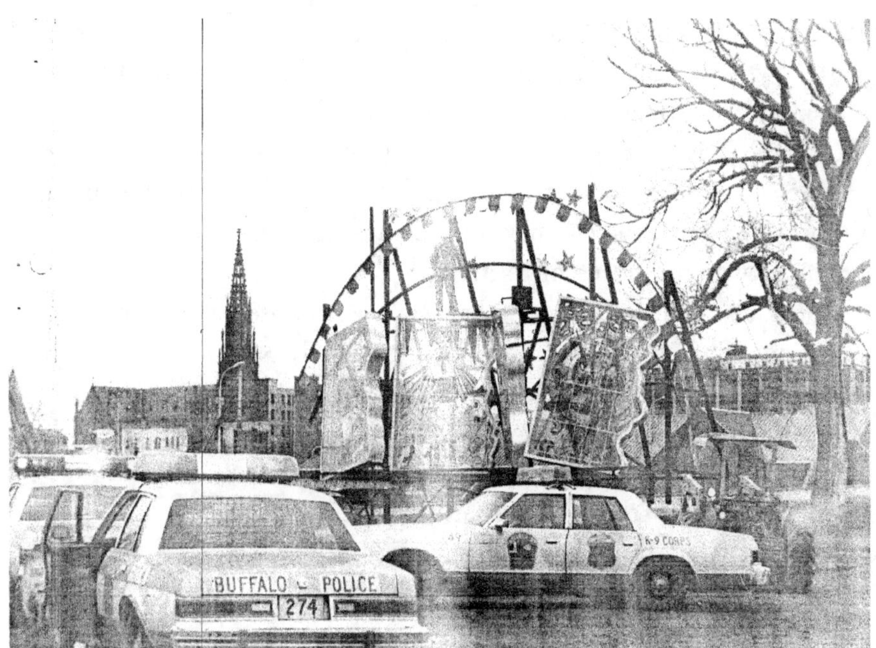

Billie Lawless stood on top of "Green Lightning," November 16, 1984, to prevent the city from destroying it. Photo courtesy of Debra Kolodczak.

Jim Militello said, "I know the outcome was disconnecting the power of the sculpture on that Friday. I remember a conversation with Wally saying that he had the power cut."[31]

• • • ● • ● • ● • • •

Green Lightning sat dark for the weekend. On Monday morning, Mike Brown called B.U.R.A. attorney Greg Dudek, but couldn't get ahold of him and left a message. "I didn't get a call back. I called again, and - - there were two or three calls. I finally reached him, and he explained at that point that... the City and he was researching the various issues and needed more time and I was to call him Tuesday morning." He talked to Greg Dudek Tuesday morning, but he said they were not ready to meet.[32]

Brown could not reach Greg Dudek again and felt they were dragging it out and nothing was happening. We ran into a "flat stone-wall," Billie said.[33]

They were concerned, but unaware of what was transpiring behind the scenes. In fact, "I was never able to arrange it," Brown said. "They never gave me a time at which I could come over to - - sit down and discuss it."[34]

Meanwhile, at City Hall, Dudek sent Griffin notes on how they could proceed. He said they could negotiate with Lawless to dismantle or agree to keep the electric off, or have him replace the neon. They could send in city crews to dismantle and destroy the sculpture and deal with the outcome afterwards. They could also have Lawless arrested on obscenity charges, or begin a lawsuit for breach of contract.

Dudek also sent Griffin two identical press releases, except for the last paragraph. The one Griffin did not choose, said "Now we hope to enter into negotiations which will have the structure standing with the exception of the existing neon light forms or replacement of those forms with others which will be less controversial."[35]

This is the press release Mayor Griffin issued.

> Because of the public clamor and the threatened public calamity that very well could arise by a continued display of the neon light component, I ordered the sculpture to be dismantled.
>
> After all, the location is on a major arterial to downtown Buffalo and the controversy that the neon lighting caused could easily have resulted in major traffic jams to nothing of potential property damage and perhaps even physical injury as a result of automobile accidents.
>
> Coupled with the apparent breach of the agreement, the final sculpture appeared to create a public nuisance, because, among other things, it had the potential of tending to obstruct and rendering a public street dangerous.
>
> Even though I ordered the whole thing taken down, Commissioner Militello, through negotiations with our legal counsel and the artist's attorney agreed that we would leave the sculpture standing based on the artist's assurance that the neon lights would be left off over the weekend.

Because it was the lighting component which caused the uproar in the City, this was a good temporary compromise.

Now we will pursue all legal remedies available to us to remove the entire structure because the final product was not what we bargained for or, in fact, authorized. [36]

The City of Buffalo, through their conservative mayor, was not messing around. Griffin wanted *Green Lightning* torn down to the ground. They really didn't care about any agreement, because those dancing dog bones had scared a couple people who were afraid to talk to their kids about genitals. And in Buffalo, Jimmy Griffin wielded a lot of power, and he did what he thought was the right thing, even if it wasn't by the books.

"I had a report from either Jim Militello or Dave More," Griffin recalled, "that the police thought it would be a danger." [37]

Their fear of cars rear-ending each other and veering off the Kensington Expressway as people gawked at the dancing neon is laughable. Of course, none of those things happened, because it was over in fifteen minutes.

In the Dark of Night

"It was going to proceed and that if either myself or Mr. Lawless tried to interfere, we would be arrested." Michael Brown

Tuesday morning, November 20, 1984, Billie had a phone conversation with his attorney, Mike Brown, and then in the afternoon went to his office.[1]

"We talked about... his position and what he felt," Brown said. There was anxiety as they tried to formulate a strategy to take on the City of Buffalo.[2]

Billie needed his attorney to know the whole story. "I had to give him the facts of the case," Billie said, "and sort of tell him what had happened. He had no idea." He explained the agreement that he and Les Foschio had worked out. Billie stayed until about 5:30, six o'clock, then went home.[3]

After Billie left, Mike Brown and his wife (who worked in his law office) headed off to dinner at Aces Restaurant next to the Statler Towers.

Behind the scenes in City Hall, things were moving at a fast pace. The City and Jim Militello believed that Billie Lawless "was making efforts to connect the power again and turn it on. I don't remember the specific dialogues, but my staff that was on it reported back to me that they had word that Mr. Lawless was making arrangements, either himself or with a contractor, to turn the power back on. It may have been Wally P., it may have been Dave More. I can't remember who specifically told me," Militello said.[4]

Militello admitted that neither he nor any of his staff talked directly with Billie Lawless to see if he was actually going to turn power to the sculpture back on. He said Greg Dudek and Mike Brown had "an ongoing dialogue at first trying to keep the sculpture up and prevent it from being lit. So at the time that we heard that the thing was going to be turned back on again, I don't recall if further communications or of what nature were made between them."[5]

Once you knew where the neon figures were, Militello said, even if the sculpture was off, "your eyes were geared to look for something, so it was very possible to see them at that point."[6]

• • • • • • • • • •

Edward Schunk founded Walt's Tree Service, Inc. in 1956 and by 1984, he was doing everything. "Bid jobs, lay out jobs, manage the office, dispense equipment, all phases of construction work."[7]

He said they did a lot of work for the City. "We bid a lot of work for them and emergency work, which they had decided emergency, a fire job, digging for bodies, taking walls down, whatever come along. Besides myself, my partner, I had eight of my men listed with the City to call in case of emergency, trees down, fires or anything that could line up a crew if I was away or something."[8]

Around three o'clock on Tuesday, November 20, Militello ordered Ned Baudo at B.U.R.A. to call Walt's Tree Service. "This job was denoted an emergency," Militello said, "so it wouldn't have to be bid. I specifically remember the discussions with Wally P. about hiring them, and him being capable of doing the work."[9]

Schunk received the call from B.U.R.A. for an emergency job to remove *Green Lightning*. He sent two of his climbers and a labor truck driver. "I told him to take a bucket truck... also stake body truck to put the stuff on, and I sent out a service truck which used ropes, torches, comealongs, anything you need for this panel, service truck and construction."[10]

The city sent Buffalo Police Lieutenant Gerald M. Donovan to the site at Elm and Oak streets because "the artist... may attempt to cause a confrontation there." When he arrived at the site, Albert Landroche and two other workmen from Walt's Tree Service were already dismantling the structure. Landroche told Donovan that they had received a contract with B.U.R.A. to remove the structure as soon as possible. Donovan said that David More was also there as the representative of the Mayor and that he was in charge of the removal of the structure. [11]

Billie Lawless was at his home on Highgate Avenue when he received a call from a business person along the Elm-Oak Arterial, tipping him off that a wrecking crew had arrived at the sculpture site. He immediately headed there.

Mike Brown was at Aces Restaurant with his wife Rita, getting ready to eat dinner. Before he could even begin, he received a frantic call from Billie, who told him to head to the site of *Green Lightning*, as a crew was demolishing his artwork.

When Billie arrived, Lt. Donovan said, he "began to become histerical (sic) and attempted to stop the work in progress." [12]

Brown told his wife there was a problem, but to wait for him, he'd be back. He took her car and headed over to the Elm-Oak Arterial, drove the car up on the grass and over to the base of the sculpture. [13] He saw several police officers, a truck from Walt's Tree Service, with acetylene equipment on it, and two workers at the base of the sculpture cutting the steel. David More stood by, overseeing the operation.

Billie was very agitated and positioned himself between the truck and the base of the sculpture. According to Brown, "He jumped up on the truck and was attempting or threatening to attempt to disconnect the hoses to the acetylene torches." The police "were preventing us from interfering with the destruction of the sculpture." [14]

Michael Brown spoke to Lt. Donovan and told him they had an agreement with the city. "This wasn't supposed to happen." Donovan said it was on direct orders from the mayor and "it was going to proceed and that if either myself or Mr. Lawless tried to interfere, we would be arrested." [15]

Edward Schunk's crew already removed the far right neon panel with an animated penis using an acetylene torch and loaded it onto a truck. Schunk declared his crew knew what they were doing. He said *Green Lightning* "was mainly built out of angle iron. The bolts were put through the angle iron first into the sign and, apparently, double nutted so no one could back these bolts out and drop the sign. We did not want to break the weather seal and take the cover off the signs or get into the neon. We had them take the torches and just cut the head of the bolt, not hurt the steel. So when it took a panel down to put it back up, it would have needed four new bolts. The nuts were on the inside. I don't know how it was on the inside, but my knowledge on that stuff, it would have been double nutted so you couldn't just back the bolt out and drop the sign. That's probably protection more for kids than grown-ups."[16]

"I got Mr. Lawless off the truck," Mike Brown continued, "and proceeded back to Aces Restaurant, where I got my wife, and we went back to the office, and she typed the affidavits and necessary papers for the Temporary Restraining Order (TRO)." It was about six thirty by then, so the courts were closed, a convenient move by the City. Brown contacted his former law partner, Justice Vincent E. Doyle, who agreed to sign the TRO.

Lt. Donovan wrote in his report that the workmen continued to dismantle the structure. At approximately 6:30 PM, Lawless and Brown arrived with the signed restraining order directing both Walt's Tree Service and David More to halt their work. [17]

The work stopped. It was then determined that the second LEXAN box was half secured and was a potential danger, so it was removed by the workmen "to protect the public safety," David More said.[18]

Lawless said painfully, "They cut it with torches and just started to dismember it." He said it felt like his child was being killed. "I don't know if Walt is a specialist in art dismantling, but all they did was sever as if it was a limb off a tree. It's a typical South Buffalo reaction," he said, in reference to Mayor Griffin. "He's a bully. I'm going to file a suit."[19]

When asked why the work was being done under the cloak of darkness, David More replied, "Why not? The mayor acts fast."[20]

Billie told someone from the press, "I don't feel bad at all. The piece is still up. Jimmy Griffin has shown his true colors. We had a verbal agreement, and he broke it. While refusing to discuss the matter in a reasonable fashion," Griffin "ordered the sculpture destroyed," he asserted. [21]

Either later that night or the next morning, Edward Schunk got a call that the court order had stopped his workers, and they got back into the yard at 9 o'clock. When the panels came into the yard, he checked to see if there was any damage to the panels. "Yeah, there was no damage to the signs" or the neon, he said.[22]

Walt's Tree Service hauled the two panels to their headquarters at 69 Cemetery Road in Lancaster, New York. Edward Schunk said City of

Buffalo Corporation Counsel Sam Houston called. "The stuff was stored in my yard, tied up next to a truck in the back so the wind couldn't blow it over or anything, and there was so many calls, including the newspapers and all, that I wasn't talking to anyone without hearing from the City that I was working for."[23]

David More said he wanted the panels "returned to the artist as soon as possible."[24]

George Howell arrived and asked David More "how it was possible that he could have followed this project through City Hall for close to two years and not be aware of what he was getting himself into." [25]

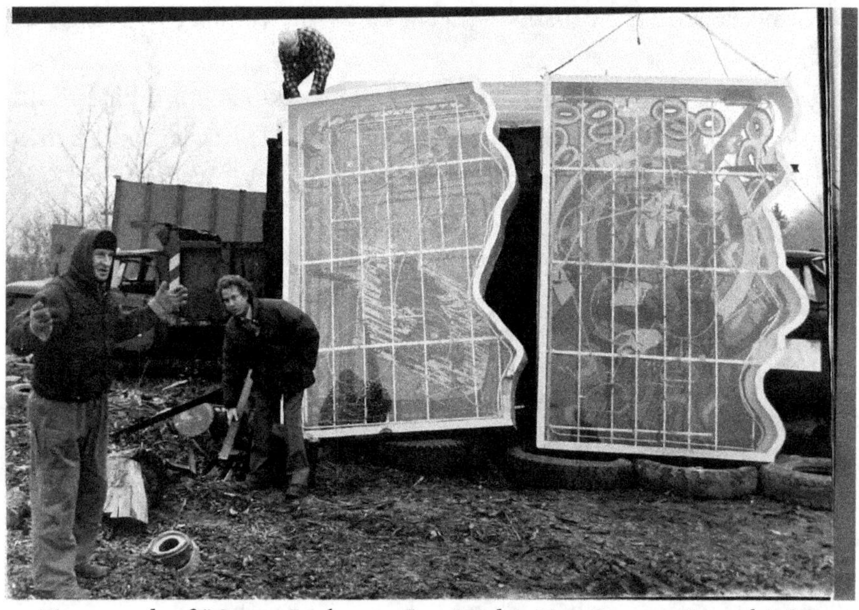

Two panels of "Green Lightning" at Walt's Tree Service. David More (bending over) and two unknown employees of Walt's Tree Service. Photo courtesy of Debra Kolodczak.

More insisted that Lawless had cleverly concealed his intentions. "To the best of my recollection, I saw no indication of anything like what was portrayed in neon once it was turned on ...it would have been an obligation on the part of Billie Lawless to come out and tell people it had a potentially suggestive nature. He did not do that."[26]

On Wednesday, November 21, feeling pressure from the media and complaints from people who said they should have known better, Arts Commission Executive Director David More submitted his resignation to

Mayor Griffin.

> By now I am sure the facts surrounding Billie Lawless' sculpture installation "Green Lightning" are clear to most of us. In short, it is my opinion that he has perpetrated a hoax on a large scale at the expense of the citizens and public officials of the City of Buffalo.
>
> In working with the artist over the past several months, I had no prior reason to believe he was other than on the level with respect to what he presented to the Arts Commission and Urban Renewal Agency. In fact, he tricked us and lampooned the City.
>
> It would be unfortunate if you, as Mayor of the City of Buffalo, should in any way be considered responsible for the artist's deceptive actions. Clearly, if anyone should be held accountable, it is the artist himself; following that, myself for failing to somehow anticipate what happened. I personally resent the unfair reflection the whole scenario has had upon your administration.
>
> I am proud to serve you in my capacity as Executive Director of the Commission. I trust you know my loyalty to you has always been and will continue to be firmly intact: Although I have no fear of conflict, in the interest of contributing to the resolution of what has now become a public controversy, I offer my resignation.[27]

It was another busy morning, as the Buffalo Urban Renewal Agency met in Room 210 at City Hall to discuss the situation at 9:30 AM on Wednesday, the 21st. In attendance were Mayor James Griffin, Acting Vice-Chairperson Daniel Kwiatkowski, Acting Corporation Counsel James McLoughlin, Commissioner of Admin and Finance Richard Planavsky, Lovejoy Council Member Norman Bakos, Councilperson-at-Large George K. Arthur, Masten Council Member David

Collins, and Gregory J. Dudek, B.U.R.A.'s legal counsel. An additional 11 people were also present.

Immediately, Dudek wanted a motion to ratify the actions of the mayor to dismantle *Green Lightning* and end the agreement with Billie, and to state that B.U.R.A. would not have given approval in 1983 if they were aware of the neon elements.

"We did not know what the finished product would look like," Dudek asserted, "from looking at the model. I hope to obtain your consensus that had you known what the finished product would have been, your approval of October 13 (1983) would have been withheld." [28]

George Arthur moved to approve the request, but David Collins said, "Have you discussed this with the Artist himself? The whole idea of dismantling..."

"No, not personally," Dudek said.

"Do we have any idea of how much is invested in construction?" Collins asked.

Mayor Jim Griffin spoke up. "He had a number of donors, Dave, and he claims something like $75,000.00. I really don't know. Dave More is here this morning, and Dave has gone through quite an ordeal over the past couple of weeks. I have Dave's letter of resignation, which I am not going to accept. Dave has done a terrific job as the Executive Director and it is just unfortunate that Dave put a lot of confidence where it shouldn't have been placed, and I want Dave to speak on this. As the Board knows, I left early that day because I had to attend a meeting. I don't remember what and that's why I wanted Dave Collins here today, because I thought he would protect my back when I leave these places."

"Always take care of you, Mayor," Collins responded.

"You fouled up once in your life. You fouled up that day. All is forgiven. Nobody is perfect, Dave."

"You're right, Mayor, nobody is perfect," Collins said.

For unknown reasons, the trial judge would not allow this banter between Collins and Griffin to be entered into the record.

The agency voted 6-1 to ratify Mayor Griffin's order to dismantle the sculpture. They went on record, saying they would have never approved the permits on agency-owned land if they had "known the neon elements would appear as they do." Voting in favor were Griffin, Arthur, Bakos, Planavsky, McLoughlin, and Kwiatkowski. Dudek didn't have voting rights.

The lone dissenting vote was from David Collins, who said, "I'd like my vote to be recorded in the negative. I think we're jumping the gun. I think we should wait until the court has a chance to deal with it and then take whatever action is necessary."[29]

Griffin later said he had ordered Jim Militello to take it down and dismantle it on Friday. "One of the TV reporters got to me last night and said, 'Well, they're taking it down in the middle of darkness.' And I said, 'What time did they start?' She said, '4:30 in the afternoon.' I said, 'Gee, that's not the middle of darkness, I don't believe.'"[30] He said, "Militello mentioned having it down on Monday and, of course, the injunction was there until Monday, so we took it down Tuesday."[31]

Whether Griffin knew if there was not a legal order or not, the city's attorneys knew. There was no injunction in place. Just a proverbial handshake deal between Mike Brown and Dudek. None of that actually mattered to Griffin, though, because in his eyes, the site was a place for development. "I did order this work of art, if people want to call it that, to be taken down," he said. Regardless of what people thought of the sculpture, "I think we've learned a lesson."[32]

David More explained there were many instances in history where artists had challenged social and moral values, "But this was not done in an ethical way. I hope the man regrets what he has done. He has hurt other artists who might want to do something similar, but in a serious vein. Billie Lawless has perpetrated a hoax on the city of Buffalo."[33]

That afternoon, both parties met in Justice Vincent Doyle's courtroom. The City's lawyers, Thomas Amodeo and Gregory Dudek, wanted the restraining order lifted so crews could complete their demolition. Michael J. Brown wanted Billie's right to flip the power switch back on. The judge admonished both parties.

The City's lawyers recognized there was "nothing that terribly objectionable" about the sculpture as it stood non-illuminated in the daylight.

Judge Doyle criticized the mayor's misplaced ideals about his authority to order the demolition without "court sanction." He considered his actions "abhorrent to my understanding of the laws of this community."[34]

Dudek argued that Mayor Griffin acted properly to safeguard the public, but Doyle was having none of it. "Could a police commissioner go into a movie house that was showing pornographic movies, tear down the screen, dismantle the projector, and hold all the pieces for you?" Doyle asked. "The proper procedure is to go to court."[35]

Doyle told Michael Brown that Billie was not to turn the sculpture back on. "There shall be no further action," Doyle told the lawyers, from either side. As a former law partner of Brown, the city's attorneys wanted Doyle to recuse himself, but he refused.

After the court appearance, members of the media asked Mike Brown to unveil the model of *Green Lightning* that Billie said he showed the city, to prove his client didn't deceive the city, but Brown refused. "The city and its officials have acted in excess of their lawful jurisdiction," he said. "There are procedures to follow here and none of them had been followed."[36]

Billie was happy with the outcome. "I think it was a great victory for the City of Buffalo," he said. "It illustrated that the mayor is not above the law, and I think it's a great country."[37]

· · · · **·**·**·**· · ·

"The suppression of sexual has always been a political act," wrote Amy Sparks. "*Green Lightning*'s neon figures are a perfect metaphor. Superimposed on other images, they represent the male dominance that has shaped Western culture for centuries. I think it's fair to say that Lawless, by making the figures cartoons that bowed and scraped in silly hats and canes, emasculated the power of the phallus in quite a witty way – - an idea the City of Buffalo didn't get."[38]

"It was not I who created a 'drama,'" Lawless said, "nor is it my intention to create a 'circus atmosphere.' I never said that I 'vow(ed)' to relight the sculpture. I did say that reillumination was one of the options open to me. I turned the electricity off voluntarily (the mayor did not 'pull the plug' as has been inaccurately reported) on November 16, 1984, and will leave it off voluntarily."[39]

Jim Militello said that the Urban Renewal Agency had started to dismantle *Green Lightning* under Griffin's direction, but said his department had nothing to do with "the damage to the thing after that, I don't know, I wouldn't have cared." He didn't mince words, either. "I'm pretty certain my organization didn't pay to store it or take it down, otherwise it would be in a dump."[40] The City paid for its removal and storage at Walt's Tree

Service.

Billie Lawless said city officials had plenty of chances to reject the idea, but David More disagreed, saying that Billie had perpetrated a "giant hoax" on the city by withholding the neon until just before the unveiling.

"I certainly hope that Billie Lawless' actions," More said, "do not adversely affect opportunities for serious artists wanting to work in the public arena. However, this whole scenario will place an extra burden on the (Buffalo Arts) Commission to go into another dimension in our review of public art projects. Clearly, we will have to tighten our screening procedures. Now, we're probably going to have to demand a lot more information from the artist. We already have pretty rigorous procedures, but who knows? Maybe we'll have to monitor the actual manufacturing process, construction, and installation every step of the way.

"The bottom line," More finished, "is that any artist wanting to work in the public domain must have respect for the public." [41]

"In my wildest dreams, I could never have envisioned this scenario," Lawless told The Buffalo News' Margaret Sullivan. When she pressed him to explain what the neon panels really were, he refused to give specifics. The beholder could interpret it as they saw, he explained - dog biscuits, Mr. Peanut, or male genitalia. [42]

"I'm not denying that interpretation," he admitted. "There's a state of ambiguity there. It's a powerful image. As a serious artist, I've got better things to do with my time than to spend two years of my life trying to pull off a hoax," by hiding part of the sculpture until the last minute. [43]

"His judgement may not have been the most mature," Sullivan wrote, "but he doesn't come off as a teen-age prankster looking for some cheap publicity."[44]

Lawless said he understood that an artist who exhibits on city-owned property had some responsibility. He said he struggled, knowing that there could be different interpretations. Like the time a 4-year-old visited his Essex Street studio in 1983 and described the neon figures as "...the little men are in the store and they're dancing because they're happy... and the stars are shooting down from heaven (swish like this), all kinds of colors, lots of pinks (one of my favorites) and the lightnings are going through the ground cause it might rain and it'll melt and it'll all be gone."[45]

"I've examined myself very closely on this whole thing, and I understand the issues of responsibility and honesty. The bottom line on being an artist is freedom of self-expression. Why doesn't everybody do a little art history?" he said. "Intellectually, (Jimmy Griffin) is just not there."[46]

Billie told Sullivan it was a "very painful experience. Another city is going to embrace this sculpture." In what may have been the first time he publicly acknowledged that *Green Lightning*, and his particular style of art, might be too much for his hometown, he said, "Maybe Buffalo's just not ready."[47]

In the immediate aftermath of the controversy, Buffalo Arts Commission chairperson Samuel Magavern was positive and on Billie's side. In the days that followed, maybe he took a better look at the sculpture, or was pressured to turn against Lawless and his sculpture. One person said maybe Magavern's age played a role in his initial view.

On November 21, 1984, he penned a letter on his law firm stationery to the funders of *Green Lightning*:

> We did not see or pass upon the completely new picture made by the use of configurations of neon lights. The picture conveys an entirely different and unrelated picture that is pornographic and vulgar. Fortunately, the lights were not turned on until the close of the dedication service. Thus, only a very few people were exposed to it.

> The average person, including myself and others familiar with art and, I believe, the general public might not have seen its vulgar connotation on first viewing. However, when pointed out and focused on by the television and press, the new picture thus superimposed is unmistakingly objectionable. It was inevitable it would be soon noticed, and I am sure you would not want us to approve the sculpture.

> Fortunately, our alert mayor, James Griffin, acted promptly and effectively to block the display of this superimposed picture to the public. The sculpture has not been injured. Maybe the artist can accelerate the taking of it on to Philadelphia… as he told us he planned to do.[48]

By this time, Billie's critics were outnumbering his allies. Other than Larry Griffis, few in the art community chose to make their opinions heard. Even though Buffalo seemed like a place unkind to local art, at least one other member of the local art community was supportive. Poet and lawyer Kastle Brill, a First Amendment purist, liked what *Green Lightning* brought to the city. "I thought it added a certain style or panache to Buffalo," she said. "It's hard to make a living no matter where you live," but once "you get hooked in (Buffalo), you're hooked in."[49]

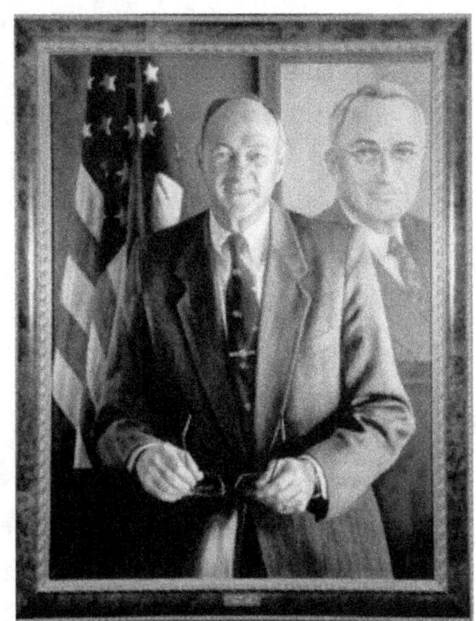

Official portrait of Buffalo Mayor James D. Griffin.

Doug Schultz, director of the Albright-Knox Art Gallery, was very angry at Billie, probably for the damage he was doing to the art community at large.[50]

Art critic George Howell opined about Sam Magavern's letter and change of course. "How else can it be interpreted except as a ploy to shift responsibility from the BAC to the artist and ensure that these donors put pressure on Lawless to take down his work? It was only after the television media exploited their news footage sensationalizing the work by labelling it pornographic that Lawless was attacked. Mr. Magavern's comments about the disturbing quality of art are probably genuinely felt, but the damning assertions that the work is 'vulgar' and 'pornographic' reflect the pressure brought to bear on him by public opinion."[51]

Whatever the outcome, Billie said *Green Lightning* was still going to Philadelphia, which was not actually the case. On November 24, 1984, he sent a letter to Marsha Moss in Philadelphia, admitting his failing:

Dear Marsha,

I could easily fill a few typewritten pages, explaining the circumstances behind my inexcusable behavior of this past summer. I really don't think you would be interested in reading through such garbage. I do want to offer my profuse apologies for the humiliation and embarrassment which I no doubt caused you to suffer.

Though I have little in terms of financial resources at the moment and am involved in a court battle, I think it only appropriate that I be responsible for the cost you may have suffered for the rental of the crane which was to help me install *Green Lightning*.

Suffice to say that I have never in my career to this point missed an exhibition or installation date. Beside missing the installation, I was negligent and unprofessional in my communications to you. The events of the last two years have been very trying, and because of my miscalculation — and because of my miscalculations you were hurt, I am sorry.

Sincerely yours, Billie Lawless.[52]

Two weeks removed from the unveiling, Billie met with George Howell, once again at his Days Park home. Howell, who Billie felt was a fair journalist, got Billie to open up on his feelings about the incident.

Howell said that "someone" (who was Joanne Posluszny) was at the Arts Commission meeting and she said that Billie received the golden treatment.

Howell: She said nobody asked any questions about the piece because of the support you got from David More. She also said she couldn't remember seeing the penises, and she was familiar with the piece. This is awkward, but did you substitute any of the elements on the maquette?

Billie Lawless: No.

Howell: It was the same all the way through?

Lawless: Absolutely.

Howell: Did David More ever talk to you about the figures or what you were doing with the installation?

Lawless: No. When I was bringing the model into the Common Council and I ran into David More, he was excited about not being consulted first. At our first meeting, we were at loggerheads. He saw the piece briefly that day, but really, the only other times he saw the piece was at the Urban Renewal meeting and at the Buffalo Arts Commission meeting.

Howell: He never went to your studio or saw the working model?

Lawless: No. He saw the piece for a total of ten minutes, which is unfortunate because, in the long run, you can't say "misrepresentation" or "hoax," but then again, no one looked at it seriously.

Howell: Nobody seems to take the work seriously or let it speak for itself. It's as though art isn't supposed to function that way. People look at public art and it either makes them feel good or reminds them of a historical event or cultural moment, but nobody goes to a piece of public art expecting to gain insight or have a question posed by it. No one assumes that that is art's role. You have a work that poses problems, but the only way those problems are going to be addressed is by going to the law. The last thing anyone would address is the artwork itself, yet it is the work that set this thing into motion.

Lawless: Yes, definitely. As far as misrepresentation goes, they're better off arguing over the backs of the panels because at the point when I made my presentations, I didn't know what I was going to play off of the neon figures. The images developed with Kathie Simonds.

Howell: Whether the panels are the same as they appeared on the maquette isn't the issue...

Lawless: But isn't the way the neon works off the panels and the rest of the piece what matters?

Howell: Kathie told me she has misgivings about the way the pieces were set up and I can see her point. When the piece was lit, I had trouble seeing the panels because the neon just jumped right off the structure. She feels the neon called too much attention to itself, that maybe it could have been downplayed or integrated more completely with the overall structure.

Lawless: But you've got to put this into a time frame. We saw it at night. It is supposed to go at 4:30 or 5:00. During the daytime, you can't see the neon at all. The piece changes: a metamorphosis is going on. I think the most exciting time for the piece is at about dusk when all of a sudden, you see the neon come on as the panels recede. And at night, it obviously becomes something altogether different.

But when it was lit that night, that was the first time for me to see it too.

I had no time to do anything after that. I have to spend time with a piece. Is it working? Is it not working? But this piece never had that time.

Howell: The thing was on for fifteen minutes and that was that. I walked by there yesterday to look at it; it's amazing, you can't really see the figures at all. The whole thing looks sad, with a big section just torn out of it.

Lawless: You know, from a critical point of view, that's probably valid that the neon called so much attention to itself, but the only way you'd be able to test that is over a period of time.

Howell: I think it's amazing that people keep saying image of "male genitalia" and "the male organ." When's the last time someone saw male genitalia with a top hat and cane?

Lawless: Exactly.

Howell: Nobody sees the joke. The figures are like a vaudeville team and that's not being seen. That goes back to what I said about nobody really being interested in the art. It isn't being dealt with as a statement. As for Magavern, did you ever talk with him about the piece?

Lawless: No, I don't even know him. I met him at the Arts Commission meeting. When you look at the power structure that this lies in, I think it's really sad that the Albright-Knox would not come out and say something. Even Bill Currie is afraid to say something. That's heavy duty, boy; what's Hallwalls all about? What are artists doing? So now Bill's saying, 'we were supposed to have this street artist doing something downtown, but now it looks like you've jeopardized it.' I'm certain there's going to be all kinds of fallout, but Jesus Christ, when is art going to get out there and whip? Isn't that what it's supposed to do? Create a dialogue - I wouldn't say confrontation - but it's out there and people are reacting to it, instead of, well, look at LIB where Beverly Pepper is putting up her sculpture [part of the new subway art program] and it looks like warmed over Brancusi to me. And Beverly Pepper is thought of as a successful sculptor in the 1980s.

Why do our supposed bastions of culture, the museums and galleries, stay away from controversial things? And yet abstraction was supposed to be the most upsetting thing at the beginning of this century. I look at work like Beverly Pepper's and George Sugarman's (another subway artist) and I think, yes, it's really interesting intellectually, but the immediate issues just seem to be put out there and people ignore them and they go away. And you wonder - what's it doing? Even the art in the subway just seems like decoration. I could be wrong about that.

Howell: I think that for the most part, no one looks to public art as a source for questions about culture. People look at it for consolation, as art that reassures you. There's the notion that questions are appropriate in one place, and a quiet respect is appropriate in public art. The George Segal *Restaurant* piece at the Federal Building on Huron and Delaware (in Buffalo) is interesting because it's not popular at all. I know people are put off by it. It's disturbing.

(Segal created sculptures with human figures. This type of sculpture was becoming increasingly popular in the United States when he installed *Restaurant* in 1976.)[53]

Lawless: Out of all his work, that's got to be the least effective because he put up that silly brick wall.

Howell: The point is that there's never anyone around it. I know people who work in that building and they say, 'Boy, it gives me the creeps,' and maybe it's a bad reflection on Buffalo. But that is the only public piece in this city that doesn't have a conciliatory tone. It's abrasive. Maybe that's a failing of public art: people don't expect?

Lawless: I think that's a failing. That's why I went ahead with what I'm doing. I think as a culture, we should examine ourselves. There's no doubt that we're schizophrenic about sex, and that's one issue I brought up here. If nothing else, I forced that issue. You brought it up before: why isn't anyone looking at the questions the piece poses? Milan Kundera made a great comment; he writes,

"I invent stories, confront one with another, and by that means, I ask questions. The stupidity of people comes from having an answer for everything; the wisdom of the novel comes from having a question for everything."

Lawless: Perhaps in the long perspective, *Green Lightning* asks these questions, no matter what else happens to it.

This interview appeared in the Winter 1984 edition of *Buffalo Arts Review* and would be referred to often during the trial.[54]

On November 29, 1984, the Buffalo Arts Commission called a special meeting to discuss *Green Lightning*. In attendance were David More, Cynthia Davis, Ann Nowak, Walter Prochownik, Jim Pappas, Ed Karnofsky, Bob Hodge, Joe Manch, Nate Barrell, and Tony Collucci.

The meeting was called in order to formulate appropriate action in response to the controversy surrounding the recent installation of sculptor Billie Lawless' work "Green Lightning." It was observed that a quorum was present and in the absence of Mr. Magavern, Nate Barrell was unanimously voted acting Chairperson. A prepared resolution was circulated for discussion purposes along with photographs of the sculpture lit up in neon at the dedication ceremony. It was generally agreed that the Commission should not involve itself in questioning whether the work is questionable. It was unanimously resolved "that a certain resolution approved by the Commission on 22 August 1983 shall in all aspects be herewith rescinded." Secondly, a motion was made and unanimously adopted that a letter to the various donors to the "Green Lightning" project prepared by Mr. Magavern be attached to the minutes of the meeting as part of its official record.

There be no further business, the meeting was fully adjourned.[55]

The Arts Commission was washing their hands of the incident. Conspicuously, Chairman Sam Magavern was missing from this important meeting. He stepped down from the Arts Commission and as president of Albright-Knox, but it doesn't appear this was the reason.

Now Billie Lawless was truly alone, with few artists defending him, and all the city agencies that had approved it now backtracking.

On November 30, 1984, the *Buffalo Jewish Review* published an editorial critical of the Buffalo *News'* November 24 coverage of *Green Lightning,* giving the impression that the *News* defended it. The *Jewish Review* said it was a "pornographic hoax attempted on the citizenry."[56]

In response, *News* editor Murray Light said he would not normally comment on other publications, but he took offense and said the *Review* "did not understand the purposes and functions of daily journalism." [57]

The *News* responded, saying, "Mayor Griffin was entirely correct in objecting to the 'Green Lightning' sculpture in downtown Buffalo. We ...have no doubt that most persons who saw the television film clip of the briefly lighted neon panels will agree with the city that they resembled male genitalia and that such an exhibit has no place on a public street." Those were harsh words from the newspaper, and Murray Light, that were supposedly "committed to a free press and free speech."[58]

The *News* said that as long as the neon was unplugged, the mayor had no reason to dismantle the sculpture. Maybe that was the bone that the *Jewish Review* had to pick with the *News*. That the *News* did not lambast Lawless more and agree with the City to tear it down like it was Frankenstein's monster.

With public sculpture, there have always been questions about what should and shouldn't be displayed; what is appropriate; whether public money should fund these projects. Today, there are ongoing discussions over statues of Christopher Columbus, Confederate generals, and others.

Alan G. Artner of the Chicago *Tribune* discussed public art in a 1985 story.

> The point no one likes to recognize is that whenever sculpture is placed on public land, it is *always* an imposition. Some pieces may be better than others. Some may be more congenial. But whether one likes a given work is a side issue. The incontrovertible fact is that a tiny group of people acting on behalf of an artist always imposes its decision on a large and powerless public.
>
> What matters is not the kind of art or even the loftiness of civic purpose. These are issues on which opinion forever will be divided. To argue that the public likes only what it knows [and what it knows, quite often, isn't good] may very well be true. But this places responsibility on the wrong side. Understanding must be fostered by those who are placing the art. It is all that will make the difference between an audience feeling comfortable or abused.[59]

The Buffalo *News* was criticized for not printing photos of the lit neon in *Green Lightning*. Murray Light said, "The *News* did not print the pictures of the illuminated neon panels because this paper does not think they should be seen in a family newspaper or should have been displayed publicly."[60]

The Cleveland *Plain Dealer* said, "Supporters felt that a major issue was the unwillingness of men to endure the kind of exploitation that has been inflicted on women. Detractors could not view the work for what it was: a witty and serious work of art."[61]

• • • • ● • ● • ● • • •

Billie headed out to Walt's Tree Service in Lancaster to survey the damage on Friday, November 30. The two panels rested on a couple of old tires and rusted junk. "They wrecked the sculpture; they've wrecked all the aesthetic work I've done. They call this 'dismantling,' I call it destruction of a work of art. This will have to be stripped down to the basic skeleton before it can be put back up again."[62]

"We had a verbal promise between two attorneys that was broken. That's the lowest an attorney can stoop. The fact is, they broke their word, and if you can't trust the people in City Hall, how can you negotiate?" Lawless continued, "Eventually David More and Sam Magavern will eat those words. I promise you that."[63]

The City of Buffalo eventually sent a payment of $2,580 to Walt's Tree Service for their work dismantling and storing *Green Lightning*.

Former *Buffalo Courier-Express* political columnist Ray Herman said in a 1984 year-ending piece regarding the sculpture, "For Artist Billie Lawless, a more avant-garde setting to accommodate his sculptures. Jimmy Griffin thinks Times Square would be perfect."[64]

In 1987, Herman again wrote about Lawless, saying, "To Griffin and his allies, the sculpture, which they claimed displayed male genitals when lit at night, was tantamount to planting Satan's flag in a morally conservative, workingman's city. When Jimmy had the thing banished, his supporters threw their hats in the air. The act was vintage Jimmy Griffin."[65]

Under the Magnifying Glass

"Billie should never have pulled one over on everybody." Matthew Bryant

THE CITY OF BUFFALO, through its attorneys, as well as Buffalo
Arts Commission Executive Director David More, insisted Billie
Lawless bamboozled them and pulled a hoax on everyone by submitting
one innocuous design, then unleashing an obscene, pornographic artwork
to the unsuspecting socially conservative city. But there were people who
knew what Billie had planned.

The entire incident did not really surprise Buffalo artist Larry Griffis.
"I'm very much amused, of course. Billie is taking a good stand, and he's
making the right stand."[1]

"To cut it down, what the hell kind of mayor do we have?" Griffis said,
"What kind of city do we have? Nobody in the art world would support
tearing it down. No matter if they hated it. I have nudes, male nudes,
genitalia, the whole thing (at Ashford Hollow) and nobody is complain-
ing. Little boys and girls come up to an 8-foot male figure. They're not
shocked."[2]

"This won't be good for Buffalo," Griffis added. "But it might be good
for Billie. It will give him a lot of publicity. I want to spend the remaining
time in my life making art. I do not want to spend my life in the public
arena, arguing with the mayor or legislators."[3]

Larry Wood, owner of Neon Graphics in Clarence, New York, said,
"There was no doubt Billie knew what it was. I accused him of trying to
pull something off. I never thought he would get this far with it." Wood

was not rooting for the artist in this case. He was hoping the court ordered *Green Lightning* removed. "I'm interested in seeing this thing come down. It's not good for my business. My friends keep asking me if I did it." [4]

And there was the real problem. Not whether Larry Wood thought it was offensive, but others might think he was okay with pornographic art.

Billie told the Buffalo *News* other neon companies did not turn him down. He said Neon Graphics was the only company he approached directly about doing the neon. "I think there are more tube benders in Buffalo that I never went to."[5]

Larry Wood, though, was not alone in his thoughts. Dennis Wilcox of Wilcox Brothers Sign Co. said Lawless told him they were dancing dog bones. "I've never seen a dog biscuit that looked like that," Wilcox said.[6]

"There was not a sign company in Buffalo that would touch it," according to Richard Houghton of Neon Display in the Town of Tonawanda. [7] It is unclear whether that pun was intentional.

Billie saw it differently. "The reason I went to Albany," he said, "was that's where I got the best price. It cost one-third of what it would have cost in Buffalo."[8]

The Buffalo *News* contacted some companies that had donated to *Green Lightning* to see if they felt they were "duped" after the unveiling.

Mary Lou Vogt of Greater Buffalo Press sent Billie a letter expressing her displeasure. "We at Greater Buffalo consider a dancing man more than his private parts. I am sorry that you consider your hometown backward in not wishing to display 'artistic pornography' in bright lights, but I'm delighted that your *Green Lightning* will not be competing with the bright lights of Christ's birthday."[9]

How did neon dancing penises compete with the "bright lights" of Christmas, a holiday of excess? One may never know.

Billie responded to Ms. Vogt saying, "We are suffering a cultural schizophrenia over the role of sexuality in our society and until we straighten out our thoughts, I suggest clothing the statue of *David* in Delaware Park or more dramatically bulldozing it into the lake."[10]

Greater Buffalo Press was the leader in printing color comic inserts for newspapers for decades. They sold the company in 1989.

Empire of America Federal Savings Bank gave a small donation, but in hindsight wished they hadn't. "I don't think we would have supported it if we had known there would be any question of it being obscene," said

Public Affairs Officer Richard D. Shaner. "Unfortunately, it could have been something very positive for the city."[11]

In 1990, regulators seized Empire of America, New York State's third largest savings bank, after it became insolvent due to bad business practices. Regulators cut up the bank and sold it.

Matthew Bryant of Bryant Machine Co. in Buffalo was definitely in the "duped" column. "I feel a little duped, yes," he said. His company had provided fabrication and some parts for the sculpture. Even though he wasn't offended by the piece, he said, "Billie should never have pulled one over on everybody." He was worried that it might discourage other businesses from supporting public art.[12]

Bryant added, "He... ought to be ashamed of himself because he really is hurting other artists who want to get help from the city." He also said the slides Billie sent to donors did not depict the final sculpture. "The slides don't show what he did. I tell you, it's not there."[13]

Every drawing that was examined for this book shows the dancing penises. Some have the original brick background, but they all show what his intention was. But did Billie send out *different* drawings or slides with his donor packages? Only he knows that for certain. On one hand, he said Buffalo was "enlightened and supportive." But he had seen censorship in his hometown before at Erie Community College, so maybe he erred on the side of caution. One of those "I'll do it and ask for forgiveness later" thoughts.

Not everyone felt Billie was entirely wrong. Allan Friedman, president of Great Arrow Graphics, said, "The fact that (the City) would send bulldozers out to destroy it before anybody even looked at it is just criminal." His company had donated the use of its copy camera. He said that although *Green Lightning* might have been questionable, overall he found Billie's work "stimulating, refreshing and sophisticated."[14]

"To treat him so carelessly is criminal," Friedman added. "There's just no excuse for it." With the Arts Commission rescinding their approval a few days earlier, he said it would discourage him from working with them, but not with another artist.[15]

Artist Larry Griffis said that he did his best to avoid working with governmental bodies. "Those guys only want to play by the rules as they go along. As time goes by, they make up some new ones."[16]

It split the arts community in Buffalo. Some thought *Green Lightning* was innovative, while others saw it as damaging to future projects.

Larry Griffis said that the slides in the donor package depicted exactly what Billie created. The Buffalo *News* decided to examine the slides and said the neon images were not clearly visible by the naked eye, but under a magnifying glass they were. Was it Billie's fault if donors didn't do their due diligence? Or did he owe them and David More the common courtesy of telling them what he was doing?

Buffalo *News* art critic Anthony Bannon was on leave when the whole *Green Lightning* incident happened. So on December 16, 1984, he gave a posthumous review after reading Buffalo *News* articles, watching video footage from WKBW Channel 7, and viewing drawings from Billie. Although his lawyer wouldn't allow him to show the model.

Bannon said that "the dancing whatever they are …is far from the sum of its parts." Where it was placed could not be read from a passing car "and defeats the understanding of it. What we are given, then, is a highly ambiguous sculpture that can only be marginally perceived. Contrarily, when its neon was lit, a full range of its suggestions probably could only be understood from a distance."[17]

He added "each of its panels like a page in a book, each neon figure, framed in neon and embedded in the panel, offering itself like a frame of film, directly alluding to motion while presumably making a cross-reference to the information upon the panels and around the installation."[18]

Bannon, like others, mention its point to "popular culture and toward a tension between the past and the future: the old-time swimmer in an other-planetary ether; the quaintly dressed little girl, the venerable figure of comic strip cop or criminal, each rendered in a design style that suggests the future, or at least a full present."[19]

He called *Green Lightning* "an old-time sideshow" and questions why the dancing girls at county fair midways don't get the same scrutiny.

"Surely it is the province of art to challenge - to challenge our individual perceptions and our collective values as expressed, among other ways, through government and law. And Lawless' work has done just that. It has raised valuable issues, exposed vulnerable assumptions and created a great deal of conversation.

"Its propositions are a jumble of voguish style, a greedy melange of too many subjects in a language too glib and slang. It is far too early for any bows." [20]

Bannon certainly seemed to get the gist of Lawless' intentions with *Green Lightning*. It was supposed to be both comical and serious, but people needed time to appreciate what it stood for. But, as we know, the City of Buffalo wasn't interested in letting time decide. They made a hasty decision, and that was that.

· · · ● · ● · ● · · ·

Billie and Kate Simonds defended their artwork in the Buffalo *News* on December 5, 1984. Whether Simonds had any input in the letter, only they know.

> Several years ago, while driving down Bailey Avenue on a search for neon signs and sign-related imagery for a sculptural project, I was struck by a powerful image which I felt, at that time, was also very playful. The image was humorous, expressive, already playing on another well-established Madison Avenue image, Mr. Peanut. As the years went by I was struck by its sticking power.
>
> And yet, year after year, it remained, steadfast – spraypaint on an imitation brick wall. There is no doubt in my mind that thousands of people saw this image and that while its original intent might have been obvious to some, I am sure interpretations ran the gamut of meanings.
>
> We jump to the present. Kathie Simonds and I are shocked by the fact that no one has dealt with *Green Lightning* in its entirety. "The shell has been fingered without reaching the kernel." Ironically, the sculpture has fallen victim to its own poetry. We had been hopeful that there would be a dialogue within the community over what we intended to be seen as a very complex sculpture. Of course, this intense reaction toward one image, only one part of the entire work, cannot be ignored because it tells us something about ourselves as a city, a people and a culture.

Green Lightning is an idea, an allegory whose symbols are our common, cultural iconography. The essence of the piece, the spider's web, is in the arrangement of these icons (girl jumping rope, space shuttle and wildlife stamp, TV with diving swimmer and a fleeing bandit) in multi-layers; a format at once billboard/display-like, both carnival and burlesque in manner, a three-ringed circus complex that aims to imitate the very nature of our daily existence.

The human animal in the 20th century operates on many levels. Like children jumping rope we seek technology that can simplify our daily lives in an increasingly complex world. We crave the security of child-like naivete and innocence and the controllable patterning of a routine that holds us together amid what seems chaotic, with patterns whose motion can distract us from the awareness that we are indeed powerless to cope effectively. We find ourselves staring blindly ahead lest breaking a mindless routine should jar our conscious equilibrium.

What are these threats to our sense of security, our individual and collective consciousness? Is it the violent energy of a restless nation with nowhere to go but up and out, literally bursting off the planet with our scientific technology?

Are we shuttling into a larger star-studded universe that yet, in its aloofness, remains secure while giving the appearance of impenetrable order? The intended poetic effect of the stars and lightning bolts around the sculpture juxtapose cosmological references against the images painted on the boxes in the main structure. They scale the statement in the same way that the old, dead tree in the Elm-Oak Arterial scales the sculpture. They refer to the fates and the ostensible role they play in each of our lives.

Minutes after the neon was turned on, a woman who was

present said something to this effect: "Originally, I had liked it until I noticed the green box where the dancing neon was superimposed over the figure of a girl jumping rope." She angrily remarked, "One more example of male dominance." Yes! Exactly! Male dominance; but burlesquing male dominance and the myths attendant to male sexuality; power and dominance. It's that simple, or is it? How is this male dominance reflected in our lives and to what extent has it affected life in our world up to this point in time?

By the natural schizophrenia toward the role of sexuality in our society. By the titillating sex of prime time television and abhorrence, of any kind, of a straightforward depiction of a penis or vagina (the squeamishness and cold language that is employed in their common descriptions). By the John Wayne bravado that led to the damages inflicted upon *Green Lightning.* By the laughter of the policemen on the scene at the sculpture's initial lighting and the subsequent police action to condemn the piece.

Is our ability to know the world we are a part of stymied by cultural myopia? There is a certain futility in knowing the sophisticated nature of our information technology (the media), and yet sensing that we, the public, see only what is set before us.

As viewers of our own history, we see it from only one side; we are like the diver on one of the sculpture's panels who is swallowed up by an ocean of events while at the same time paying homage to the bearer of those events.

Right now, an effort toward a peripheral view of history is as futile as turning the television upside down to get a better perspective. The quickness to pass judgement on anything and everything in lieu of grappling to understand has become a way of life for most of us, leaving us as a discontented civilization poised on the brink of self annihilation.

> *Green Lightning* is about perception, how we learn to inter-
> pret our world in its many layers of meaning and intention.
> Ours is a responsibility, not to set our minds on automatic
> patterning, like a child skipping rope, but to be able to dis-
> cern, search and question beyond the surface.

> So now that we have spoken, has *Green Lightning* been com-
> pletely defined? Of course not. We hope not. There is much
> to be harvested in the work, and we reject unequivocally the
> media's superficial attempts to define the meaning and depth
> of this artwork through one image, taken out of context.[21]

Simonds and Lawless presented "Green Lightning, Just Possibly an Idea" on Sunday, December 16, 1984 at Unitarian Universalist Church in Buffalo, where they must have discussed the entire event.

Simonds said there was something she should have asked Billie, but never did. How soon did she exhibit again? She came back into the light with a show at Hallwalls in July 1985. They gave her a pass, and she came out of the affair far less dirty than Lawless did, and rightly so. The sculpture was his and in the end, the final presentation was his. Simonds work, although important to the piece, ended up playing second fiddle to Lawless' neon penises.

Could it have anything to do with gender differences? Artwork by female artists makes up a much smaller percent of permanent gallery collections in the U.S. and Europe, and at auction art created by women sells for significantly less than men, even though they are the subject for a large percent of artwork.

According to an article on Artsy.net in 2019, people don't value art by women artists like men. They barred women from artistic professions and training until the 1870s. "Untangling the reasons that this inequality persists today is more difficult. Differences in gallery representation; the cultural biases of art interpretation; the cliché of the art world 'bad boy'; the sexism of aging; the imbalanced weight of parenthood; the proportion of curators, collectors, and gallery representatives who are female; and the lack of assertiveness among female artists have all been proposed as hypothetical causes."[22]

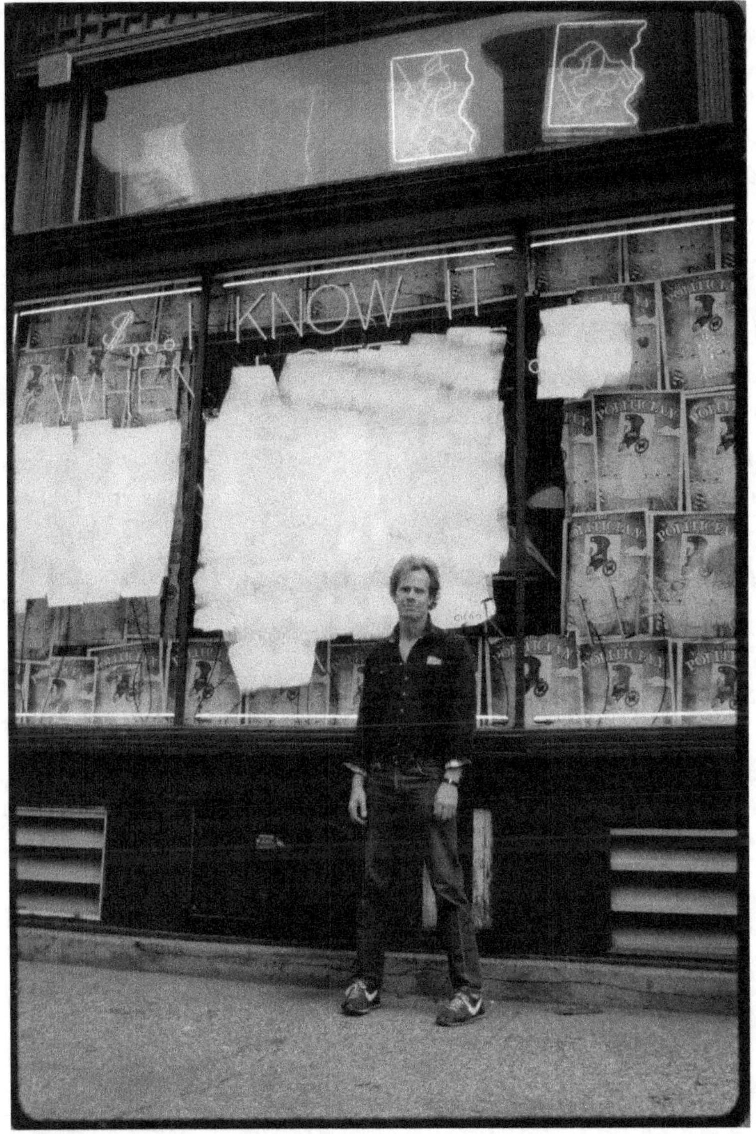

Billie Lawless standing in front of his exhibit at SPACES gallery in 1985. Courtesy SPACES Archive Collection, Kelvin Smith Library Special Collections.

More research is necessary, according to them. They acknowledge that gatekeepers, dealers, critics, and curators prefer male artists. Maybe this was why Kate took less flack from the *Green Lightning* events than Billie did.

When the trial for *Green Lightning* took place in 1992, Kate wasn't called as a witness by either side, which seems unusual. She would have had a perspective and inside look into the creation and design that probably no one other than Bille could provide.

Kate would go to have a career as an art teacher for years at Buffalo Seminary in Buffalo, a private girl's school. From all accounts, it looks like she was an amazing influence on many young women throughout her career. The incident with Billie Lawless may have been a blemish on her life, but Kathie Simonds came out on top and continued producing and teaching art.

More than one person spoken to for this book said that Billie Lawless was manipulative. He would develop close relationships with people, who then felt they couldn't betray that friendship. Or he'd ask for a favor, maybe a reduced fee, claiming he couldn't afford it. Was that really the case?

In 1985, Mitch Flynn interviewed Lawless for *Buffalo* magazine. In the story, he mentions that Lawless had a new BMW in his driveway. Without knowing all the details, it would not appear that he was a starving artist. [23]

BLIZZARD

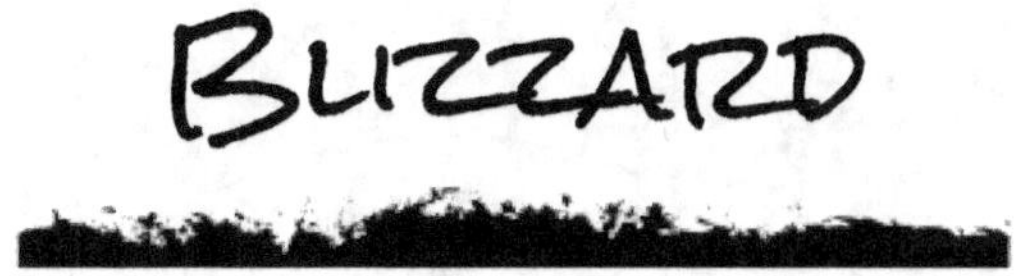

"A cop came up to me and said, 'What are you doing down here? You're gonna get mugged.'" Billie
Lawless

A BLIZZARD STRUCK BUFFALO on January 18th, 1985, leaving 33.2 inches of snow and winds reaching 53 mph. Most people in western New York can handle snow, but 33.2 inches of snow is a lot. The last major storm had been in 1977. This was not a usual occurrence, and they shut the city down. There was a driving ban, so city plows could clear the streets. It was during this storm that Mayor Jimmy Griffin uttered what is now one of his infamous quotes when he told Buffalonians to "Stay inside, grab a six-pack and watch a good football game," meaning the Superbowl that weekend.

Green Lightning found itself covered by mounds of snow piled there by city plow crews. Mayor Griffin, also serving as acting streets commissioner, instructed city dump trucks to pile snow around the sculpture in the Elm-Oak Arterial, nearly burying it.

Billie's attorney, Michael J. Brown, said he called him about it on Saturday, February 2. They discussed it, but they were not worried, since the city was careful not to interfere with the primary structure. "We have some thoughts as to why it was done, but this was an emergency situation, so we're not going to argue about it. We can't see the lightning bolts at the front of the structure, so we won't know whether there'll be any damage to it until the snow melts. We'll reserve all our rights in case there was some damage."[1]

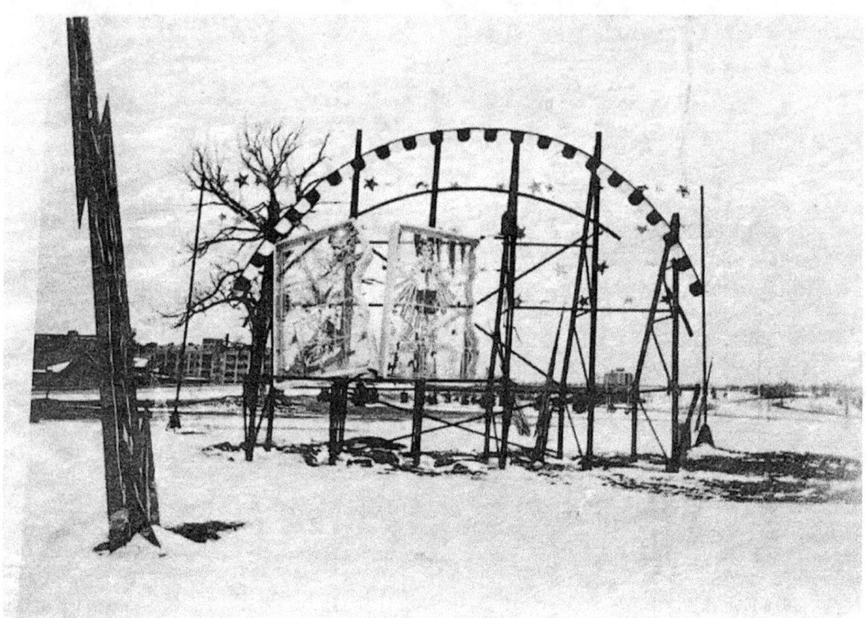

Green Lightning, winter 1985. Photo by Bonnie Chimes from Buffalo Arts Review.

The sculpture was dark and covered in snow, but now Erie County was investigating Billie. On February 13, 1985, Roger A. MaGill, Special Investigator for Erie County, sent a letter to David More saying that he was investigating if Lawless had committed fraud against the taxpayers of Erie County. [2] David More provided a list of Billie's donors on February 22, 1985 and said he didn't think there was any fraud against the City. But, he told him about a low interest home improvement loan he got from the city. [3]

Lawless filed a Notice of Claim, February 13, 1985, less than three months after the dismantling took place. The claim said Walt's Tree Service and the City of Buffalo Urban Renewal Agency owed $100,000 for trespass and punitive damages; plus another $100,000 for its negligence. The Buffalo Urban Renewal Agency was liable for breach of contract for $600,000 with interest on $100,000, and the City of Buffalo for breach of contract and tortious interference with plaintiff's contract.

The following day, February 14th, 1985, the City responded to the suit and served Lawless with a summons and complaint. The City of Buffalo wanted to prevent Lawless from illuminating the sculpture, and maintained that *Green Lightning* "is obscene, lewd, lascivious, indecent or disgusting and is therefore in violation of the law." They also wanted an order preventing Billie or "his agents and servants" from displaying the structure, and to surrender *Green Lightning* to the Sheriff of Erie County and allow the Sheriff to destroy it.[4]

The City of Buffalo wasn't messing around. They wanted disgusting *Green Lightning* torn down immediately, and would use the County as cover to destroy it.

Gregory Dudek, lead counsel for the Buffalo Urban Renewal Agency, filed a $1 million counterclaim lawsuit against Lawless. "We want a jury to decide the issues," Dudek announced, "because we feel that what Billie Lawless did was not only directed toward City Hall."[5] The suit accused Lawless of "fraudulently misrepresenting" his sculpture through bad faith actions. The City was also asking for $2,000 to defray the cost of dismantling *Green Lightning* in November.

To avoid any claims of favoritism, they assigned Wayne A. Feeman Jr., Acting New York State Supreme Court Justice from Allegany County, because Billie's father was a former judge in Buffalo.

Michael Brown said he would ask Judge Feeman to dismiss the city's countersuit. Gregory Dudek said the Griffin administration wanted the judge to lift the retraining order filed in November to "let us take the rest of the sculpture down or make Billie Lawless take it down or award us money damages."[6]

Michael Brown said that attorneys for the city agreed to stipulate that Lawless "properly presented" his sculpture concept to city officials before building it.[7]

Billie went to Walt's Tree Service to look over the pieces they dismantled in February or March 1985. "I was concerned, and (Michael Brown) arranged for me to go out and take a look at them with the City's attorneys." He said the boxes "looked like they were propped up against some tires and they were just left outside. There wasn't (any protection), they were left uncovered."[8]

On April 24, 1985, Billie Lawless sat down for a deposition in Room 1108 of City Hall. Attorney Henry Wyman (from the same office as Mike Brown), represented him. Rosemary Bis and John J. Murphy, Chief Legal Investigator for the City of Buffalo, also were present. Now he could make his case under oath.

During the questioning, Murphy asked Lawless what the contract with the city called for. "Well, I don't think I should sum up the contract because it's very specific and detailed," Billie replied. He said he had worked on the sculpture on and off at three different locations. "I raised funds and materials for it, but I did not make any money from it." He claimed he lost between three and five thousand dollars and admitted he had never made money off his projects.[9]

They asked Billie about the damages he was asking for. He estimated there was $30,948 for the sculpture, plus $165,000 in lost sales, and another $30,000 for emotional trauma. He said he lost rowing coaching jobs at St. Joseph's Collegiate Institute and the West Side Rowing Club. They excluded him from the "Western New York Exhibition." He claimed there was a loss of reputation. The event led to an inability to take *Green Lightning* to Philadelphia because of adverse publicity and loss of credibility. The total loss was $299,948.[10]

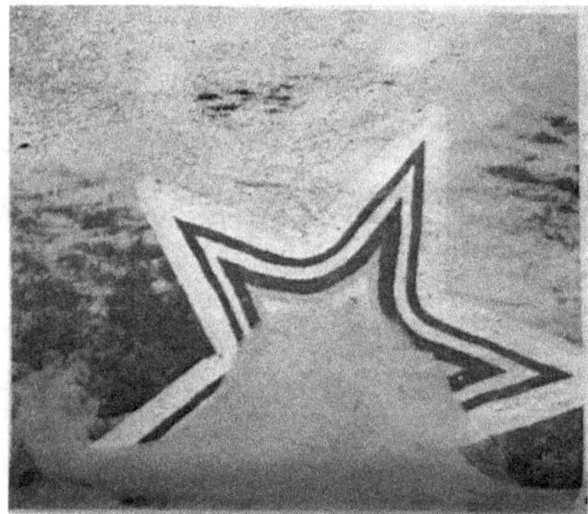

Fallen "Green Lightning" star, winter 1985. Photo by Bonnie Chimes, Buffalo Arts Review.

He told Rosemary Bis he had promised Jim Pitts he would try to place the sculpture in the Elm-Oak Arterial, yet his intention was to put it on Broadway. "I didn't have any idea of where it was going to go," he said. "I was just interested at that point in just building the piece. I was working on the sculpture" and didn't care where it ended up at that point.[11]

David More submitted an affidavit on April 8, 1985. In it, he stated, "I understood that neon would illuminate certain silk-screened lyric imagery applied to the back panels of the sign structure as designed by Kathy Simonds. I was never shown any specific neon image proposed. Mr. Lawless advised me that the neon light would blink in the completed sculpture, but I was totally unaware that the neon light would move until I saw the neon images on November 15, 1984."[12]

He insisted if he had known about the images, "I would have been compelled to bring the photographs and slides to the attention of the Buffalo Arts Commission and B.U.R.A., since the images contained in the panels show a form that could be interpreted as highly offensive particularly because of their phallic nature."[13]

By May 1985, there were questions of whether Billie could continue to make a living as an artist in Buffalo. Lawless told the press "They've created a situation in Buffalo where it's difficult to sell work and be exhibited here." He said he was "defamed."[14]

"Since most of his artwork is sold outside Western New York, Lawless doesn't see *Green Lightning* as having much of an effect on his financial well-being. Most of his sales are made in places like Philadelphia and Boston." He said that "Buffalo's shortage of Yuppies is the problem, because young people in Buffalo just don't buy art as they do elsewhere."[15]

But would he continue to live in the city that destroyed his artwork? He wasn't bitter and had no plans to leave. He loved Buffalo. "You just have to take it as it comes," he said.[16]

Billie said when he started working on *Green Lightning*, "A cop came up to me and said, 'What are you doing down here? You're gonna get mugged.' Nothing ever happened to me or my work." He called the comment stereotypical "lower East Side lingo."[17]

The City of Buffalo wanted Billie and his sculpture to just go away, so they offered a settlement in May 1985. "Their financial offer was $15,000," Lawless said, "and I had to agree to never bring (the sculpture) back into the city limits. I found (the offer) totally unacceptable." [18]

On May 15, 1985, Lawless finally showed a model of *Green Lightning* to the porn hungry press, claiming it was the same model he showed to the City multiple times in 1983. Gregory Dudek, attorney for the Urban Renewal Agency, said the model shown to the press was not the same model displayed to city agencies. "Our position is that is not the model (he originally displayed)."[19]

The legal bills were starting to add up for Billie, so his friends at the Artists Gallery on Essex Street decided to host a fundraiser for him on May 18, 1985, in the grand lobby at Carl Paladino's Ellicott Square Building. There was live music by local bands Nullstadt and the Splat Cats, and art installations by John Toth, Henry Jesionka, and Billie. One person claimed Billie made three times what it cost to build the sculpture.[20]

• • • ● • ● • ● • • •

Lawless needed proof that the city of Buffalo had damaged *Green Lightning*, and to what extent? He called 34-year-old Steve Wisenbaugh, who was living in Harrison, Ohio. He was an art conservator with extensive experience with outdoor pieces. "The majority of the pieces that I am particularly interested in are like bronzes and steel structures."[21]

Wisenbaugh was also co-owner of a small foundry and did castings for various artists, including George Segal's *Restaurant* piece. "That was the first piece that George created out of bronze. We did that for him in 1975."[22] Segal installed it in 1976 in front of the Dulski Federal Office Building in Buffalo.

According to Wisenbaugh, he had worked on thousands of outdoor sculptures, including 75 to 100 steel sculptures.

"I received a phone call from Mr. Lawless. I believe it was June or July of '85," Wisenbaugh said. "He had informed me that there was a piece that he wanted me to take a look at and wanted to know if I was interested in doing so and what my fees would be, etc. I told him how much it would cost for me to come up, what he would get for the money. We decided to meet, and I flew to Buffalo."[23]

They visited the Elm-Oak location and Billie explained how someone had damaged the piece. "It was obvious the piece had been altered, so I asked him, 'Billie, obviously there's some panels missing or what have you.'"[24]

"We proceeded to look at the piece of sculpture, assess the damages, talked about the possibility of what it would take to restore the piece, talked about time frames, expenses ...how much ...I thought it would cost for the restoration of the piece, what we thought would be entailed. I was in Buffalo for a better part of the day."[25]

They took photos and examined the sculpture, then went to Walt's Tree Service to examine the panels that had been taken down.[26]

"It was strewn around. We found a piece here, a LEXAN panel there, pieces all over," Wisenbaugh said.[27] "They weren't crated, they weren't covered, they weren't being taken care of in any manner, with any care.

Pieces were tilted back. Water had entered the pieces. There were all types of watermarks in it from the water that had came up in the piece. It dried out, you could see water marks going through it. Large LEXAN panels were completely ruined." Wisenbaugh said the LEXAN was scratched and there were burn marks where they'd cut through, and embedded into the LEXAN. "There were little burn marks all over. I mean, the piece was taken down hastily, and there was no protection to the piece itself, and so both panels were just laying."[28]

"I mean, there was just no concern for it at all. We couldn't assess the complete damage. I could do a visual inspection, but it didn't have power, so we couldn't test the fluorescent lighting or whatever, so that was something that would have to be done at a later date. Until you get into the piece, you won't be able to tell …what else isn't damaged."[29]

After spending some time examining the pieces, they departed. Wisenbaugh returned home to Ohio and wrote a report and estimate. He said that it was several pages with an estimate for repair costs.

When interviewed in October 2022, Wisenbaugh said he liked Billie's artwork and had a print or two of his work. "Billie was a nice guy," he said, "cool."[30]

Sculpture Chicago '85

"When we dismantled the thing, we dismantled it
because it was unsightly." Mayor Jim Griffin

B ILLIE GOT AN ANONYMOUS phone call on April 30, 1985, about a
missing *Green Lightning* bolt. He contacted the Buffalo Police, who
learned from a woman on South Ryan Street that her husband and several
of his buddies took it as a prank. Lawless then rented a truck and drove
to the house with a small crew, where they picked up the 500 pound steel
bolt of lightning. They took it back to the site at the Elm-Oak Arterial and
reconnected the $3,000 lightning bolt back into its concrete base.

When asked if he planned to press charges, Lawless said, "For today, I'm
just happy to get it back."[1] It probably should have been grand larceny,
but the police hemmed and hawed about charging the South Buffalo men
(where Mayor Jimmy Griffin hailed from) with any crime.

• • • • • • • • • • •

In the early 1980s, Carolann Haggard circulated an idea for a sculpture
symposium in Chicago. About the same time, the Burnham Park Planning
Board was seeking ways to make the isolated South Loop area culturally
attractive. Chicago real estate developer Robert A. Wislow brought up the
idea of a sculptural symposium that would occur over several weeks. This
would become "Sculpture Chicago."

The first year, "Sculpture Chicago 1983," took place in the Printers'
Row district, with 12 artists from a 150-mile radius of Chicago taking
part. For two years, the spectacle of sculptors making their art in public

drew crowds to one of the then-less-traveled neighborhoods of the city. Complaints ensued, which forced the exhibit to move west to Wells and Harrison Streets near the River City complex.[2]

They accepted applications for the 1985 event, which would run from September 1 to October 6, starting in mid-February 1985. The panel of judges were Howard Fox of the Los Angeles County Museum of Art; Mary Jane Jacob of the Museum of Contemporary Art, Chicago; and John Chandler, Director of Supervision, Art Consultancy and Management, Boston.

The intent of the show was to have the artists make new works of art on the site for five weeks in outdoor tent studios. They invited the public to watch and interact with the process. In addition, they scheduled a lecture series and panel discussions.[3]

Each artist received a $1,500 honorarium, travel, a condo rental, as well as $1,500 for materials. Sculpture Chicago had a budget of $150,000 and artists had access to arc welders, cranes and other heavy machinery necessary to build their sculptures.[4]

Billie Lawless, after spending a long snowy winter of 1985 fighting Buffalo's City Hall, was ready for a change. He had seen a notice for "Sculpture Chicago '85" in late 1984. To submit an entry, he would need to submit a scale model, a dimensional drawing, a list of materials, eight slides and an application. He had a model but built a new one, which he started around the third week of December 1984, and finished the primary structure before February 19th, and the base in June 1985.

Lawless said the neon in the fourth panel he submitted to Chicago looked no different and was the same as in Buffalo. [5]

They chose ten proposals out of the over 200 submitted for "Sculpture Chicago '85." Of the sculptors chosen for this symposium, five were from Chicago, one from New York, one from Detroit, one from the Netherlands, and lastly, Billie Lawless from Buffalo.

On May 21, 1985, Chicago Mayor Harold Washington held a press conference to announce the winners of "Sculpture Chicago '85."

Good morning ladies and gentlemen.

We are here today to announce and recognize the 10 outstanding winners of Sculpture Chicago 85.

Sculpture 85 is a unique, exceptional program organized by the Burnham Park Planning Board, with the Mayor's Office of Special Events and support from the private sector.

This innovative program brings prominent sculptors from around the world to Chicago. These sculptors are fully supported as they work on and complete their creative, thought-provoking, inspirational sculptures. The unique sculptures from last year's program are currently on display along State Street and they are indeed the talk of our town.

Chicagoans have a deep appreciation for the arts and cultural affairs. Sculpture Chicago 85 provides Chicagoans with a golden opportunity to meet exceptional artists as they complete their work. And this highly rated program impacts positively on Chicago and helps to sell Chicago as a city that promotes, supports and encourages the development of art and artists.

I want to congratulate the 10 winners of this year's program and also thank the diligent staffs of the Burnham Park Planning Board and the Mayor's Office of Special Events for organizing an excellent program. [6]

The Chicago *Tribune* called it "a unique opportunity to witness the ongoing construction of 10 large-scale pieces in a new sculpture park in the South Loop at Harrison and Wells Streets. More than $200,000 has gone into material, housing, and an honorarium for the artists, with almost $70,000 for the re-construction of the site into a 3-1/2 acre Illinois prairie."[7]

When asked about choosing *Green Lightning* after the controversy in Buffalo, Bette Cerf Hill, president of the Burnham Park Planning Board, said, "Maybe Chicago has more guts than Buffalo."[8] Because *Green Lightning* was already a completed work, she said they still expected Billie to produce as much as he could on the site. With needed repairs, there would be plenty he could do in Chicago.

John Chandler, one of the judges, said, "The question came up about the controversy that it would cause and we were willing to risk it. It seemed like a delightful piece, because of its carnival atmosphere, and it was very attractive to the jury because of its controversy, too." He characterized the work as "lightweight, but fun."[9]

Billie spoke with Christine Ingraham in May 1985 about the piece. Ingraham was the exhibition director and Frank Lloyd Wright's great-granddaughter. She asked if he would consider "just a modification of the piece."[10]

He explained it's a commentary on society "and our values in society" and he could come up with many different kinds of images, but he wasn't really going to change any aspect of it. [11]

• • • ● • ● • ● • • •

On Friday, June 7, 1985, Justice Wayne A. Feeman Jr. made the first major ruling in the Buffalo case. Feeman said that Billie had gained access to the Elm-Oak property through an approval process, therefore possessed certain rights.

The City said they had the right to abate nuisances, without judicial process or proceedings. But Feeman wrote in his decision that the City "may not invoke its police powers... as a pretext to assuage strident community opposition." It must be an actual emergency measure. He added that the City never said the unilluminated sculpture was a public nuisance. "It is clear that the Mayor considered the sculpture a public nuisance only when the neon light component was illuminated. It is therefore this Court's opinion that the sculpture, in a non-illuminated state, does not create a public nuisance. Because the sculpture is not a public nuisance in an unlighted state, the respondents are prohibited from further dismantling or interfering with the reconstruction of the sculpture as long as it remains non-illuminated."

He further wrote, "The illuminated sculpture, located near major arterials to downtown Buffalo, is capable of creating substantial annoyance and discomfort to, and endangering the health and welfare of those motorists who view it."[12]

Billie was thrilled. "I'm going to go ahead with putting it back up here and getting it turned on," he said after the ruling. But, he knew the sculpture was going to Chicago shortly, so why he would continue to antagonize the City is baffling.[13]

Mayor James Griffin praised the decision, saying the judge "showed some common sense. When we dismantled the thing, we dismantled it because it was unsightly. Most of the people that saw it felt it was just a blot on our city."[14]

B.U.R.A. attorney Greg Dudek got a restraining order issued by state Supreme Court Justice Joseph Ricotta to prevent the relighting from happening. "The court has now ruled. And although (Judge Feeman's) decision was a fair one, it apparently failed to be effective enough to shut off the opportunity for another act in a drama that has already embarrassed Buffalo enough."[15]

Billie's attorney, Michael Brown, asserted, "We do not intend to try to provoke an incident. That is not our intention."[16]

The Buffalo *News* wrote an editorial on June 12, 1985, saying, "A great many people in Buffalo and elsewhere are not comfortable with displays as garishly suggestive as this one. That's why they don't normally appear in such prominent places – anywhere. If Lawless had placed *Green Lightning* in an art gallery or sculpture park, that might not have presented a problem. But it is on public land, in the center of one of the city's busiest traffic corridors. The city was left with the choice of offending many of its own citizens or opening itself up to charges of prudishness and parochialism by suppressing an artwork."[17]

They added, the dismantling of *Green Lightning* contributed to the drama. And "the arts advisers who were supposed to have approved the sculpture for the city must take much of the blame for whatever trouble it causes because they allowed the problem to be created in the first place. After all the publicity *Green Lightning* has received, any relighting would be conducted in a circus atmosphere, with Buffalo the butt of plenty of jokes."[18]

• • • • ● • ● • • • •

Christine Ingraham from Chicago called Billie again on June 12, 1985. "I'm just calling to see what kind of progress has been made on modifying your piece?"

"Yea, I'm working on some drawings right now, as a matter of fact ---" he told her.

Ingraham asked him if he considered adding more neon light within the boxes to take emphasis away from the "figures of the penises." He had no intention of changing anything. He later admitted that he was not working on any drawings and had lied to her. "Ha, ha. It looks like that way," he admitted.[19]

They spoke again on June 17, and she tried to get him to change the piece. He then sent her a letter and said that he felt he had met the exhibition guidelines.

When Buffalo Urban Renewal Agency attorney Gregory Dudek was told that *Green Lightning* might leave Buffalo, he said, "We'd love for him to move it. We certainly aren't going to require him to leave it here for a year. It would bring tears of joy to the mayor and certain members of the Common Council."[20]

Like Buffalo *News* editor Murray Light, Billie took offense to editorials about him that weren't entirely true. He responded in a rebuttal to the *News* in a June 12 editorial.

> Editorials are designed to express opinions, but they must be predicated on facts. I will not argue in great depth ...over whether or not *Green Lightning* belongs in the Elm-Oak Arterial as this is entirely subjective. The idea that 'a great many people ...are not comfortable' with such a 'garishly suggestive' image cuts both ways. Since the Great War, Hitler, the Bomb, TV dinners, Jim Jones and our alleged collective consciousness, there has been, indeed, little to be 'comfortable' about.
>
> Art does not come wrapped up in neat little packages, nor

should it be constrained/confined to defined spaces. New thoughts are constantly occurring. The mayor and other public officials involved in this controversy have made statements which are untrue. But because of their positions of public leadership, these statements are reported as uncontroverted facts. Tape-recorded comments will prove that public officials involved with approving the exhibition of *Green Lightning* had a complete understanding of the work. There will be a 'sequel' to *Green Lightning*. It will occur in a courtroom where the statements are made under oath and subject to cross-examination.[21]

On Thursday, June 20, Lawless stated he would not relight *Green Lightning* and declared he would break it down and send it to Chicago for its display in "Sculpture Chicago '85."

Before *Green Lightning* and Billie Lawless even arrived in Chicago, a "concerned" Buffalo citizen sent a letter to Mayor Harold Washington. "I'm writing in the hope that you, like Mayor James D. Griffin, are opposed to pornography and want to protect the good citizens of Chicago from it." This person wasn't even a resident, but felt they should impose their definition of pornography on the 7.2 million people that lived in Chicago in 1985. They went on to say they hoped "this monstrosity will not be shown in your fair city."[22]

To be sure they covered all bases, the mayor's office spoke to their Cultural Affairs office and the Burnham Park Planning Board, but decided *Green Lightning* posed no risk to the citizens of that "fair city."

The Chicago *Tribune* prepared its citizens for *Green Lightning* by writing, "There may be some fireworks at September's 'Sculpture Chicago '85.'"

After mentioning that Buffalo found it "lewd, obscene and disgusting," they added it meant that "Chicago should love it." [23]

On July 22, 1985, Edward Schunk of Walt's Tree Service received a letter from attorney Michael Brown, stating they would like the panels back, with instructions to let Lawless supervise the loading and return to the site. He also received a letter from city attorney Sam Houston acknowledging same.

They asked Schunk if he ever saw the panels lit. "No. They come out with Mr. Lawless, and ...they wanted to light the panels, and I wasn't too anxious in getting involved, but I said I would furnish cord enough and plug the cord in my shop so they'd have electric. They went in the back, they come back in the office and told me they lit, they were all right. In fact, that day Mr. Lawless accidentally forgot and left his briefcase in my office, so he come back later that afternoon and got it, and he was there when we loaded the panels out and took them back to the site."[24]

Billie Lawless began disassembling the sculpture in late July 1985. He made temporary repairs on the neon artwork since it had suffered damage from weather and minor vandalism. The city damaged the electrical wiring when they cut the power, and several of the stars above the sculpture had been stolen. He estimated it would cost more than $30,000 for repairs. [25]

He intended to "dismantle it as it was meant to be," a reference to what he thought Walt's Tree Service did.

They loaded the sculpture onto a flatbed truck and sent it to Chicago. "I'm really optimistic about Chicago," Billie said. "People there are saying that this sculpture is one of the most exciting pieces in the show." But he wasn't giving up on Buffalo yet. "I was born in Buffalo, and I have all good feelings for the area," he said. "Some people here really did like the work, and some day I would like to bring *Green Lightning* back here."[26]

They installed the sculpture in the downtown South Loop area in Chicago and it could be seen clearly from Eisenhower Expressway, the Sears Tower, or the Midwest Stock Exchange Building.

The grand opening of "Sculpture Chicago '85," the third year of the event, took place on Sunday, September 1.

Chicago artist David Simons said, "for the artists who were picked it's really fortunate. They give you materials, space and money, and there's a certain freedom in that, and a certain responsibility. We get a chance to work outside, to make something big. But it also allows a town like the city of Chicago, which is not really accustomed to interacting with art, the chance to get involved. If we can get people down there, regular people who aren't normally involved in art making, I think it'll open them up to an experience they will really gain something from."[27]

The Chicago *Tribune* added, "The whole issue of a community's relation to public art is, in fact, a hot one at the moment."[28] In New York City there was a "bitter wrangling" over relocating *Tilted Arc* by Richard Serra.

In Chicago, Irene Siegel outraged people over a fresco. And in Buffalo, there was *Green Lightning*.

Christine Ingraham said the five-week symposium aimed to bridge the gap between the artist and the public. "I think it's important for the community to understand what art is supposed to be. This program makes people aware of how sculpture is put together. And to be able to watch the building process and to talk with the artists, I think, helps to answer a lot of people's confusions and frustrations and questions."[29]

"It's really a good idea," Billie said. "That was one of the problems in Buffalo. If people had had a better idea of what this was about, maybe all this wouldn't have happened. Maybe what this work needed was a more sophisticated audience."[30]

· · · · ● · ● · · ·

In 1987, United States Attorney General Edwin Meese, under President Ronald Reagan, released the Meese Report, the results of an long investigation into pornography in the country. The committee gathered what it considered a panel of experts, including police officers from five cities: Buffalo, Chicago, Los Angeles, Houston, and Miami.

From Buffalo came the one-man vice squad, Lt. John Dugan, and from Chicago Lt. Thomas Bohling. The two men met during the hearings and became friends. When Dugan heard that the highly offensive *Green Lightning* was heading to Chicago, he called his friend to warn him.

Bohling visited the site where Billie was working on his sculpture. "He was in a small little park, not much of a park at all, where the expressway entered into the downtown area. You could hardly miss it. It was right there if you're driving in and he had those neon tubes that would light up. They would go from being sort of like it was almost a horizontal flaccid, and then it would step up to be what implied being erect."[31]

Before they got any complaints, Bohling said, "we took it and ran with it right away. You realize that I was the obscene matter investigator at that time. I think I was the only one in the city, and I was handling, we used to call them the dirty bookstores. There was, 50 or 60 of them at that time, and a good dozen adult theaters. So I was kinda busy with that. Of course, it was just a state misdemeanor, it wasn't a big fine. It was a $1,000 fine or something like that. It wasn't even considered a big deal. And prior to my involvement in enforcing the obscene matter statute of the state, the city used to prosecute under a city ordinance. So it was the prosecutors for the city that ...would handle it. Essentially, what I'd have to do is I'd have to get a hold of the material, in a legal way. I'd have to purchase the stuff and then find out who the guy was and then present it to a state's attorney for approval for a search warrant, and then go before a judge and then arrest the guy."[32]

Bohling said he would have had to take a video of *Green Lightning*, then present that evidence to a judge. So, Bohling, a special prosecutor from the state, and his commanding officer all went and interviewed Billie. "We weren't, and he wasn't, confrontational. There was just a discussion. And he explained what it was supposedly representing, male dominance, I think, or something. And the state's attorney, and also the corporation counsel, deemed that it wouldn't be necessary to prosecute him."[33]

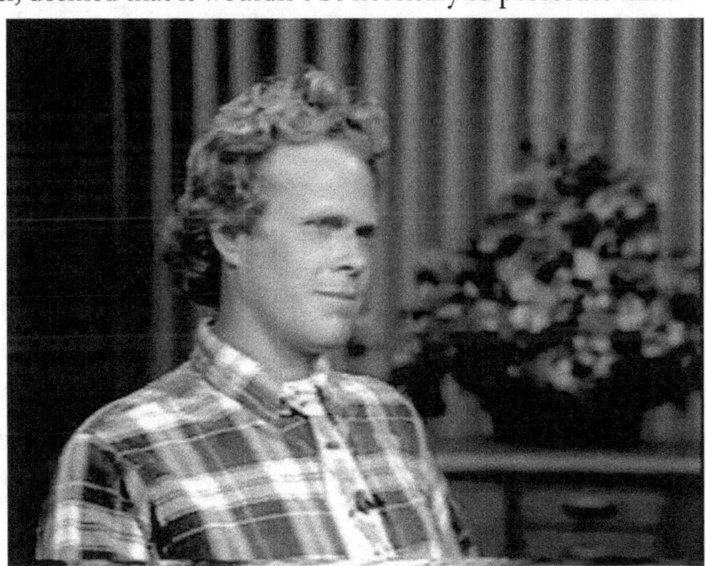

Billie Lawless on "Chicago Tonight." Courtesy of WTTW, Chicago.

"If it was up in Grant Park or someplace like that," Bohling said, "maybe there would be trouble. I'll tell you, some high-ranking officials in the Chicago Police Department thought it should be prosecuted." [34]

The local press was more curious than usual because of the Buffalo controversy and gave the sculpture and Billie plenty of airtime. WBBM news radio reported Jimmy Griffin's reaction. WTTW Channel 11, the local PBS station, did an in-depth look at public art and public controversy on "Chicago Tonight," September 17, 1985.

The host of the show, John Calloway, did an excellent job of getting a city of Chicago alderman to describe how he thought they should create public art. There was a controversy about a fresco by Irene Siegel installed at a new library and a group was suing to have the artwork removed and ultimately destroyed.

Like Buffalo, Chicago had an arts commission and a committee for every piece of public art, yet the public still said they didn't have enough input. Here, they felt Irene Siegel should have worked directly with the public to create a work of art they wanted, not what the artist created. Siegel admitted if that had been the case, she would not have taken the commission.

In the second half of the show Calloway said the year long "Sculpture Chicago" exhibition would include "One nationally controversial piece, *Green Lightning*, by Billie Lawless. When this symbolic neon work of art was unveiled last year in Buffalo, it was called obscene and pornographic and was quickly dismantled," while the camera panned across the sculpture model.

"I think actually, it was actually just one person in Buffalo, and that was the mayor," Lawless said, as he stood outside behind the model wearing red sunglasses, a bandana headband, a yellow t-shirt, and a blue and white plaid long sleeve shirt. "Because actually the people weren't upset by the piece at all. His problem was that he objected to the neon. He thought it was, I don't know, he just thought it was obscene. The three jurors that put together the show were taking a risk, and I think that's what's gotta be done."[35]

In the studio segment, Billie and Mary Jane Jacob, chief curator of the Museum of Contemporary Art in Chicago, (and one of the three members of the selection panel for "Sculpture Chicago '85,") discussed public art with host Calloway. Billie wore the same blue and white plaid shirt, a whimsical yellow tie, and a hat did not hide his curly sandy blonde hair.

John Calloway: What happened finally in Buffalo? You got kind of banned in Buffalo?

Billie Lawless: Well, no, I wasn't banned John. What happened was the mayor went in without due process and he destroyed part of the sculpture and I think that that was really more of the controversy than the subject matter of the sculpture itself. And I was more than reasonable in terms of dealing with the city, and if they had objections, I said I would leave the lights off. But nonetheless, they went in three days later and they wrecked the sculpture.

Calloway: Were you able, could you have gone into court and stopped that, or...

Lawless: I did.

Calloway: ...would you need a lot of money?

Lawless: No, I did stop them and it did take a lot of money. (Laughs) And it's unfortunate, and I think though it does reflect upon Sculpture Chicago, that they're willing to take this kind of a risk on a sculpture that I think poses serious questions as to the public and I think these are questions that should be posed.[36]

Calloway then asked Jacob if this was something new or if it had been going on all along.

Mary Jane Jacob: This is something since the 1960s has become more part of our consciousness with the legislation through the National Endowment for the Arts and programs and General Services Administration, and even the Veterans Administration. Doing public art and having it in places where we didn't have it before. A program like Sculpture Chicago is something which comes out of a local initiative not through one of these federal programs but which brings artists nationally together in a kind of workshop situation, open air situation, and something which hopefully addresses the kind of issues in which you were talking about in the first part of the segment here. Because it allows people to see how artists work for months. They're there, every day from 9 to 5 like regular old business-people, working seriously and we can see how they make the art.

Calloway: Billie Lawless, what do you think the public's right is? Clearly, you would think that you have a right to create, to be shown. What do you think the public's right is?

Lawless: Exactly. Well, I'll tell you. Listening to the alderman, I think that he's got something a little askew, and that is that he believes the public should be involved in the process, and I don't think that's correct. I think the public should be involved as an observer, but making art is a one-person job. It does not take a committee to make art and I think that's where the priorities have to be set straight.

Calloway: Well, what if it's public art supported by public dollars? Does that make a difference? Don't I have a right over my tax dollars?

Lawless: No, I don't think so because we, neither of us, has the right over our tax dollars. So there's many things that our tax dollars are spent on that none of us agree upon. So I think that it's important that a select number of people from the art community representing the art community, be empowered to make these decisions and I think that they have to, at times, take risks.

Calloway: So the appropriate thing would be, that if we don't like, say that I just really don't like most of the art that's coming out, that I'd have to work to remove the people who created the public art legislation in the first place.

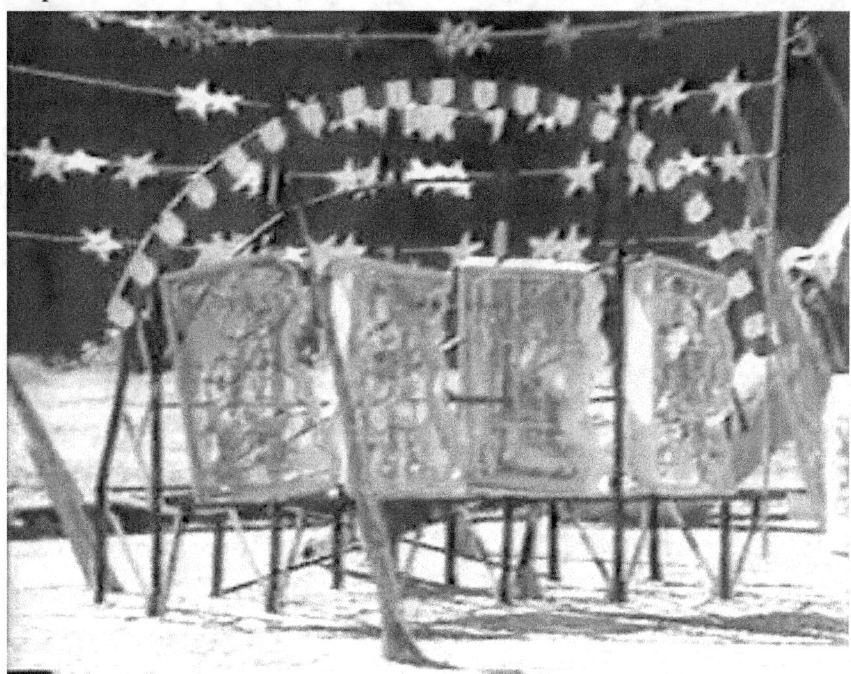

Model of "Green Lightning" on "Chicago Tonight." Courtesy of WTTW, Chicago.

Lawless: Or you could work to increase your knowledge of the piece. And I think that Arlene Siegel touched upon, I think it's very important, our society...

Calloway: Irene.

Lawless: Yes. There is not a very great emphasis in our society on art education, and I think that the first thing that gets tossed out of the budget is music or art education. Here is part of the problem and it has to be addressed.

Calloway: So, is this a constructive thing that's going on? Do you look at this flap over art in public art in any way as a constructive thing for art?

Mary Jane Jacob: Yes, on the one hand, I think it's sad because we realize perhaps the disrespect for the experts in and for the artists themselves in such a process, but it does make people aware of the situation. And hopefully when we have new pieces come about, people will be a little bit more sensitive to it. And I wholeheartedly agree with Billie that in terms of the public's involvement, it can't be in selecting art. It can hopefully be in communicating with the artist and with the piece in the future. But we do need to have the people who are educated in those areas to make those decisions as we would in medicine or in any other field where expertise is necessary.[37]

When Mary Jane Jacob was contacted to comment on "Sculpture Chicago," she said she "was not there then." When reminded that she was actually one of the judges, she said, "oh, maybe, but in that case, remember NOTHING."[38] An interesting take by the former museum curator who appeared on "Chicago Tonight" with Billie and stood by her decision to choose *Green Lightning*.

According to Nick Rabin, deputy commissioner of cultural affairs in Chicago, "It didn't stir up any dust one way or the other. I've heard nothing negative on Lawless, and the critics found the whole show stimulating and gave no indication that any work was inappropriate."[39] Quite anticlimactic after Buffalo.

Bette Hill of the Burnham Park Planning Board added, "It's not as if people don't look at it. There are people on the site all the time. The majority of people I talked to think it's terrific."[40]

Billie found the whole experience in Chicago "uplifting. While I was building the piece, I must have talked to hundreds of people, a lot of them there because they heard of the Buffalo controversy. They'd say, 'where is it?', meaning the 'obscene' part, and I'd say 'you're looking at it.' Usually they'd laugh. Many found it unfathomable that the piece caused all the controversy it did in Buffalo.

"My experience in Chicago when I put that piece up was one of the nicest of my life. I think I only got one negative comment from a drunken soul that was walking through on opening night. He kept coming back and he would yell things at me and I would ignore him."[41]

Although *Green Lightning* was a finished piece, the damage by the City of Buffalo through Walt's Tree Service was extensive. Billie said, "The electrical work was just cut from the box. It was designed to all bolt together and whatnot. When they cut this with the welding torches, it created a flashback into the box and destroyed a lot of the contents of the brain as well. The box is heavily damaged. I had to recondition the entire box, the brain; and, I mean, this was useless at that point. It was cut, and ...I repaired this part in Chicago."[42]

"I'm not sure why ...they cut the bolts on the bunting. I think they were having a hard time getting the box off, because this tin bunting up in this area, it was very tight fit at the box. So this was all cut up in this area and which necessitated replacing this part of the bunting, this curved angle up on the top."[43]

So even though he wasn't building the entire sculpture, Billie could do repairs in Chicago, where the people got to watch him work and rebuild *Green Lightning*.

Christine Ingraham remembered when Billie was a participating sculptor. "I remember his piece---but don't really know much more about Billie or his work after that summer." When pressed about why Chicago took *Green Lightning* in stride while Buffalo tried to destroy it, she said, "Yea, there was no controversy — like Buffalo." When asked if there was a difference in the people in each city, she agreed that it's possible that Chicago in 1985 was "maybe more sophisticated---who knows."[44]

Unlike Buffalo, *Green Lightning* was a hit in the Windy City. The city signed a one year extension to allow the sculpture to stand for an additional year. At the time, Billie said he was going to move to Chicago, "an environment free of obsession with a subway."[45] This was probably a reference to the new light rail in Buffalo. Chicago already had an extensive subway system in 1985.

After *Green Lightning* had been on display for two years in Chicago, it had become a focal point of "Sculpture Chicago" and a city landmark of sorts, according to Barbara Lynne, the new executive director of the Burnham Park Planning Board. "When we try to tell people where Sculpture Chicago is, they say, 'Oh yes! You mean where the sculpture is? When we have friends in from out of town, we take them to see it. We go after dark.'"[46]

When talking with a *Chicago Reader* reporter, Buffalo Arts Commission Executive Director David More said he was far enough removed from the incident to laugh loudly. "The model," More said, "how will I say, was not a particularly elaborate rendition of the full-scale figures that were eventually illuminated."[47]

The sculpture was a hit in Chicago, so Billie knew it was an opportune time to sell one of his models. On December 7, 1985, he sent a letter to Niagara Falls arts patron and founder of Tops Friendly Markets, Armand Castellani.

> Dear Armand, I have just received the maquette of Green Lightning back from a gallery in Chicago. At one point, you mentioned an interest in purchasing this model and asked that I drop it off at the Buscaglia-Castellani Art Gallery.
>
> There has been interest in the maquette expressed by other parties. I feel obliged because of your past support to contact you.
>
> Please advise me of your position.
>
> Seasons greetings to you and your family.
> Best regards.[48]

They gave *Green Lightning* three extensions on its exhibition in Chicago. Exhibition founder Bob Wislow was asked about *Green Lightning* in 2023. He couldn't recall it. The negative impact in Chicago was negligible.

• • • ● • ● • ● • ◆ ◆ •

What a difference a year makes. In May 1986, after his success in Chicago, Billie announced he was moving there and would never bring *Green Lightning* back to its birthplace in Buffalo.[49] He finally left Buffalo in May or June 1986 after selling his house on Highgate Avenue, and moved not to Chicago, but to Baltimore, Maryland. He only stayed until the fall and moved to East Orleans, Massachusetts, then in late December 1987, he moved to Cleveland.

The February 4, 1988 edition of *Chicago Reader* published a letter from Billie in which he made some "observations" about an article by Michael Ervin. In his response, Lawless said only two of 90 articles written about him were accurate and he called it a "sorry state of journalism." He corrected the fact that Walt's Tree Service only came on Tuesday, November 21, to dismantle *Green Lightning*, after the courts were closed.

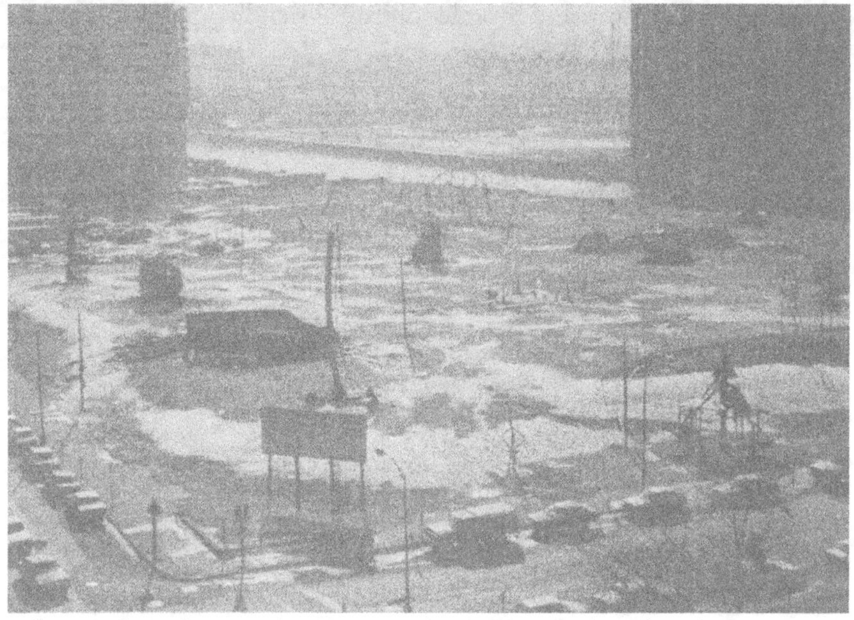

The site of "Sculpture Chicago" in January 1986. Photo by Al Kovacs and F Newsmagazine.

"Sure enough, in the four hours it took my attorneys to get a temporary restraining order, the sculpture was almost entirely destroyed. In the area of $100,000 worth of damage was done to the piece in what was later described by the New York State Supreme Court as actions 'abhorrent to the (court's) understanding of the laws of the community.'

"To win this case in the New York State Supreme Court, I had to pay attorneys' fees approaching $20,000. This eventually required the liquidation of my home and studio. Personal relationships were lost. I lost my job as a rowing coach at a local high school, and I was repeatedly subjected to death threats. I left Buffalo because it became impossible to live and work there. I now live in Cleveland after giving strong consideration to

Chicago. Both cities have in common a warm, generous, and supportive populace."[50]

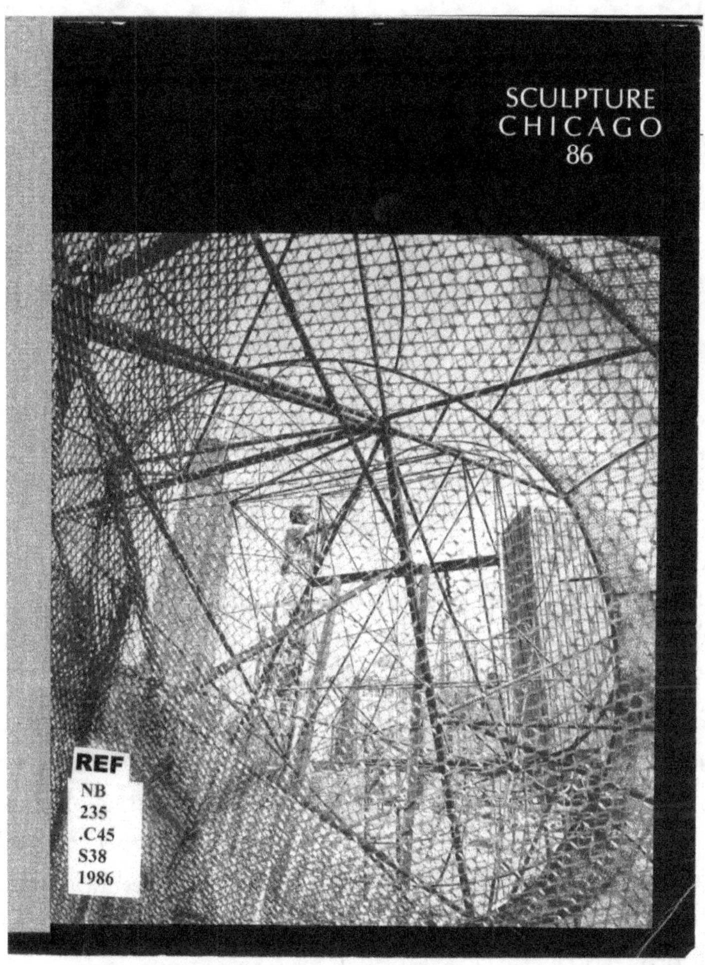

Cover of the 1986 "Sculpture Chicago" pamphlet. Courtesy of the Chicago Public Library.

I Know It When I See It

O N FEBRUARY 12TH, 1986, Richard M. Schaus, secretary of the West Side Rowing Club in Buffalo, (where Billie was a coach), sent a letter to Billie advising him that the board of directors voted not to make him a rowing coach for the 1986 rowing season.[1]

On March 10th, 1986, the City of Buffalo answered the amended complaint from February 17, 1986. In it they said they rescinded the contract with Lawless, the "Court lacks jurisdiction over the subject matter," and any actions "were done in the exercise and performance of a governmental function of its police powers in order to preserve the public order, welfare and safety and are thereby immune from suit in these proceedings."[2]

The City claimed they acted in "good faith" and used no unnecessary force, and did not cause any damage or injury to the plaintiff's personal rights or property.[3] Case closed in their eyes.

It wasn't until August 26, 1987, that the Buffalo Urban Renewal Agency answered the February 1986 complaint. B.U.R.A. had begun using an outside law firm, Moot & Sprague and partner Richard F. Griffin, to represent their interests.

Was the city purposely dragging this case out in the hopes it bankrupt Billie Lawless so he would drop it, or was this typical?

B.U.R.A. denied most of the allegations in the lawsuit and instead blamed Griffin in his capacity as mayor. They said the doctrine of sovereign immunity barred it, meaning Lawless could not sue the government without its consent, because the King could do no wrong. In reality, it rarely applies to municipalities.

B.U.R.A. also said, "If it is proven at trial that this defendant engaged in any culpable conduct... those actions were undertaken in good faith, with proper justification, without unnecessary force and without malice," much like the City's response.

They said because Judge Wayne Feeman had ruled in 1985 that *Green Lightning* was a nuisance, collateral estoppel barred the entire complaint, meaning they could not sue them for that prior action. Because Billie knew that the neon would depict male genitalia, they relied upon his "oral misrepresentations," and he committed fraud by omission and they had suffered monetarily. [4]

They said because "the sculpture ...did not fully resemble the scale model presented to B.U.R.A.," they exercised their right to end the Agreement by letter. Once again, this would be a contentious point during the trial, as no one knew who delivered the termination letter to Lawless, and he said he never received it.[5]

The multiple parties would continue to respond to each claim and counterclaim for months. On November 4, 1987, Billie's lawyers denied the claims that the maquette he presented to B.U.R.A. "did not, in fact, constitute a complete depiction of the *Green Lightning*." [6]

As an artist, Billie needed to continue making art. It was his source of income and in his blood.

· · ● · ● · ● · ● · · ·

James Rosenberger graduated from York University in Toronto, Ontario with a graduate degree in theater and moved to inexpensive Cleveland, Ohio, in 1976. In January 1978, he and Robert Mihaly created Aeolus, an artist run workspace. Mihaly had a MFA from Kent State University in Ohio.[7]

In 1979, Rosenberger left and took the organization names with him, so Mihaly took the helm and they renamed the organization SPACES. They became an art gallery that challenged the status quo and presented artist-driven works. (In May 2018, SPACES celebrated its 40th anniversary.)

In July 1987, they created an exhibition called "UNCENSORED," which they called "An uncommon show for uncommon times, UNCENSORED--a show of previously censored paintings, sculpture, photography, videos, installations and performance by regional artists." The show ran from Friday, October 16th through Saturday, November 14th. They included documentation and press coverage of the censorship incidents, as well as new works by some artists.

There were about 28 various media artists in the show. They also showed four controversial films originally banned in Ohio.[8]

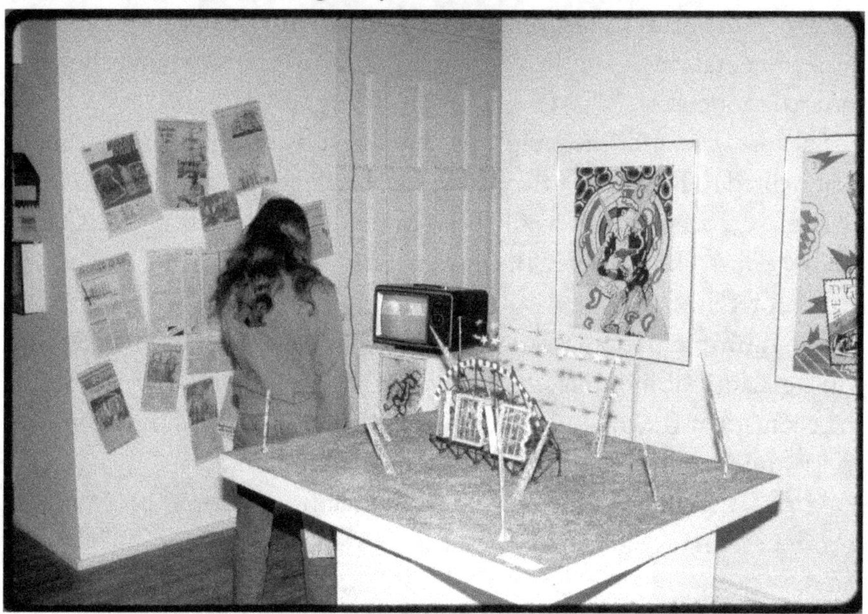

"Uncensored" exhibit, SPACES Gallery, 1986. Courtesy SPACES Archive Collection, Kelvin Smith Library Special Collections.

This is an exhibition of work allegedly censored from public, private and university galleries, traveling exhibitions, television broadcast and public spaces throughout the region. We use the word 'alleged' because some of the cases have either no documentation or the situations were not clearly defined. All of the artists represented here, however, feel that their work was censored when it was removed from exhibitions, shut down, damaged or not allowed to hang or stand. In several cases we raise the question, 'Is this really censorship?' and leave it up to the viewer to decide. We are not necessarily advocating the work itself, but believe strongly that it should be exhibited as originally intended. Because we support artists and not individual works of art, we have included new work by five of these artists. Financial support did not come from the usual sympathetic sources. We are grateful, however, to Art Matters, Inc., for support in this endeavor.[9]

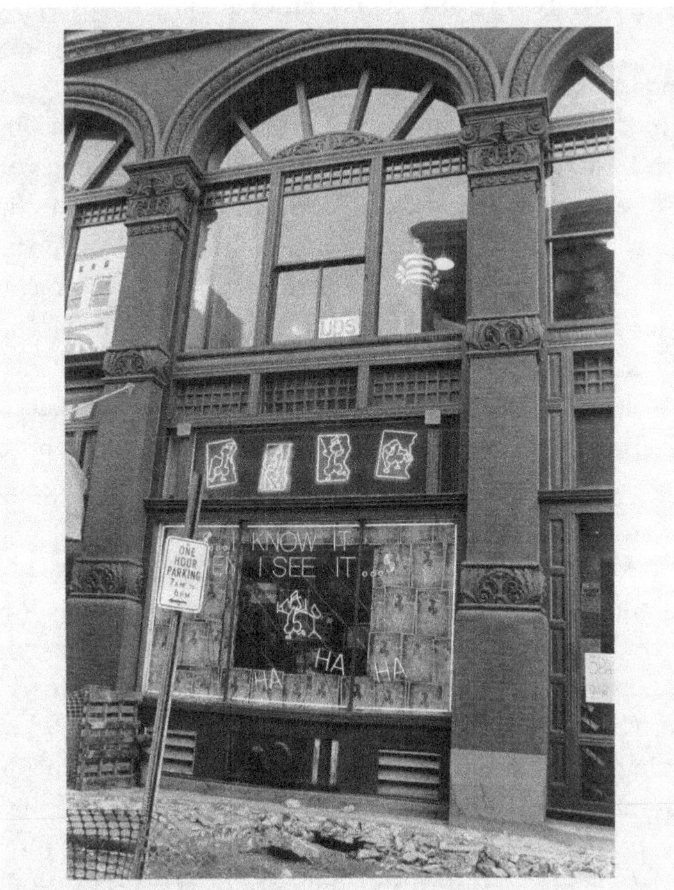

Front window of SPACES gallery in Cleveland for I Know it When I See It display, 1985. Courtesy SPACES Archive Collection, Kelvin Smith Library Special Collections.

For this exhibit Billie created *$...I Know It When I See It...$ (Uncensored*

Einstein to Uncensored Bork). It was a multi-media installation, including neon, video, and sound. It would take the front window of SPACES at 1216 W. 6th Street and include small versions of the four *Green Lightning* panels that created the controversy in Buffalo.

Cleveland writer Amy Sparks wrote, "Armed with inspiration in the form of Walter Kendrick's *The Secret Museum* and Walter Percy's *Message in the Bottle*, books dealing with the history of pornography, its suppression, and the nature of language and man, Lawless created a complex, multimedia installation at SPACES, a key work in the gallery's important *UNCENSORED* exhibit in 1987. Although smaller than *Green Lightning*, this work confronted many of the same issues, resurrected the 'offending' images and incorporated video technology."[10]

The piece "rips political statements out of their contexts and illuminates them with biting irony." The title comes from United States Supreme Court Justice Potter Stewart who, in 1964, tried to describe his threshold for obscenity. He also included passages from the 1968 Meese Commission on Pornography. Lawless used conservative music and "comments in the frequent censorship in art as compared to music and science."[11]

There was a timed sequence of the same neon penises from *Green Lightning*, and "although much of the work is tongue-in-cheek, it addresses the issue of censorship, tries to define the weird line between pornography and art and wrestles with the urge for communication under government suppression."[12]

Sparks said, "On the one hand, Lawless satirizes the Meese report, a compendium of dirty books, as a farce putting the Government Printing Office in the pornography business. He's also saying music and science (Mozart, Einstein) traditionally have not experienced the censorship art has. He also takes a poke at Judge Robert H. Bork."[13]

Interestingly, Mozart encountered censorship during his lifetime. The ruling class often imposed censorship, and suppressed some of his operas, such as "The Marriage of Figaro," which criticized nobility. The uneducated rejected the ideas of scientists and philosophers as they seemed absurd to them. Billie comparing himself to those great people shows his continued level of egotism. He would say, although he was a homebody, he "confesses to a fondness for the limelight—at least where his art is concerned." To him, creating his large sculptures was "very much like being on stage, and definitely an enjoyable part of the overall process."[14]

In 1985 Tipper Gore, wife of Vice President Al Gore, was upset by a Prince album her daughter bought. She then helped form PMRC, the Parents Media Resource Center, which forced the music industry to put parental warning labels on music. And in the 21st century, science has become politicized. So, maybe Billie Lawless felt alone and attacked, but in the grand scheme of the arts and science, he was not.

The Cleveland *Plain Dealer* in 1997 called the UNCENSORED show a "neon penis extravaganza." The dancing neon penises danced across the front window of SPACES, but nobody complained, except a guy who worked in the porno shop across the street. "He goes, 'You're really pissing me off, man,'" Billie said. "'If I put that up in my store, I'd get busted.'" [15] He was probably right.

From November 12 to 14th, Billie offered a daily audio-visual window piece involving five video monitors "best viewed after sunset."[16]

Highway to Hell

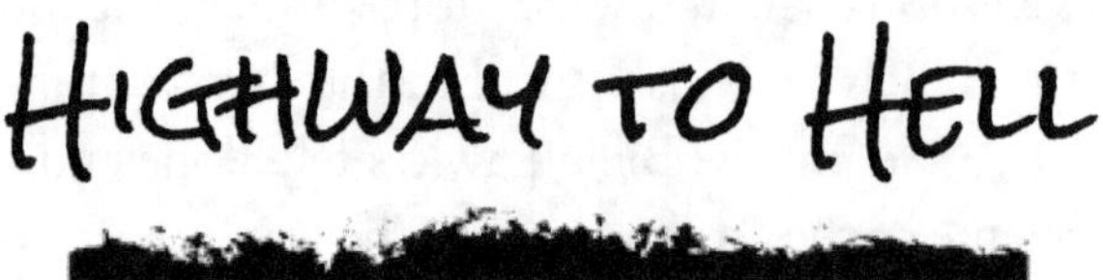

"I believe that there is something going on in
Columbus that is detrimental to outdoor art and
artists." Billie Lawless

*G*REEN *LIGHTNING* WAS STILL a hit in Chicago in 1988. "*Green Lightning* is a nice piece, it really is," said the new "Sculpture Chicago" director Robin Franklin. Rumor was that anytime the power turned off *Green Lightning*, people complained that "their sculpture is off."[1]

"We usually write one-year display contracts," Ms. Franklin said. "The artist retains ownership of the piece. A lot of the constructions are abstract. *Green Lightning* is one of the few that is quite representational."[2]

"I think that Buffalo never really saw the statue for what it was," Lawless said. "Of course Buffalo never got a chance, and the media in Buffalo generally missed the whole point of the piece."[3]

After the final year of exhibiting *Green Lightning* in Chicago, Billie Lawless had it taken down in late December 1988.

Lawless submitted an application for "Sculpture at Heritage Village" in late February or early March 1988. Columbus Jewish Foundation d/b/a Heritage Village was a retirement community at 1151 College Avenue in Columbus, Ohio, that had run a yearly sculpture exhibition since 1985. The husband and wife team of Marty and Pauli Greenberg curated and coordinated it. The Columbus arts community knew Marty as an enthusiastic patron and supporter of artists. They accepted 32 entries out of the approximately 90 submitted for submission in the 1988 show.

On April 16, 1988, Lawless received a letter from Martin L. Greenberg advising him they had selected him to exhibit at the 1988 show.

"We are pleased to advise you that you have been selected as an exhibiting artist in Sculpture at Heritage Village 1988. The selection committee felt your entry, *Didy Wah Didy*, was a powerful statement relevant to contemporary society. They further felt your slides demonstrated a body of work of exceedingly high quality and integrity."[4]

They must have believed the piece was worth displaying in a high-profile location, and selected a site visible from busy Interstate 70 in Columbus, which would become contentious.

Lawless named *Didy Wah Didy* for the last stop on the mythical railroad bound for hell in Black southern folklore. The 1988 "Sculpture at Heritage Village" contained earthworks, installations and traditional sculpture by regional artists.[5] Billie said his sculpture was about Chernobyl and Three Mile Island, and a message about nuclear power and weapons.

As part of the agreement that Billie signed, the sculpture was to be installed by May 20. The show itself ran from June 6 to September 11 and sculptures were to be removed by October 10. One reason for the install date was so they could photograph the art for a program and a juried competition worth $1,000. The judges were Sarah Rogers-Lafferty, curator, Contemporary Arts Center, Cincinnati; John More, artist, Manhattan resident; and Penelope Walker, editor, *Sculpture* magazine, Washington, D.C.

According to Billie, he made a verbal agreement with Marty Greenberg on April 6, 1988, to keep his sculpture up and lit until April 1989 so he could get as much exposure for a future sale.

"With extremely simple imagery and few words," Amy Sparks wrote, "the piece is a timed neon sequence that shows a mushroom cloud forming over a boy's head. With the words 'Atomic Playground Ahead' and 'Kids, Ride the Big One!' it is a piercing send-up of typical American roadside attractions. In three of the four corners, constantly flashing are the words 'chills,' 'spills,' 'thrills.' When the 'kid,' who starts out smiling, then becomes alarmed, is finally 'nuked,' 'death' with an alternating skull and cross bones flashes in the lower right-hand corner. Each of the three flashing words are surrounded by the icons common in Lawless' work, lightning bolts, dollar signs and stars. In all, it is a timed sequence of approximately sixty seconds."[6]

Jacqueline Hall wrote in the *Columbus Dispatch*, "Billie Lawless' *Didy Wah Didy* may stop traffic on I-70 with its flashing mushroom-shaped neon lights talking of destruction in a rather satiric manner. It also speaks of billboards' defacement of nature."[7]

Even though Marty Greenberg knew what the piece would look like and placed it next to a highway, he said he asked Billie about potential zoning problems and asked if he would need zoning or building permits. According to Greenberg, Billie assured him that no permits were required because "this was art." Greenberg was still concerned, so he telephoned Columbus' development department to inquire about the need for permits for a temporary sculpture.

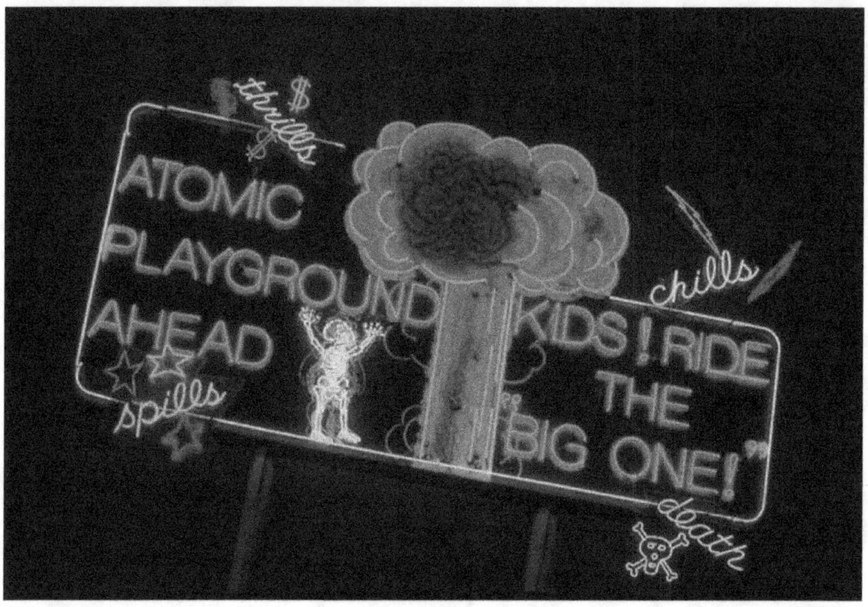

"Didy Wah Didy," Columbus, Ohio. Photo © and courtesy of Barney Taxel, photographer, Cleveland, Ohio, USA.

Lawless did not complete installation by the required date in May, but in late June or early July. Because of this, he missed the photo opportunity for the program and it was not operational in time for the gala organized by Heritage Village. Almost immediately after installation, on July 7, 1988, the city of Columbus cited Marty Greenberg and Heritage Village with a zoning code violation for prohibited graphics along the Interstate. Greenberg said he did not receive the violation until July 19 and when he tried to contact Lawless about the violation, only reached his voicemail.[8]

A letter dated August 3, 1988 contained a second notice sent from the City of Columbus attorney stating, "This is a criminal offense. Failure to comply with the notice of violation is a misdemeanor of the 3rd degree which carries a fine of $500.00 and/or 60 day's imprisonment." On August 11 Heritage Village appealed the violation.

"We asked the city if a permit was needed for a neon sculpture installation," Greenberg said. "They said no." But apparently someone complained to the city and city officials had to cite them.[9] Lawless and Greenberg disagreed on where the complaint originated.

Billie received pro bono legal representation from the Volunteer Lawyers and Arts Program in Columbus. Through them, attorney John S. Marshall took the case.

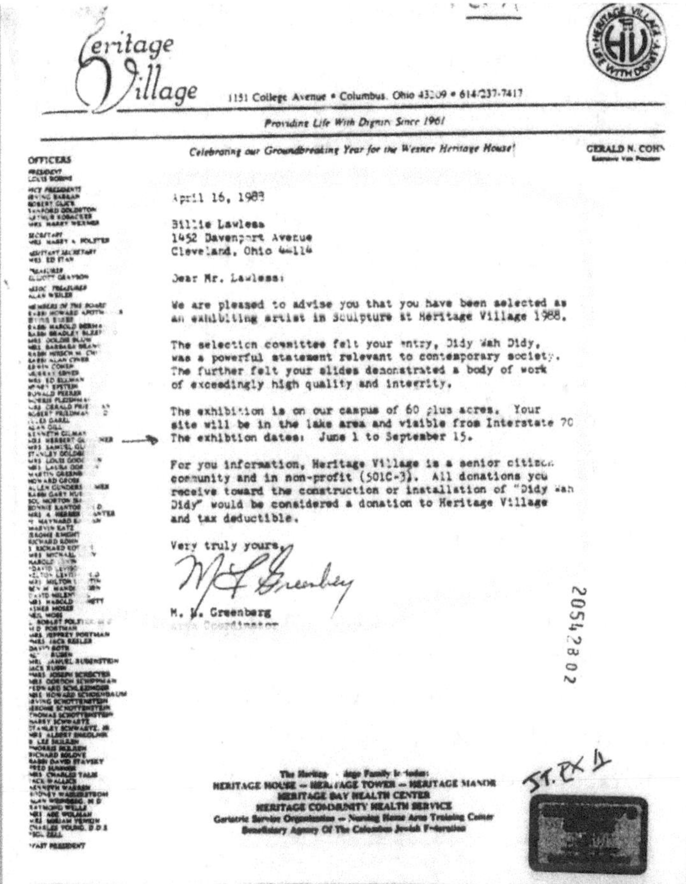

Heritage Village

1151 College Avenue • Columbus, Ohio 43209 • 614/237-7417

Providing Life With Dignity Since 1961

Celebrating our Groundbreaking Year for the Wexner Heritage House!

April 16, 1988

Billie Lawless
1452 Davenport Avenue
Cleveland, Ohio 44114

Dear Mr. Lawless:

We are pleased to advise you that you have been selected as an exhibiting artist in Sculpture at Heritage Village 1988.

The selection committee felt your entry, Didy Wah Didy, was a powerful statement relevant to contemporary society. The further felt your slides demonstrated a body of work of exceedingly high quality and integrity.

The exhibition is on our campus of 60 plus acres. Your site will be in the lake area and visible from Interstate 70 The exhibtion dates: June 1 to September 15.

For you information, Heritage Village is a senior citizen community and in non-profit (501C-3). All donations you receive toward the construction or installation of "Didy Wah Didy" would be considered a donation to Heritage Village and tax deductible.

Very truly yours,

M. L. Greenberg
Arts Coordinator

The letter from Heritage Village congratulating Billie.

The *Columbus Dispatch* received inquiries asking where the "Atomic Playground," was located, so reporter Robert Albrecht looked into it. "All of you westbound drivers on I-70 east will have to look elsewhere for a new place to take the kids. There is no Atomic Playground, contrary to what you've imagined after seeing that tall neon sign along the banks of Alum Creek. That's art, freeway commuter," he wrote.[10]

"Tens of thousands of people can see it from the highway," said Lawless. "But it's not a sign. It's a sculpture in a sculpture garden."[11]

After the exhibition ended on September 15, 1988, Lawless ignored his contract and kept the artwork standing and lit.

On September 19, Fran Resch, administrator of Heritage Village, tried to fix the problem by placing a tarp over the sculpture. When they could not do it safely, they just covered the rear of the sculpture, still causing damage to the piece, according to Lawless. "That was upsetting," Billie said. "One day I went down there to work on the piece and it was shrouded in black plastic." The following day, they removed the tarp.[12] Marty Greenberg claimed wind did the damage.

"Seeing as the exhibition was officially over September 15th, we don't feel the need to talk about it anymore," said Greenburg. "It's over." [13]

Not according to Lawless, who stated, "I was led to believe the sculptures would stay up throughout the winter." [14]

Yet to have his day in court in Buffalo for *Green Lightning*, Lawless went to battle for the right to keep *Didy Wah Didy* standing in Columbus. On October 12, 1988, he filed a complaint naming the City of Columbus and Heritage Village, which ended their cooperation with him. Lawless' attorney John S. Marshall got a restraining order barring the city of Columbus, Ohio, or Heritage Village from tearing the sculpture down.

What seemed to tick Billie off was that Heritage Village wanted to keep the concrete base he built for the piece intact, presumably for a less "controversial" sculpture to be shown the following year.

According to Mary Jo Kilroy, a Columbus attorney who represented others under this code, the City Graphics Commission exercised its power discriminately. She said, "The city uses it to prohibit peace and anti-nuclear demonstrations. However, the graphics code isn't used against club owners, anti-abortionists, or mainstream politicians."[15]

At the October 19, 1988 meeting of the Columbus Graphics Commission, they declared by a unanimous vote, Lawless' sculpture a sign, not artwork. Then the City of Columbus cited Lawless for erecting a sign without a permit (and said that he was not an artist but a "sign maker"), hoping to shut it down.

"You start looking for entrails, omens," said Lawless, who said he received letters and calls of support from around the country, including one from Athena Tacha, whose sculpture was destroyed by city workers at the Columbus airport. "I believe that there is something going on in Columbus that is detrimental to outdoor art and artists," he continued. "Somebody has to take a stand."[16]

Amy Sparks wrote in 1989, "It should not be taken lightly that Columbus, Ohio, which is the home of the Ohio Arts Council, had just previously been embroiled in a controversy over a Lichtenstein sculpture at the airport. In both cases, there was not one word of support from the Ohio Arts Council for either of the artists."[17]

"They offered me what they thought the damage to the piece was--$100," said Lawless. "But they didn't call in a curator to estimate the damage. They called a sign maker. So I can take $100 or sue. If I win, the piece stays up until April (1989), turned on. If I lose, the sculpture comes down."[18]

According to an unknown Columbus artist, "I suspect the content of the sculpture is at the root of the problem."

Marty Greenburg admitted that he'd gotten some complaints about the content of the sculpture. But, he said, "we're trying to play it low key here. The arts community enjoys a nice relationship with the city's zoning committee. If we create a furor over this, it will kill future temporary shows like this." In Greenburg's opinion, Lawless was "a super-sensitive artist, or he is looking for trouble."[19]

"I'm tired of fighting and getting attorneys," sighed Lawless. "When I talked to the building inspector who cited me, he led me to believe someone complained about the subject matter. I was also told I was going to have to prove it was a sculpture, not a sign. I've been a sculptor for fifteen years. What else do they need to know?"[20]

On October 28, Lawless filed an appeal to the violation. In his legal filing, he incorrectly said that Heritage Village was a party to the appeal.

• • • ● • ● • ● • • •

On November 4, 1988, Billie sent a letter to the board of directors of SPACES gallery in Cleveland, unrelated to this event.

This letter is long over due.

As some of you may know, since coming to Cleveland to do an installation at SPACES, I have decided to make my home and studio here which has kept me busy and unfortunately delayed my writing these comments to you.

I have dealt with commissions, curators, galleries both profit and nonprofit and individuals of all kinds related to the art world throughout the country. I have until SPACES never dealt with a group that worked so well together as the three individuals who you have chosen to run the day to day affairs of the gallery.

My installation was made all the easier by the support and hard work which went, I thought, beyond any reasonable expectations. This was done with a 'we can succeed' frame of mind that was accompanied by a positive and uplifting attitude spiked with just the right amount of humor.

This is such a rare occurrence in the art world that I felt obliged to let you know my feelings.
Best of luck![21]

It wasn't just the city of Columbus that objected to Billie's artwork. Phyllis M. Redshaw took exception in a letter to the editor in the *Columbus Dispatch*. She said, in part, "It is a particularly poor specimen of workmanship. The symbolism and design is the tritely conventional type... and any artist that uses... 'day-glow' pink for anything deserves, in my opinion, to have his artistic credentials severely questioned."[22]

Franklin County Common Pleas Court referee Harold Paddock heard testimony about the sculpture dispute in November and December 1988. In mid-December attorney John Marshall told Paddock that Columbus' efforts to dismantle the work before Lawless had intended to take it down the following spring was an unconstitutional assault on art as non-commercial speech.

Eileen Pruett, an assistant Columbus city attorney, told referee Paddock the city considered *Didy Wah Didy* a sign because he built it like a standard roadway sign. Ms. Pruett said the "sign" was also a safety hazard because its neon lighting distracted motorists.[23]

Court referee Paddock ruled on February 8, 1989 that *Didy Wah Didy* was art, but it was also subject to the Columbus graphics code. He concluded that the city of Columbus could enforce its sign regulations and require dismantling of the sculpture because its code dealt with sign safety and location, not with the material depicted.[24]

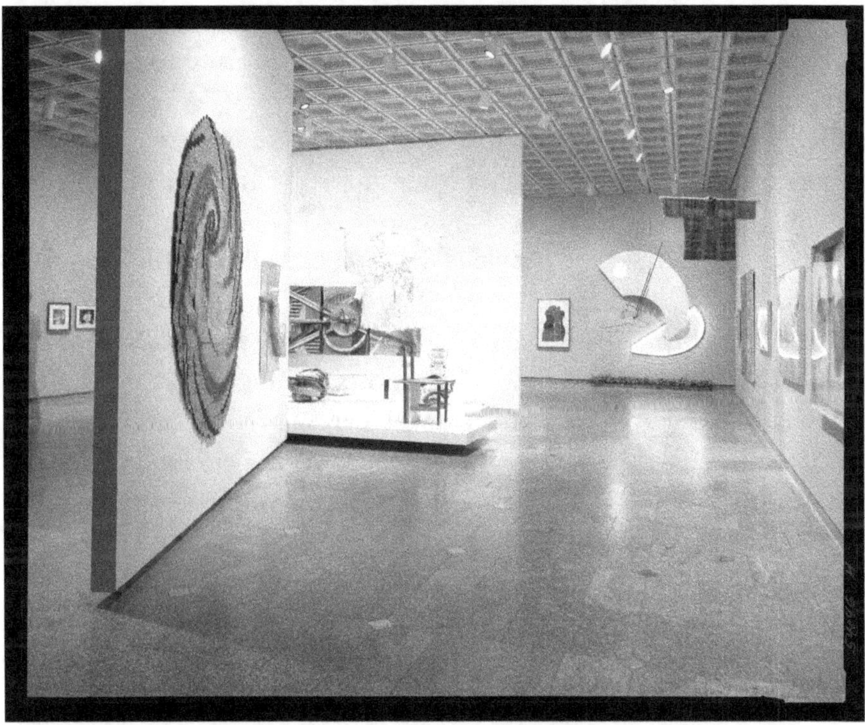

"Danger: Do Not Touch! High Voltage!!" from 1981. Mounted on far wall at Special Exhibition Gallery - May Show, 1988, E5406H. Courtesy of the Cleveland Museum of Art Archives.

Unrelated to this, ten days later, Marty Greenberg announced that the outdoor sculpture show would take a two-year hiatus while construction took place on the grounds. He said they were "always gambling on people who had ideas," but couldn't always follow through. As for the controversy with Billie Lawless? "Actually, the publicity was good for us," Greenberg said. "I guess it wasn't good in terms of fundraising, but it won't hurt us, because we're not raising funds this year. ... As far as I'm concerned, that had nothing to do with this."[25]

The referee's recommendation established a precedent supporting city control over artwork falling under the graphics code. Michael Shannon from the Columbus Department of Development said because of the ruling, "I'd be much more inclined to hardball it in the future."[26]

According to Lawless, "they started playing hardball last year when they tried to get rid of my piece. This is a political decision. Everyone is more or less protecting themselves. Columbus is the biggest loser in all of this. I'm a sculptor, not a sign maker."[27]

Through a compromise, they allowed the sculpture to stand for a month, albeit unlit.

Billie's attorney John S. Marshall said, "It wasn't going to cause any more accidents than any billboard does." But they still ended the case in April 1989.

One wonders what the people of 1989 would think of the video billboards of today.

Billie moved *Didy Wah Didy* to a salvage yard on Pearl Road in Cleveland in 1990, where a new crowd of motorists heading eastbound on I-480 at the Pearl Road overpass wondered where the playground was.

"You'd be surprised how many people come in here looking for the Atomic Playground," said Myron Kaplan, owner of the salvage yard and an art patron. "Who the heck would want to go to the Atomic Playground?"[28]

His son Mike said, "It's poetry in light. It's funny in a scary way."[29]

In an interesting twist, Mike Kaplan left the family salvage business to start a glass blowing shop and welding shop.

Billie took *Didy Wah Didy* down in September 1996 for 28 months to dismantle and repair it. He restored it in April 1999.

It is in storage at Lawless' Cleveland shop at the time of this writing.

Spearfish

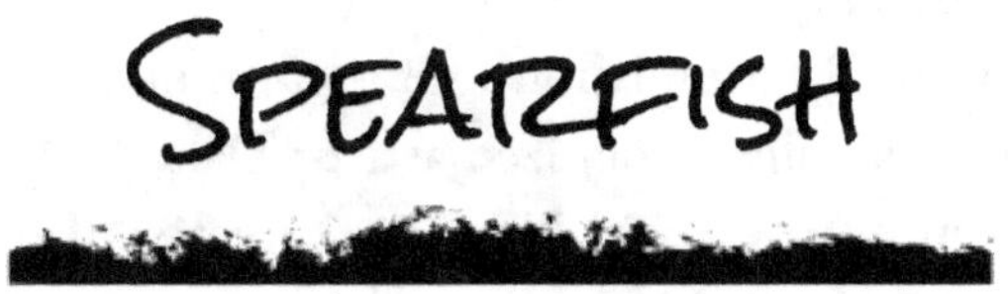

"I don't know art, but I know I don't like it." Dennis Walkins

THE STORY OF SPEARFISH, South Dakota, is as bizarre as all the tales of Billie Lawless. By 1985, he was living in East Orleans, Massachusetts, where his mother and six of his siblings had moved after his parents' divorce. This is a small town in Cape Cod, an area known for its summer partying from the 60s through the 80s. "Party-hearty times when the booze flowed freely and a group of performers ruled the local bar scene," wrote one writer.[1]

This took Lawless away from the controversy that had taken over his hometown of Buffalo. He paid his next-door neighbor in Buffalo, Charles Daniels, to watch over his garage studio and after he sold his house a few years later, he would store some of his belongings in Daniels' garage.

In February 1986, Jerry Boyer, a member of the Outdoor Sculpture Committee in the small town of Spearfish, South Dakota (population less than 6,000), requested city participation in an outdoor sculpture competition. Boyer, also chairperson of the Spearfish Area Council on the Arts and Humanities (SACAH) asked the city to furnish the location at the median at North Avenue in the RSVP Garden. SACAH allocated $4,000 and applied for federal funding through the National Endowment for the Arts. They approved it at the February 6 Common Council meeting and the city council approved $1,000 in funding as an incentive that would cover site location, physical installation, as well as electricity and lighting.[2]

SACAH nationally advertised the competition and started a call for work on a sculpture. In response, Billie submitted a model of a ten-year-old abstract sculpture he called *Hungry Fish* for consideration. "It came from my dying goldfish," he said. "He couldn't get to the top of the tank, so I'd raise him up so he could eat."[3]

SACAH received 481 submissions. Of that number, 71 were juried by a committee of nationally recognized artists: Dale Lamphere, a Sturgis, South Dakota sculptor; George Neubert, director of the Sheldon Art Gallery at the University of Nebraska; and John Day, dean of the College of Fine Arts, University of South Dakota. Representatives from the city, public schools, Black Hills State College, business community, and the SACAH Board of Directors also consulted and decided the winner. They would award the winner a $20,000 commission.

On Monday, June 20, 1988, the Spearfish Common Council had a town meeting where they unveiled the winning design. "They sent me a letter saying I'd won the competition," Billie Lawless said. His abstract fish design had beaten 70 other entries, and almost immediately set off a firestorm of comments. They announced they would unveil the final sculpture, 18 feet wide and high and made of black metal, the following year at the Festival in the Park.[4]

Jerry Boyer, after taking the city's temperature, said, "Many people it will grow on. Many people it will never grow on."[5] Oddly familiar words, reminiscent of Sam Magavern on the night of the *Green Lightning* unveiling.

"They want to know why it doesn't look like a real fish," Lawless complained, "because that is what they really want. The officials also want to know if their letter of acceptance is considered a contract." With so many voices having a hand in the decision making, Lawless was understandably upset. "It becomes art by committee," he said, "which is not art at all. Did Picasso need community input?"[6]

Again, Billie's ego showed as he compared his work to Picasso.

Former Spearfish Mayor Joe Jorgensen said that the plastic trash bag that had protected the model from the rain was "the appropriate container" for the piece. "Why not have a fish that you can see is a fish?"[7] Maybe because it's boring?

Spearfish councilperson Dennis Walkins, masquerading as an art critic, said, "I don't know art, but I know I don't like it."[8] This sounds like a lot like Jimmy Griffin.

SACAH committee member Stuart Bellman suggested they should get additional public input, but Boyer reminded them that because of the

NEA involvement, "it's this sculpture or no sculpture."[9]

"What confuses me more," wrote David Townsend in the Spearfish *Daily Queen City Mail*, "is that the suggestion that Spearfish is not sophisticated or imaginative enough to accept or appreciate a different viewpoint when it comes to public art."[10]

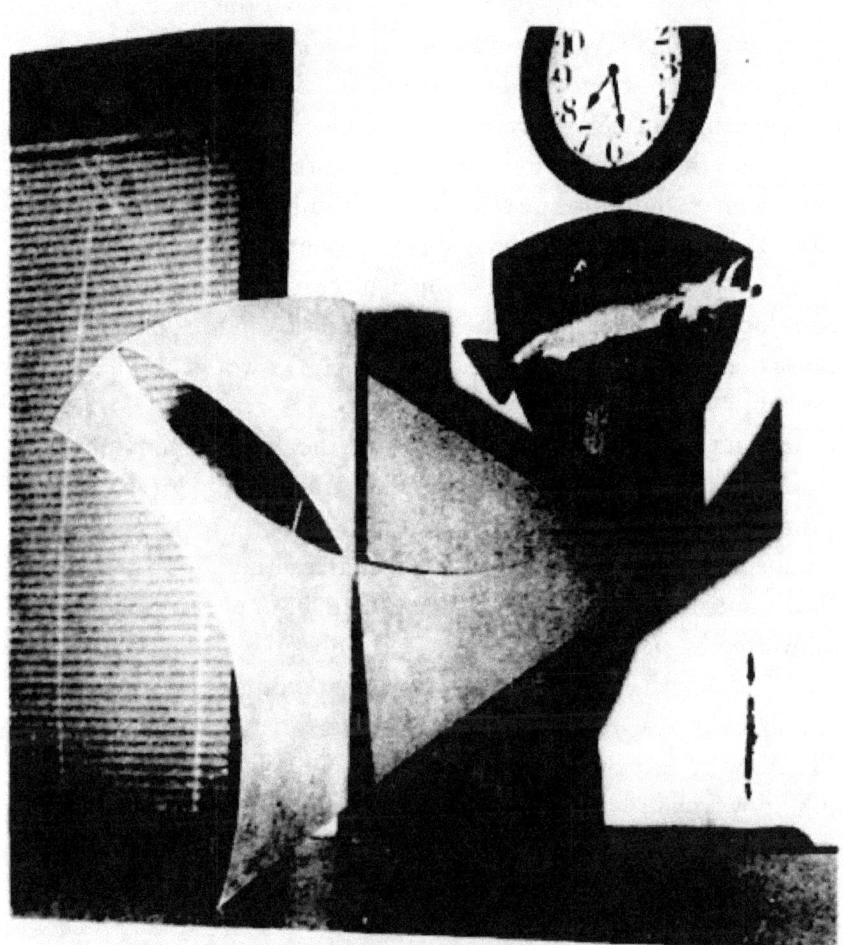

"Hungry Fish" model, as displayed in Spearfish, South Dakota, 1985. Photo by David Townsend.

He listed several projects that were not without detractors. "What I may view as a refreshing change from the mundane, the trite and the commonplace, will be labeled as 'garbage' by others. It is absolutely necessary that a variety of views be allowed to co-exist side-by-side.

"The energy and emotion being spent in opposition to *Hungry Fish* would, I believe, be better spent in doing the planning, research and fundraising needed for an alternative art piece. Not to replace the one which is planned, but to be erected in another public place. There's room for imagination in Spearfish and room, I believe, for two sculptures." [11]

At the August 15, 1988 Spearfish Common Council meeting, Councilperson Dennis Walkins said the board opposed the placement of the sculpture in the RSVP Park and made suggestions in its place. [12]

The issue was not resolved by March 1989. So Billie started legal proceedings against the city to accept the commission he had won. Spearfish did not want the abstract sculpture. They negotiated with Lawless and his attorney to have the sculpture placed in Centennial Park, near the entrance to D. C. Booth Fish Hatchery. He agreed not to litigate for the original site. At the March 6, 1989 Common Council meeting, they approved moving the site location and rescinded the original location in the RSVP Garden. Because the location was being changed, the NEA would also have to be consulted. [13]

In the end, the city of Spearfish rejected the piece. When one of the jury, sculptor Dale Lamphere, was asked about the incident in 2022, his response was, "I don't recall anything specific about the incident. I vaguely remember choosing the sculpture, but don't recall anything after that." [14]

With controversial art-related incidents like the ones that Billie Lawless was involved in, no one ever seems to remember the details. Is it just the passage of time that erodes the mind, or is it that the incidents were a blight, a stain on their past and they would rather just forget about it?

"These were sort of like Garrison Keillor people," Billie said. "They didn't know what to do. They wanted me to disappear." The city offered to pay him the commission anyway, but he refused to take it. "I told them that was unacceptable. You can't pay people not to make sculpture. That just seems stupid." [15]

The D. C. Booth Fish Hatchery does not have the sculpture. No one in Spearfish remembers the sculpture, so we don't believe it was installed there. Billie says the city of Spearfish paid him $12,000 to "go away," but there is no mention of Lawless, the sculpture, or a payment in common council records after March 1989. [16]

According to Billie's 1986 VITA, the city of Harrisburg, Pennsylvania, agreed to construct *Hungry Fish* in a waterfront park in the summer of 1987. Officials there could find no record of the sculpture. Carrie

Wissler-Thomas said she was on a committee for a temporary art exhibit then and doesn't remember it. In 1986, they permanently placed another sculpture there.

So, did *Hungry Fish* ever get constructed?

CLEVELAND

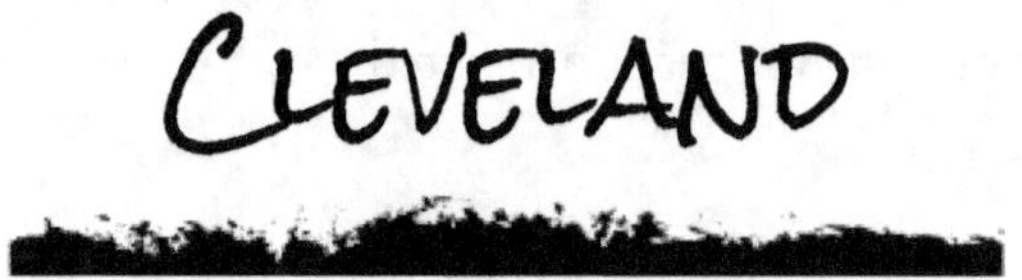

"He was out there a little bit. He was a different kind of artist." Alan Rossman

CLEVELAND, OHIO, IS NOT much different from Buffalo. They are about 190 miles apart. Both are former manufacturing scions that had seen successful booms during the industrial era. Both cities also seem to have a similar religious and political makeup, and tend to be on the conservative side of things.

It was here in the late 1980s that Billie Lawless had moved. He exchanged one small rust-belt city for another. It was also here where Alan Rossman lived. He was born in Canada, but he attended law school in Cleveland. There he met Svetlana Schreiber, a patron of the arts in Cleveland.

"I used to hang with the art community pretty good," Rossman explained. He liked to attend gallery openings, including at SPACES, where Billie had exhibited in the 1985 "UNCENSORED" show. The art community in Cleveland was tight, according to Rossman. There were non-artists that hung with the artists. It was open and everybody knew everybody. Rossman was pretty sure he first met Billie at that 1985 show. "He was out there a little bit," he said. "He was a different kind of artist." But because they ran in similar circles, they had mutual friends, like Schreiber. [1]

After Rossman passed the bar exam, he began working as a county public defender. He then went into private practice and shared space and worked with Svetlana, who had gone into immigration and civil practice. They shared similar interests in defending people in need and in the arts. "I'm not sure whether I met Billie personally through her or whether it was through the art community. But it was clearly in the context of him being an artist," Rossman added. [2]

They may have met at the "UNCENSORED" show or this new one, "Billie Lawless: Lightworks," which was an exhibit that opened on January 6 and ran until February 18, 1989 at the Cleveland Center for Contemporary Art, 11427 Bellflower Road. Much like the 1982 "New Works" show in Niagara Falls, Lawless said this show of smaller works "all have to do with children's memories."[3] He included *Senor Mouse, Lunar Watch, Danger: Do Not Touch! High Voltage!, Caged Souls to the Moon, Swizzle Sticks,* and *Dancing All Night at Z's Place*. These were old pieces for a new audience.

The Cleveland *Plain Dealer* called it a "collection of innovative constructions by frequently controversial neon/multi-media artist Billie Lawless." [4]

For the show, Cleveland poet and writer Amy Sparks wrote the text for the 12-page catalog. "Like a crusader on a mission, Billie Lawless has spent the last six years not only planning and constructing massive sculpture/installations, but defending them against politicians and the media, going to battle with words, with his body, with outrage. Lawless knows his way around a courtroom battle with the same ease he makes neon curl around steel. He talks of whimsy and lawyers, sexual suppression and plexiglass in the same breath. Everything is of utmost importance and a sense of urgency pervades his life and studio."[5]

Sparks' writing was reminiscent of George Howell in 1982.

This 38-year-old Buffalo, New York native, is a sculptor for whom nothing and everything is sacred. Ours is a world ready to be plundered, mechanized, highlighted, driven home, shaped, or stylized. But before the word 'censorship' began appearing in daily conversations, Lawless was sculpting fluid wall constructions punctuated by curvilinear neon, graceful lines of steel and flat tempered plexiglass.

These works embody the very roots of Lawless's work: the use of formal, or traditional aesthetics combined with wit and humor; the easy grace of modern materials; the sign as cultural icon; the strength of the image to convey emotion.

Wherever Lawless's crusade may take him, these pieces remain as set-points in his career, nostalgic, evocative buttons
that, when pushed, exude the elegance underlying passion-
ate, political commitment.[6]

Did they include *Broasted Babies Brew-Ha-Ha* in this exhibition? In the
show catalog, they listed it as being located outside, but there is no text
related to it. Is it possible he planned it, but he did not complete it?

Although Amy Sparks wrote extensively about Lawless during the
1980s, she did not keep up with his career and did not feel comfortable
talking about him for this book.

• • • • • • • • • • •

In 1989, SPACES presented a new exhibit, "Ghirardo & Roberts, Lawless,
Wolfe," which opened on February 17.

This show was different, with three separate but intertwined exhibits.
Helen Cullinan wrote in the Cleveland *Plain Dealer*, "Urban waste, geno-
cide and death are themes visualized with powerful impact." The other
artists, Cleveland artist Beth Wolfe, and Ithaca, New York artists Raymond
Ghirardo and Megan Roberts, created three different works that "express
deeply felt concerns in environmental sculpture that ranges from almost
playfully sardonic to macabre, and in one instance brutal and possibly offensive. Simultaneously, the gallery space becomes a junkyard playground,
the scene of a funeral pyre and the post-mortem of a civilization."[7]

"The walls of Lawless' installation are painted bubble-gum pink," Cullinan continued. "The centerpiece is a funeral pyre of railroad ties supporting a cross-shaped coffin affair; inside are neon letters that spell 'Broasted
Babies Brew-Ha-Ha' which is the title of the piece."[8] Inside the coffin were
babies being roasted in flames. Billie covered the pink walls in recipes for
cooked children.

"Little is left to the imagination," she continued, "in this elaborately
decorated tour-de-force of silkscreen and collage imagery (including icons
and flags), drawn on plexiglass, panels, video screens and paper rats. (Col-
laborators were Melissa Craig, Laszlo Gyorki, Steven B. Smith and Beth
Wolfe.) The sound track is African drums."[9]

Once again, Billie Lawless used layers, lightning bolts, imagery, and icons (as well as hot pink) in his creation, as well as paper rats, dating back to his home on Highgate in Buffalo.

Wolf's piece was called *Waterfront Development in Progress* and was "composed mostly of found objects including wooden beams, chain link and chicken wire fencing, theater curtains, rusty bedsprings and skeletons of car seats. The elements are reminders of the obsolescence, destruction and decay that surrounds us."[10]

Inflated Ruins by Ghirardo and Roberts represented "the remains of a vanquished civilization in air-inflated white cloth boulders and bodies. Mounds of crushed marble contain tiny video sets showing the same figures, moving in what appears to be the last stages of death by some unseen force."[11]

The show ran until March 17, 1989.

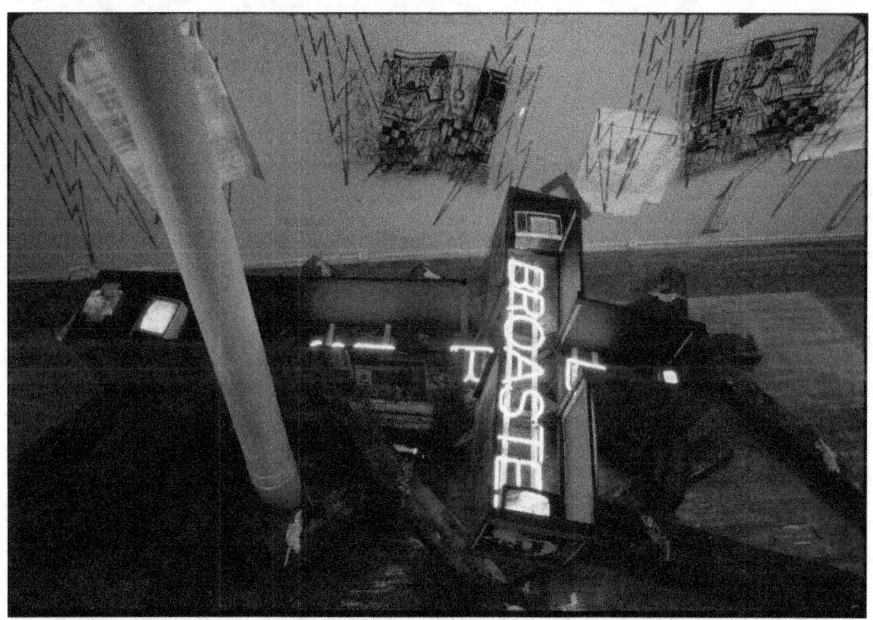

"Broasted Babies Brew-Ha-Ha" at SPACES Gallery in Cleveland, 1989. Courtesy Kelvin Smith Library Special Collections, Case Western Reserve University.

Billie would exhibit *Broasted Babies Brew-Ha-Ha* once again at CAGE (Cincinnati Artists Group Effort) in Cincinnati, Ohio, from October to November, 1994. They founded CAGE as an alternative arts gallery in Cincinnati in May 1978.

"I painted the walls a shocking pink and then I pasted these recipes on the walls," Billie explained. "Here's 'Fetus Delight.' 'Here's Golden Brown Toddlers.' I took recipes from *Good Housekeeping* or *The Joy of Cooking*, I forget, and just substituted baby parts. Here's 'Broasted Babies for 24.' Then I took a big lightning-bolt stencil, and I stenciled over everything. You know, building up layers."[12]

"I worked on that piece for three years," he said. "It made me angry, because I think it was really good, but so what? Maybe 150 people saw it. I was the sound in the forest that nobody heard."[13]

Many artists, musicians, or writers have been in this position of working on a project or planning an event and have no one show up. It can be very disheartening.

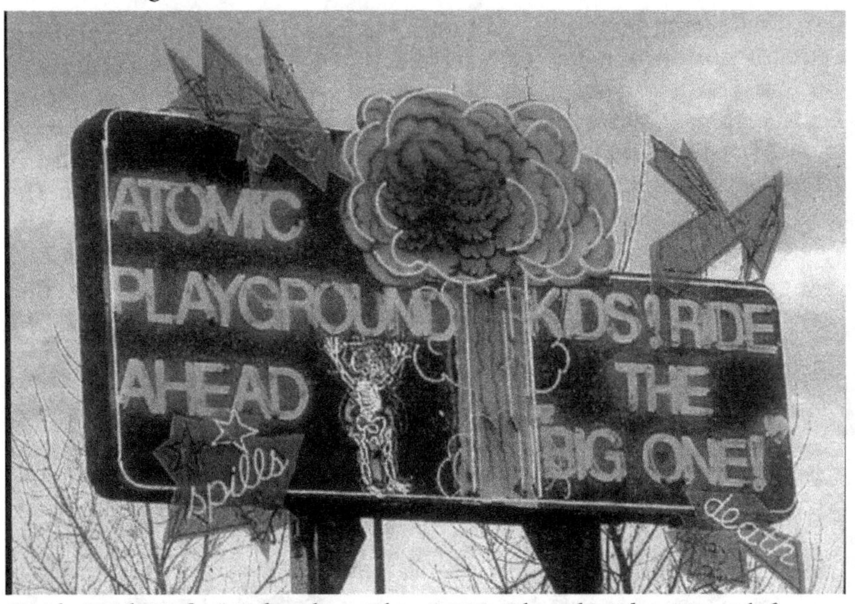

"Didy Wah Didy," Columbus, Ohio, 1988. Photo by Clay Herrick from the Cleveland Press Collections, courtesy of the Michael Schwartz Library Special Collections, Cleveland State University.

Pre-Trial

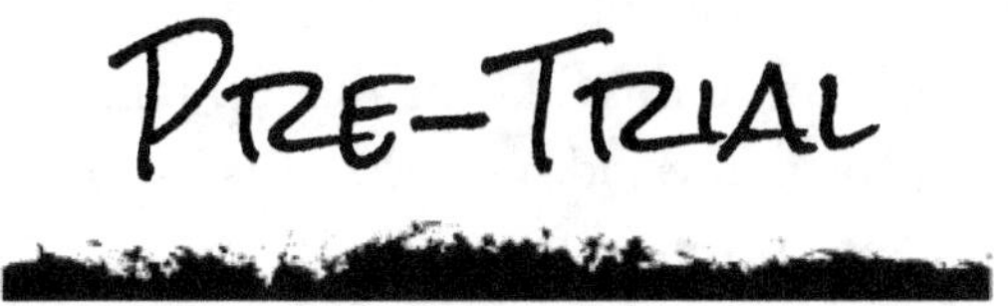

"Animation of dog bones,is that what you intended
to show?" Richard F. Griffin

ON THE MORNING OF November 2, 1989, Billie Lawless sat for a second deposition to prepare for his trial against the City of Buffalo, Walt's Tree Service, Inc., and the Buffalo Urban Renewal Agency. They met at his attorney's office, 1500 Statler Towers in Buffalo. In attendance representing him was Irwin Ginsberg of Diebold, Farmelo, Gorman, Ginsberg & Miller; Lillian A. Anderson, Assistant Corporation Counsel for the City of Buffalo; Richard (Dick) F. Griffin (no relation to Mayor Jimmy Griffin) and Linda A. Kaumeyer of Moot & Sprague for B.U.R.A.; and Edmund S. Brown from Maloney, Gallup, Roach, Brown & McCarthy, representing Walt's Tree Service, Inc.

In the 450-page transcript, you can see Lawless' combative attitude. Dick Griffin questioned Billie's experience, which led to the creation and building of *Green Lightning*. It surprised Billie when he took a sheet of paper from a folder and Griffin asked to see the folder, then marked the entire folder and its contents as an exhibit.

Griffin focused a lot on what the City and Jimmy Griffin deemed the obscene aspect of the sculpture, the ten foot tall boxes with the neon Mr. Peanut figures. When asked questions, Billie would often interrupt Griffin and sometimes may have offered more than necessary. Griffin tried to get Billie to admit that the model he brought to City Hall in 1983 was not the same as the final product. "You're asking me if, if it's the same outline," Lawless said. "I'm telling you it's of different materials, though it's all the same."

"So, what you ultimately built did not completely match the scale model; isn't that correct?" Griffin asked.

"Yeah, it did," Billie answered, "yes, it did match very closely and if I had put all of the neon onto this drawing that I put into the final box you wouldn't even have the faintest idea of what was happening here. For the sake of clarity, I put one position."

Griffin asked Lawless to identify a photo of what would be box four on the far right if you looked at *Green Lightning* from the front.

"Is Exhibit K... a picture of the fourth box, fourth frame as you built and installed on the B.U.R.A.'s land?"

"Not exactly," Lawless disagreed. After some back and forth, he finally admitted the neon figure looked like the same figure he created. Griffin asked him if the figure in the photo was the same as the model he showed to B.U.R.A. He admitted it was not. This is the first time Lawless said he showed the city something different from what he created.

They then argued about the neon being illuminated or animated and Billie tried to muck the waters by saying he could illuminate them all at one time and not show motion. But when asked how they worked when he installed it, he said it *was* animated. But because a photo showed all the elements illuminated at one time, Billie quibbled over the details since he didn't take the photo and it showed *Green Lightning* in a way that he didn't intend.

As this back and forth took place, Irwin Ginsberg said, "Let the record show that Mr. Griffin is beginning to raise his voice to a seriously high pitch, standing up within six feet of the witness."

Griffin then tried to get Billie to admit it was dancing anatomy, which he differed with. "That's your choice of words," Lawless said. He called it an "image."

"Dog bones?" Griffin proposed.

"I don't know. What's the question? Dog bones is a statement. What is the question?"

"Animation of dog bones. Is that what you intended to show?"

"We talked about intention and I'm saying I didn't intend anything in terms of image," Lawless said.

"Was it your intention that the figures be totally abstract?" Griffin pressed.

"I had no intention—I found the image. How could I have an intention about something that I find?"

Griffin asked if he understood B.U.R.A. could end the agreement if what he displayed did not represent the model. Lawless said that was a question for attorneys, but in his opinion there wasn't a right to terminate it.

They moved on to a photo of box two compared to the model. Billie refused to admit they were basically the same. "I don't know. It's like about five times the size," he said. In addition, he said the hat band was different, so to him, they were not the same.

The deposition ended close to five o'clock.

When they reconvened a month later, on December 5, Griffin asked Billie if the images on the acetate panels were present when he submitted the model to Artpark in 1983. He said yes.

"And these panels," Griffin asked, "have they ever -- since you first made this in October of '82, have they ever been changed?"

"No, they come off, I tape them back on. I taped the one back on just last week when I came up."

Griffin inquired if Billie had ever substituted them or if there was a different outline on them.

"No, those are the originals."

Did Lawless have any other models and did he ever show B.U.R.A. or David More any other models? "No," he said, and he said he never replaced the panels.

Lawless said he gave a set of slides to David More, which he said depicted the model exactly as he constructed it. More has insisted he never received nor saw any slides before the unveiling.

They asked Billie if he had ever illuminated the sculpture before the dedication ceremony on November 15, 1984.

"No, not that I can recall," he said.

Griffin tried to get Lawless to detail his income in 1984. He said he'd have to check his tax returns, so Griffin said he would like Billie to produce his tax returns going back to 1982.

The tax returns and whether he had lit the sculpture before the dedication, would later come back to bite him.

Griffin asked Billie if he thought he could sell the sculpture, even though most of the parts were donated to him.

"I wasn't really interested in selling it," he said.

"In connection with soliciting these donations for this sculpture, did you feel you had some fiduciary duty as to continuing to exhibit it in a public place?" Griffin asked.

Lawless said he just wanted to display it, public, private. It didn't matter. His creative ideas and process should be worth something, even if he built the sculpture with donated parts. After all, a lawyer sells their experience by the hour.

Dick Griffin asked Billie about "Sculpture Chicago '85" and conversations he had with Christine Ingraham. "Was it your practice to record conversations that you had with people relative to your work?"

"After people started saying things to me privately that they wouldn't say public," Lawless said, "I had a discussion with my attorney (Michael Brown)."

Who was saying things privately that they did not say publicly? Members of the art community? The Buffalo Arts Commission? Was the wrath of Jimmy Griffin too much to allow people to speak up publicly about how they actually felt, or was Lawless lying under oath?

Griffin asked if, when he designed *Green Lightning,* did he have the phallic images in mind?

Lawless said no, but "Probably after all the controversy in Buffalo when I was placed in what I felt was just a defensive posture that I had to come up with some kind of -- I had to make a verbal explanation. I don't know what was going through my mind. I just found a graffiti image on a wall. What I do in my work, I collect images and I hold them out to society, it's that simple."

Griffin asked Lawless if he ever "took an abstract penis figure and put it on top of the panels as a symbol of power?"

He may have, he said.

"When you drew it out on the panels and had it done in the neon, it was an abstract penis figure in your mind, was it not?" Griffin asked.

"You could say it was an abstract penis character," Lawless said. "You could refer to it that way. It doesn't make any difference."

They eventually went over all the repair and restoration costs. Griffin disputes much of it, saying that because he took the piece to Chicago, he would have incurred many of the costs anyhow.

"Did anyone in Chicago raise any question about you putting up a used and damaged piece?" Griffin questioned.

"I don't know if anybody did. I don't think so."

Billie also admitted he didn't remove the foundations in Buffalo because he was in litigation.

Griffin asked about the costs and Billie shot back, "The whole piece was damaged. Whether one part of a painting is damaged or not, if you take a Picasso painting and put a scratch on it, the whole piece is worthless. Ninety-nine percent of the painting might be intact, but it's still damaged. You could break down a small painting like that inch by inch and say, is this part damaged or this part? What I'm saying is the piece was made worthless by the actions of Walt's Tree Service in Buffalo. What I'm saying is the thing was damaged totally."

Billie also said that he had other costs related to the incident in Buffalo. "Well, I lost my job at St. Joseph's Collegiate Institute. I was the rowing coach."

Apparently, the athletic director said one of his concerns was that students were "drawing penises on their desks and using pictures of penises on their desk relative to the sculpture."

"It did surprise me when Mr. Wolf informed me of that," Billie said. "I was pretty surprised that the students would do that." When asked who decided to terminate him, he said, "I would love to know, I don't know."

Lawless explained that he applied for pro bono legal representation through the Volunteer Lawyers and Arts Program

Original "Green Lightning" shirt by Billie Lawless from 1985. Author's collection.

in Buffalo. "I believe Art Development Services has a number of people who are well renowned and respected in the community, were on the board of directors who I don't think wanted me to have pro bono." So he hired counsel to represent him. The director of Arts Development Services, Maxine N. Brandenberg, was also on the Buffalo Arts Commission, which could explain why the Volunteer Lawyers did not provide services to Lawless.

One of the last claims Lawless had was with sending *Green Lightning* to Philadelphia. Even though there was no way he was ready to ship the piece to Philly in 1984, he said that he planned on sending it there after the show in Chicago. But because he bungled it and was not there when the show opened in 1984, they wanted nothing to do with him.

Again, nothing related to Buffalo, as he didn't have the sculpture done in time.

As they neared the end of the deposition, Griffin asked, "Did you ever anticipate that there was going to be controversy about this *Green Lightning* sculpture before, let's say, before it was dedicated?"

"No, I didn't," Lawless said. "I really didn't think there would. I mean, there's a possibility for controversy on any sculpture that's always in the back of your mind. There was controversy over my sculpture at State College, *Cock-A-Doodle-Doo*, because it's an idea and people were scared of ideas."[1]

· · · ● · ● · ● · · ·

In 1990, the City of Buffalo was battling a budget deficit. But the legal fees related to the protracted lawsuit the city was fighting against Billie Lawless were mounting.

At a meeting of the Buffalo Urban Renewal Agency board on Thursday, April 12, 1990, they approved paying up to $43,129 to defend the city agency against the lawsuit filed by Lawless.

Community Development Commissioner Laurence K. Rubin said its law firm had billed the agency $18,129, and expected future legal fees charged by Moot & Sprague and attorney Dick Griffin could cost up to $25,000 more.[2]

The trial against the City of Buffalo was ramping up. Billie's attorney Michael Brown left Buffalo in 1986 for Kennebunk, Maine.

In 1990, Lawless' attorneys may have seen the case could be hard to win simply on the claim of damage, so they filed a motion that declared "a violation of his constitutional rights." But, since the civil rights action is subject to a three-year statute of limitations, it had already expired.

On May 14, 1990, Judge Mark H. Dadd denied the amended complaint, another blow to Billie's case. Dadd was the Wyoming County judge that was chosen to preside over the trial.

Irwin Ginsberg appealed the decision on June 11, 1990, to the Appellate

Division, Fourth Judicial Department. "Essentially, the decision allows the City of Buffalo to use the notice of claim as a sword rather than as a shield, and such is contrary to the intent of the statute." [3]

In order to avoid expensive litigation, Walt's Tree Service, Inc. made an offer of $15,000 in late 1990, to be removed from the lawsuit. Billie accepted, and Walt's was no longer a party to the suit. But that didn't prevent the company from being subpoenaed to testify against Billie.

On November 15, 1991, Billie's new Cleveland-based attorney, Alan C. Rossman, won the appeal, reversing the ruling by Justice Dadd from May 14. The justices said that Lawless was not time-barred from filing the additional complaint of civil rights violations. [4]

Rossman was friendly with the art community in Cleveland. As a public defender, he was working on civil rights cases. He ran with a group of radical lawyers in Cleveland. He said that like everybody else, artists had no money. There were starving artists, but a lot of them were mutual friends. He was still at the front end of his career. And he saw it as one guy against the institutions and the way things worked and pushing limits, and he needed a lawyer. "I'm not sure what his relationship was with Svetlana at the time," Rossman said, "but she was part of the legal community, and part of the art community as well." She was doing civil and immigration law and he was doing criminal defense, and Billie fell in the middle. He also saw it as a First Amendment issue. [5]

Rossman said he understood *Green Lightning* was controversial, but Billie went through the process and got permission to build. He said he thinks nobody paid Billie much attention until it was too late. Then they had egg on their face and had to blame someone.

He always respected the art community and that their view was to push envelopes. "We were all young and pushing envelopes of our own in our own way. I mean, there was a lot of pushback going back in a lot of different areas against institutions. It was really kind of pushback on the establishment because all of Billie's art work was sort of satirical and politically based in its own way. Everyone was looking to push limits." Then it came crashing down and he needed a lawyer. Rossman said that Billie had little money to hire a real lawyer. So, he decided, "Hell, I'll go to bat for you." Billie paid him with a couple of pieces of art. "It was very much him against the establishment." [6]

In 1991 Rossman said the appeal "gives a new and interesting perspective to the case." Now Lawless could bring claims of First Amendment, free speech and due process violations against the city of Buffalo. They could view it in court as a "work of art."[7]

On May 6, 1992, Judge Dadd issued an order that said "The mayor's legal authority clearly includes sufficient discretionary functions and duties to justify governmental immunity for his actions in any appropriate case. However, not every act of such an official would be entitled to immunity."[8]

On May 14, 1992, Judge Dadd dismissed the City of Buffalo's claims against Billie Lawless. He rejected the city's claims that *Green Lightning* was a public nuisance and that it and the Urban Renewal Agency were immune from damages. But he also dismissed Lawless' claim that it entitled him to financial damages for "personal emotional injuries in the form of mental anguish and humiliation."[9]

The judge faulted the city for its "absence of proof as to what reasonable basis supported the mayor's belief that his actions were lawful," Alan Rossman explained.[10] Dadd also dismissed Lawless' claim for unspecified punitive damages against the Buffalo Urban Renewal Agency, but retained the freedom of expression, trespass and breach of contract claims on which Lawless now centered his lawsuit.

After winning the appeal, Rossman sought to get a judgement in Billie's favor, while the City sought to have the complaint dismissed. The City and B.U.R.A. asserted they were absolutely immune because of the Mayor's discretionary authority under the Charter of the City of Buffalo to "maintain peace and good order" under circumstances he perceived to be a "public emergency."

Dadd said the City and B.U.R.A. never contended that such an emergency existed after the sculpture had no source of electricity. He added that the city's "attempt to enforce the contractual rights of the parties were not protected by such immunity." [11]

James Militello recalled that Judge Dadd "was very thorough. He read everything. Looked at everything."[12]

Attorneys for Lawless planned to subpoena Buffalo Mayor Jimmy Griffin and force him to explain why he ordered *Green Lightning* torn down.

"The mayor's state of mind or beliefs are an important element of the case," said Henry E. Wyman, a lawyer who shared offices with Mike Brown. "It seems to me the mayor is well known for being able to express his beliefs."

The mayor is "a pretty important witness," Alan Rossman added.

Mike Risman said no one talked to him about Griffin testifying. This "is just a further attempt to create publicity and name recognition for Lawless as an artist," he said.[13] Risman added that Lawless "did not really lose any money" on the sculpture, "and it helped promote him as an artist. His modus operandi is to market his work. We feel a jury will ultimately see that was his intent with *Green Lightning* from the beginning."[14]

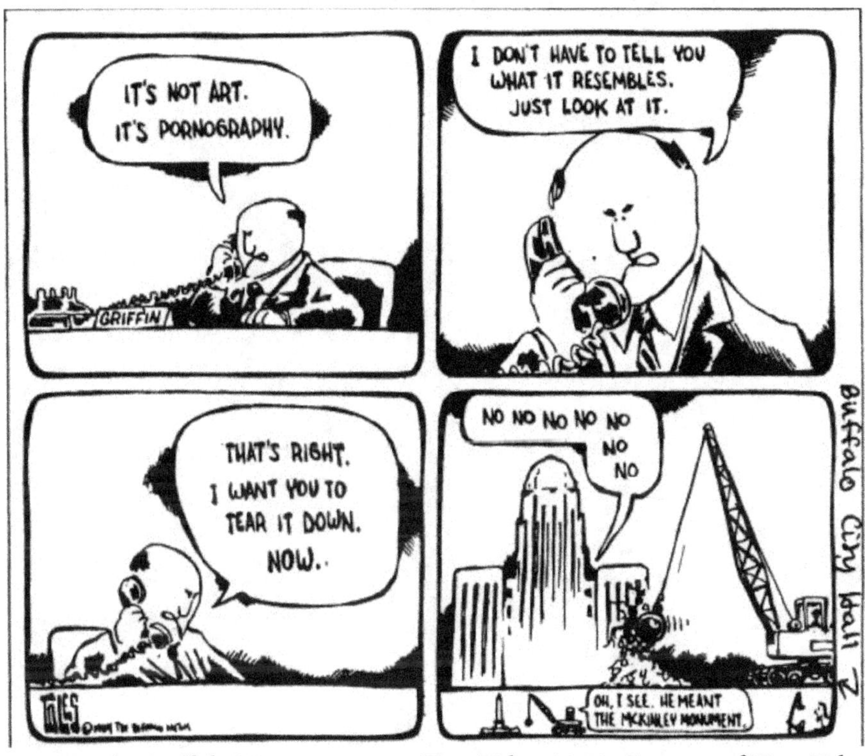

Cartoon by Buffalo News cartoonist Tom Toles, 1984. Courtesy of Tom Toles.

As both sides gathered to begin jury selection in Justice Dadd's courtroom on June 2, 1992, the judge delayed jury selection and ordered attorneys for both sides to meet to try to resolve an evidence dispute. He threatened to impose financial sanctions against the City of Buffalo if city attorneys didn't turn over 1984 police and government documents to the artist's attorneys before the trial began.

Wyman also told the judge that Mayor Griffin agreed to appear as a witness in the trial, but City attorney Michael Risman refused to say whether the city would allow the mayor to testify.[15]

After the two sides met, lawyers from the City tentatively agreed to provide the documents that Lawless' attorneys requested.

That afternoon, June 2, 1992, after they settled the evidence dispute, jury selection began. When they were done, a jury of four women and two men were prepared to judge the merits of the case.

The trial would continue to be played out in the media and in the court of public opinion as the wheels of justice turned.

Opening Statements

"A hoax has been perpetrated on the citizens of
Western New York." Michael Risman

I T WAS EIGHT YEARS later, but everyone still had a recollection of seeing *Green Lightning* as they exited the Kensington Expressway, or watching Channel 7 news anchor Irv Weinstein discuss it. It was long gone from Buffalo, but the memories lingered, and Jimmy Griffin was still mayor.

Michael Risman had risen to become Senior Deputy Corporation Counsel of Buffalo by the time the trial began. The Buffalo Urban Renewal Agency was still trying to find a business to fill the lot where the sculpture had once stood.

They relegated Gregory Dudek, B.U.R.A.'s counsel, to bystander for the trial, and Dick Griffin, an experienced trial lawyer now with the law firm of Philips Lytle, handled the B.U.R.A.'s aspects of the trial. Billie Lawless had a connection to Dick. In 1962, Griffin successfully argued for Black Muslim prisoners in front of Billie's father, then a New York State Supreme Court judge.

Attorney Mark J. Mahoney stated that Henry Wyman and Michael Brown shared space at the Statler Towers. Mahoney said that Wyman "worked hard on that case." [1] Wyman would serve as Billie's Buffalo counsel. His other attorneys were Alan Rossman and Svetlana Schreiber from Cleveland.

Wyman's hard work during this trial would unravel in his personal life not long after the trial ended.

Alan Rossman reflected almost 40 years later that a lot of the controversy was that Billie had gone through the process, and then everyone was outraged that somehow he took advantage of them. "But I think they were embarrassed, and they were angry," he added. "They were angry at him, and I think there would have been less anger if he had just... done this on the sly. But it was the idea that they had to take responsibility because they had approved it."[2]

The trial ran from June 8 to June 25, 1992. Billie himself was no longer a Buffalo resident after moving to Cleveland in 1988. But this was still home, and in his mind, the events that took place in November 1984 forever changed it.

Thirteen total witnesses were called. All except two were called by Billie's legal team. Not that they didn't try to get others to support Billie's case. Although she hasn't specifically said it, it's believed that Kathie Simonds was supposed to be a witness. She and Billie were no longer talking, and she had moved on, so she didn't testify.

People in town were abuzz about the trial. The Buffalo press started airing daily coverage, leading up to the trial and rehashing the incident. The fresh exposure did not make everyone comfortable. Billie and his attorneys tried to convince Joanne Posluszny to return to Buffalo from New York City to testify. She had attended the Arts Commission meeting in 1983 and says she saw the neon images. She could be crucial to Billie's case.

But she was also receiving pressure from her parents, who told her not to come home. It would have been shameful. As the trial got closer, the pressure was too much and made her sick. She got a doctor's excuse to not testify, and that was it. Posluszny and Simonds both felt the public and private pressures and were frightened to get caught up in the turmoil, so Billie would be the best witness he had.

Curious onlookers attended the trial, as did reporters for the Buffalo *News* and local television and radio stations. It was a media circus of sorts.

In his opening statement on June 8, 1992, Alan Rossman said that the Buffalo Urban Renewal Agency only expressed concern about vandalism when they approved the sculpture in 1983. "The evidence will tell that this piece was vandalized," Rossman told the jury, "and it was vandalized by representatives of these defendants."[3]

He said that Lawless suffered from post-traumatic stress disorder, after witnessing Walt's Tree Service dismantle his artwork under orders from the City. They would have a psychologist testify as to his state of mind after the

1984 incident, and he would seek monetary damages for such suffering.

Mike Risman said in his opening statement, while the City was a corporate entity, it was made of people like David More. "He and his family have been very active in the art community for many years, perhaps even before Mr. Lawless was involved in the art community. And a hoax has been perpetrated on the citizens of Western New York."[4]

He said that Billie wanted to build in the Elm-Oak Arterial, which was not his original plan.

"People were concerned about the impact the structure would have on children driving by going to the Aud, coming from the Aud, going down to the circus. We're going to call a number of witnesses, not the least of which will be Mr. More who, unfortunately for him, has been thrust into the middle of this controversy."[5]

Risman said he would prove that media attention was all Billie had sought.

Dick Griffin said in his opening statement, "At no time ...did anyone suggest that there was any particular sexual type of message. At no time did anyone, either in a model that we saw or in a description, say that there was going to be animated male figures simulating the erection of the male penis as a burlesquing idea, as a symbol of male power vis-à-vis or in contrast to female figures that would be put in the back. At no time did anyone suggest or did that ever dawn on anybody who was sitting there."[6]

After eight long years, Billie Lawless finally took the stand for what would be four grueling days of testimony. During testimony, he detailed the costs of repairing *Green Lightning* after the damage by Walt's Tree Service. He said "There was major structural damage to the piece," and it would cost at least $63,000 for future repairs.[7]

Lawless said he charged himself at a rate of $75 an hour, based on "the works I've sold in the past." The defense disagreed with Billie's cost estimates, and Judge Dadd sent the jury out. For unknown reasons, Dadd asked if *Green Lightning* was presently being exhibited.

"No, it's not," Alan Rossman said.

At some point Billie had said that the four panels from the six-foot model were in a nightclub in Cleveland, while the sculpture was in storage in Chicago.

Rossman said, "I guess I'm still a little unclear, Judge, that if Mr. Lawless can't assess the work required to repair the sculpture, I don't know who can. He built it. Clearly, there was nobody better than him to indicate what needs to be done and assess the time and means to do that. I mean, it seems to me that we are prepared to show – and it's never been denied the piece was exhibited. It was exhibited in a damaged condition. We're talking damages to the sculpture, and the damage is real and exists and some yet exists."[8]

Dick Griffin argued that, as an attorney, he could say he was worth $500 an hour with no point of reference. "If my house burned down, I'm entitled to say it's worth a half a million dollars, and that's a prima facie case," meaning the evidence suffices to establish the fact in question.

Henry Wyman said, "The damages are very extensive. This is not one burned-down house." [9]

Judge Dadd said, "as to this business of having the right to value your own property in court and have it a prima facie case, I think the answer to that is yes."[10] The burden of proof was on Billie's team to prove the evidence.

We know Billie performed some repair work on the sculpture in 1985 for its exhibition at "Sculpture Chicago," where it ran for over four years. "I was just trying to show it to the best degree I could," he told the jury.[11]

When they asked Lawless about the damage to the LEXAN panels, he said, "You can see how the LEXAN has been pitted and marked and damaged. Lots of marks. The whole sheet looks like it's covered with... pits from the sparks of the welding torch."[12]

That was what art restorer Steve Wisenbaugh had said when he testified about examining the panels. They asked Wisenbaugh whether they could restore the sculpture to its original state.

"The piece can possibly be restored," he said, "to somewhat of the original intent of the artist, but the piece could never be restored to its intent. It's already been altered." Wisenbaugh explained that any time a piece is damaged or altered, it changes either the piece, or the value of the piece. The piece changes. "The artist's intent at the time he created the piece is one thing, and later on, when a piece is altered, it's completely different."[13]

They asked Wisenbaugh if he assessed whether they could restore *Green Lightning* to its original condition before it got damaged. He said his estimate was primarily for materials, but there could be other costs involved. "I believe this cost estimate to be very conservative and low." [14]

He said when he made the estimate, there were probably items that were overlooked or unknown damage. "There's also expenses that will be incurred that the artist isn't aware of. To reiterate what I previously covered, the idea that the piece has, in fact, been damaged and, in fact, is not the same piece, nor will ever be the same piece."[15]

When asked if Billie charging $75 an hour for labor was out of the question, Wisenbaugh said no. "In a case like this dealing with a piece of art and not just an object and the artist's sensitivities and this particular quality that he brings to the work, I mean it's his brush stroke, his sensitivity to the angle, I mean he would have to be there overseeing everything exactly, so there's no reason for somebody else to be doing it, I mean you have to have hands on."[16]

"Every ... artist has his own unique style of working," Wisenbaugh added, "that's why there's various types of art. The sensitivity that Billie has in a particular piece, or what I may have in a particular piece, would be different. When I restore a piece, I have to copy as much or as closely as I can what the artist intended and how the artist works. Not everybody can do that."[17]

Finally, they asked Steve Wisenbaugh what the total cost for the complete restoration of *Green Lightning* would be. He said it was $103,418.81. But when pressed, he again said he thought the estimate was low. He told the jury that it would cost $200,000 to $225,000 to fully restore *Green Lightning*. ($438,000-$493,000 in 2023 dollars).

Under cross-examination for B.U.R.A. by Dick Griffin, Billie Lawless said the cost of restoring the sculpture was $13,352. But because *Green Lightning* had exhibited in Chicago, and they covered some costs during that show, Griffin reduced the cost of repairs to $7,200. He even questioned a line item for transporting the two panels that were stored at Walt's Tree Service.

Griffin said, "Now, actually, Walt's through the City returned those two panels to you at the site, did they not?"

"Yes, they did," Lawless replied.

"And they didn't charge you 300 dollars for it, did they?"

"I don't think there were any charges."

After that line of questioning, Griffin asked about the foundations that were poured for *Green Lightning*. Per Billie's contract with B.U.R.A., he was to restore the land to its original state. "I think your initial estimate was something under $2,000 dollars, correct? And you haven't paid that or done that work; is that correct?"

"No," Lawless replied, "the foundations still are there."[18] This was eight years later and the concrete foundations were still in the ground.

Griffin asked if Billie remembered testifying at his deposition that he paid a Chicago firm to replace two or three neon elements for $500? He did. But in his lawsuit, he was trying to collect $1,600.

"There were only 11 pieces broken," Billie admitted.

"But you say here replace 30 --"

"Correct."

Under intense questioning by Dick Griffin, small holes were slowly forming in Billie's case, as the jury watched in utter amazement. The expert legal work of Griffin dismantled the high costs to repair or replace parts.

Billie didn't recall questions about the neon in his interview with George Howell for the *Buffalo Arts Review*.

"You don't remember that?" Griffin asked.

"No, I don't," Lawless stated.

Question after question, Lawless gave the same response. Either he couldn't recall, didn't remember, or didn't read something.

Billie Lawless had moved on since the *Green Lightning* incident. He had created new art and displayed in other cities. But he had waited eight years for his day in court, and he was floundering on the stand. Much like the goldfish that he based *Hungry Fish* on.

They asked him about his response to George Howell regarding the Mr. Peanut image he saw on the deli wall on Bailey Avenue. He said he didn't recall it.

Billie couldn't remember if he had said he hoped there wouldn't be a controversy or that he hadn't duped anyone.

His behavior contradicted the confident Lawless that was quoted in the press when he wasn't being squeezed for the truth. Billie claimed to have all these costs, pain and suffering, trauma, but now he said he couldn't recall anything.

Griffin asked Lawless about the donation letters he had sent to prospective donors. "In these letters, you make reference to the fact that your *Green Lightning* would continue the exploration of sign imagery begun with the work exhibited a year ago at the Buscaglia-Castellani Art Gallery; is that correct?"[19]

"That's correct," Billie replied.

"And, incidentally," Griffin asked, "never in any of your letters did you say you were going to use male penis images for social satire, did you?"

"I had a press release, but no, I did not say male penis. I didn't use those words, no."

Griffin asked how much he made for *Cock-a-Doodle-Doo* and *Lament.* "I wasn't paid anything," Billie said.

Griffin then asked, "In layman's terms, could we describe these ... as somewhat abstract pieces?"

"Somewhat abstract," Lawless said. "I would say that *Cock-a-Doo-dle-Doo* is an abstraction. I was dealing with formal issues in that. And I would say that *Lament* is ... if I were to use layman's terms, I would say figurative. There's a woman's head, and I'm not sure how I would describe *Señor Mouse.* I would say it's fairly representative." [20]

Billie described how he felt regarding the fallout from the incident. "The public knows that such a controversy is a death knell of your career. Public commissions and whatnot are not given to people or to sculptors or artists who create controversies... they don't want to deal with you."[21]

When asked if that differed from a work being controversial, he said it was. Because, to a great extent, his livelihood depended on commissions. "Sales were ...crucial to myself to... make a livelihood." In 1984, he made approximately $24,000. "I was getting better every year."

So Dick Griffin turned the questioning to Billie's tax returns. He had turned over 1984, 1985, and 1986 tax returns during discovery, and on the stand admitted that he never actually filed them. "I filled them out, but I never filed them," he said.[22]

Judge Dadd halted the trial. He sent the jury out and Lawless' attorneys revealed he hadn't filed federal taxes for the previous nine years until that week. He had an accountant prepare his taxes the weekend before the trial.

Attorneys for the city demanded the lawsuit be dismissed because of his alleged tax fraud. "It all goes to the credibility of this witness," Richard Griffin told Judge Dadd.

After careful consideration, Judge Dadd denied the city's motion to dismiss Lawless' claims that he paid himself $75 an hour to repair his sculpture. But he also dismissed damages for "claimed mental suffering or emotional harm based upon either loss of income or damage to professional reputation." [23]

Because Billie had not filed federal taxes until right before the trial began, the Court would not restrict the defense from using it against him in any way they wanted. His case was becoming more difficult for his attorneys and Lawless was proving to be a terrible witness.

During another line of questioning, Dick Griffin showed a photo of the fourth panel of the sculpture, called "The Fleeing Bandito."

"Now, do you see that part up at the — about two-thirds of the way up where there's two lines that look like arms going out? Now, it is true, is it not, that on the model that you presented to the Buffalo Urban Renewal Agency, that that portion of this exhibit above the arms, we'll call it the head, so to speak, that was not drawn in, illustrated or marked in any respect, was it?"[24]

Reluctantly, Billie admitted, "No, it was not."

Griffin then produced a photo that showed the fourth panel neon illuminated with all three positions of the dancing penis. Like the previous question, Griffin made Lawless admit that the model he showed B.U.R.A. did not include the neon design.

This was the first time Lawless admitted he didn't show B.U.R.A. the neon as he intended it all along.

Griffin read through parts of the 1984 interview with George Howell and questioned Billie. Between that and asking questions about his deposition, Billie said he could recall nothing. He didn't recall the interview or anything he said during it. He recalled nothing he said in his deposition. It did not look very good for Mr. Lawless at this point.

Michael Risman questioned Lawless about the 1983 Buffalo Common Council resolution.

"... You described it as colorful and lighthearted, but there's no reference to any political statements in there; is that correct?"

"That's correct," Billie said.

"Now, do you recall, you've read the Howell article, have you not?" Risman asked.

"You know, I've never really read that whole article."

"Well, I mean, didn't you just review it outside in the hallway just before Mr. Griffin continued his questions?"

"Not that I can recall."

"And you didn't review it after I made reference to it in my opening statement?"

"I looked at that section, but you asked me if I'd read it, and I've never really read the whole article."

"Even to this day?" an incredulous Risman asked.

"Right."[25]

If Billie Lawless couldn't recall something from 15 minutes ago, how was the jury to believe anything else he said? Once again, the layers of Billie's onion were slowly being peeled away in front of the jury, and that was not good for his case.

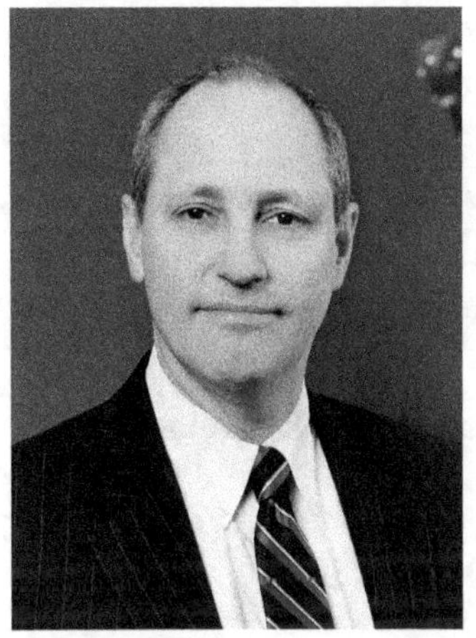

City of Buffalo Deputy Corporation Counsel Michael Risman provided some "gotcha" moments during the trial. Photo courtesy of Michael Risman.

When asked if he told George Howell he told Jimmy Griffin, "Tis the Irish in me," he couldn't recall.

Risman started digging into the details related to the four panels. This would, again, prove somewhat embarrassing.

"And the 'Jump For Your Life' was the one with the young girl; is that correct?" Risman asked.

"Correct."

"And I believe this young girl, that Kathie Simonds added some spikes around this image?"

"She did," Lawless continued. "We collaborated on the images. I'm not sure exactly who did what."

"And I believe on your direct you mentioned something, there were some figures, sort of roundish figures below her dress; is that correct?"

"Correct," Lawless said.

"And I think you said they were meant to be something that you might see under a microscope?"

"Well, they're amoeba-like, I guess, yeah."

"Well, I guess my question is," Risman prepared, "are you stating that they were in some way meant to be sperm or suggest something along those lines when you say something under a microscope? Is that what you were suggesting?"

Risman's "gotcha" moment took the jury by surprise. He said he noticed a look of shock, which was the response he had hoped for. [26]

Billie replied, "No, I don't think so."

"That was not an image that you thought about at all?"

"Not at all, no," Billie answered.

"It was something under a microscope, an amoeba?"

"I wasn't even thinking of a microscope. They seemed to have like an amoeba shape. I'm not even certain what an amoeba is, to be honest."

"These were your words on direct, an amoeba-like figure, something under -- like something under a microscope," Risman pressed.

"I guess I was thinking of like a cell. Have you ever seen a cell dividing under -- you know, something on TV, like nature, they would show cells dividing, I was thinking of that."

"Now, I believe you told the Urban Renewal Agency that this was supposed to be lighthearted and whimsical and contribute to the revitalization of downtown; is that correct?" Risman asked.

"That's correct."

"And in one -- in 'The Fleeing Bandito' there's an image of an Afro-American male; is that correct?"

"No, I don't think so, not at all," Billie said.

"Well, was he dark-skinned?"

"I think the skin is like a lemon yellow."

"Okay."

"You're talking about 'The Fleeing Bandito,' right?"

"Absolutely," Risman said.

"I think that 'The Fleeing Bandito's' skin is like most a fluorescent lemon or yellow."

"And he was supposed to be a bandit. Is that what you mean by like a robber?"

"Yeah, Dick Tracy, cartoonish," Lawless said.

"And he had a gun in his hand; is that correct?" Risman questioned.

"Right."

"And I think you said it was suggestive of violence and unsafe, like an urban neighborhood?"

"Well, I don't recall exactly what I said, but it was a symbol of sort of violence, of Dick Tracy, cartoonish."

"And is it your feeling that this would contribute to the revitalization of downtown by having an image of urban violence?"

"Well, the revitalization of downtown is not my responsibility," Billie shot back.

Risman asked him if the 'Space Shuttle Attacks' panel was contributing to the revitalization of downtown.

"Well, again, I'm not trying to contribute to the revitalization per se, but I was trying to do a contemporary sculpture."

"And would you also say that these two themes, the fleeing armed robber and the attacking space shuttle, are whimsical and lighthearted?"

"Looked at in their cartoonish way, I would say that they do have some of those elements, yes, particularly with the dancing character in front of it, absolutely."[27]

As Mike Risman continued to cross-exam Billie, he asked him about a 1982 tax return he used to apply for a low-interest loan with the City of Buffalo for home improvements. The tax form Lawless used to apply for that loan had sales of $11,879, but the amended form he filed just days before testifying had sales of $24,535. So Billie used the lower gross sales tax form to apply for and receive a rehab loan for his house on Highgate Avenue.

On re-direct, Alan Rossman had Billie go through the proposal that was submitted to the Buffalo Urban Renewal Agency in October 1983.

"Now, at that B.U.R.A. meeting, did anybody ask you about the silkscreen images?" Rossman asked.

"No, they did not." He said no one asked about the blinking pattern of the neon. He said he hadn't even finished the silkscreen designs when he made the presentation to B.U.R.A., so he couldn't have explained them, he told Rossman. [28]

B.U.R.A. and the City were trying to suggest that Billie knew what the images were going to be when he made his presentation, since he had detailed them in his "Sculpture Chicago" submission. But that application came after *Green Lightning* was already constructed and displayed in Buffalo.

In another line of questioning, Alan Rossman asked Billie if he knew about the B.U.R.A. meeting on November 21, 1984, where they canceled his contract. "Were you notified of that meeting?"

"No, I was not."

"Did anyone from B.U.R.A. indicate that your permit with them was going to be discussed at that meeting?"

"No, they did not," Billie said.

When asked if anyone from B.U.R.A. asked for a response from Billie in relation to that meeting, he also said, no. And how about the mayor directing Jim Militello to demolish the sculpture? Another no.

Rossman asked, "Did there come a time when you found out that that action had been taken by B.U.R.A. at that meeting?"

"Yes," Billie said. "My attorney informed me, Michael Brown."

Rossman then asked him about the permit agreement with B.U.R.A. After reading two paragraphs regarding Termination, Billie was asked, "Mr. Lawless, to your knowledge, did the Elm-Oak become part of a development project during the period of time that we've talked about for the last couple days?"

"No, it did not," Billie said. [29]

Dick Griffin later asked Lawless if he had "committed to erect and exhibit *Green Lightning* in Philadelphia during the period of time from early August 1984 till the middle of September of 1984?"

"I made a commitment, yes, I did," Lawless replied.

He admitted it was the same time frame in which he had agreed to start and finish the erection in Buffalo within a 90-day period.

After Lawless told the jury he was emotionally upset at missing the 1984 Philadelphia art show, Griffin asked if the fact that he didn't file tax returns cause him any emotional disturbance?

He said it did.

Masten Council member David A. Collins took the stand. He said he believed the B.U.R.A. "jumped the gun" in approving Mayor Griffin's decision to dismantle the sculpture.

Jonathan Thornton, a professional art conservator in Buffalo, told the jury that Lawless' description of the removal led him to consider the dismantling of *Green Lightning* "a destructive process."[30]

Billie's lawyers called Buffalo *News* art critic Richard Huntington to the stand. The reason? In 1982 he was the director of visual arts at Artpark, when Lawless submitted the model for *Green Lightning*.

Huntington wrote in the *News* that he was a bit nervous. "I imagined myself in court discussing the controversial... sculpture and slipping into phrases like 'the lively configuration of the forms' when I really meant to say something more precise, such as 'four penises in top hats doing the cakewalk.'"[31]

"Lawless' lawyer had me get out of the witness chair," Huntington wrote, "to inspect the model close up. I gave it a long, hard look and determined that it indeed was the same model with the same dancing 'phallic figures.'"[32]

"Artpark proposals in those days were just as apt to come as magic-marker scratchings on butcher paper as elaborate models. *Green Lightning* stuck out in the heap. The clincher, I thought -- my assistant and I, both possessing refined erotic sensibilities, made numerous off-color jokes that afternoon involving Fred Astaire, top hats and *Green Lightning*."[33]

That seemed to be a big win for Lawless' team. Under cross-examination, the defense wondered how Huntington could remember such details ten years later. Huntington said he "was a highly trained art expert whose visual memory was so acute that he remembered every detail of his first toothpick sculpture executed in the third grade under the watchful eye of Miss Feelock."[34]

They tried to impeach his testimony and asked him a zinger: "What color tie did you have on that day?"

"I didn't have a tie on that day," he shot back. "Little did he know that I never wore a tie at Artpark, and if I had I would have been greeted with 'Where's the funeral?' eight or nine times before I reached my office chair."[35]

Huntington said, "During the parts of the trial that I observed, everyone seemed almost desperate to avoid the 'P' word." They avoided the word penis at all costs. The jury apparently couldn't handle the word. "They must have feared that they would be associated with those naughty folk on 'Saturday Night Live,'" Huntington wrote.[36]

As it goes in many trials, the momentum swings back and forth, depending on the testimony. The defense was stopping at nothing to impeach Billie Lawless, and his legal team was doing their best to swing back.

Testimony

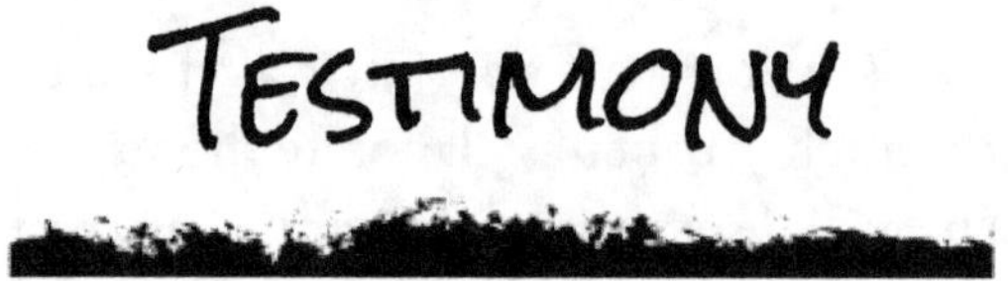

"It's an injury, in a sense, to his soul and identity as
an artist, and I think that was a devastating blow."
Dr. John P. Wilson

D R. JOHN P. WILSON was called to testify on Billie's behalf. Wilson was an expert and pioneer in identifying post-traumatic stress disorder as a disorder in Vietnam veterans.

"My research in the late '70s identified a constellation of symptoms that's now known as post-traumatic stress disorder. In 1980, posttraumatic stress disorder or PTSD for short became a diagnostic category in the psychiatric manual. As a member of that task force, I participated in the writing of the diagnostic criteria in establishing the scientific basis and rationale for those criteria."[1]

If anyone should know about PTSD, it should be Dr. Wilson. When asked if he saw Billie in the courtroom, he identified him as "the gentleman at the table in front of me wearing the dark gray suit with the red tie." He said he had been called to evaluate Lawless before the trial began and saw him for about two and a half hours total. [2]

He had reviewed Billie's medical records from several institutions and formed a diagnosis related to that. "The diagnoses are that Mr. Lawless suffers from depression... and he also suffers from posttraumatic stress disorder. The criteria on which I base the diagnosis of depression is that Mr. Lawless meets the diagnostic criteria for dysthymia as specified by the Diagnostic and Statistical Manual-III-Revised of the American Psychiatric Association." [3]

"And you've been made aware of the *Green Lightning* incident; is that correct?" Alan Rossman asked.

Wilson said yes. He then explained that following the *Green Lightning* incident, he could see symptoms of depression. Billie was restless, irritated, agitated and felt worthless, and his sense of identity as an artist had come under attack. Billie had trouble sleeping, difficulty focusing, and struggled to express himself. Wilson also believed Lawless experienced a traumatic event, with the prospect of his sculpture being torn down twice. He said that he continued to brood and obsess and ruminate and had many thoughts about himself and his sculpture. [4]

The doctor discussed the time in 1986 and 1987 in which he moved to East Orleans, Massachusetts and "withdrew to his mother's home. In fact, he did not work as an artist during that point in time," Wilson testified.[5] He recommended outpatient psychotherapy to Billie. Outside stressors, including Billie receiving threatening phone calls, contributed to it.

Dick Griffin immediately objected, Judge Dadd sustained but sent the jury out. Griffin wanted all of Dr. Wilson's testimony regarding Billie's treatment stricken. Wilson had given a deposition the night before his testimony, on June 16. Griffin said the good doctor mentioned no treatment or cost, and the lawsuit never mentioned the same.

Henry Wyman said on February 8, 1988, a Bill of Particulars was delivered to B.U.R.A., which included a quote for continued counseling. Judge Dadd agreed, denied Griffin and allowed the testimony to continue. When the jury returned, he told them that Wilson's mention of threatening calls was stricken from the record.

Who was calling Billie and threatening him and why couldn't they talk about it?

According to Mike Risman, Lawless tried to say that he had emotional distress, "that he was so emotionally involved in the work that when the city damaged it, this affected him emotionally." [6]

Risman said Billie's legal team had called the psychiatrist to testify about his emotional damage. And one claim was that he couldn't have relationships with women anymore. Risman said he could tell from the medical records and watching Lawless that it seemed like he was dating Svetlana Schreiber. He questioned him and asked if he was having relationship trouble with women. Billie said "Yes," and that was when Risman said, "Well, are you having a relationship with someone now? In fact, isn't she in the courtroom, isn't she at the table? In fact, isn't that her?" as he pointed to Schreiber. Another "gotcha" moment from the attorney that seemed to shock the jury.[7]

Svetlana Schreiber served as co-counsel and was at the plaintiff's table for the entire trial.

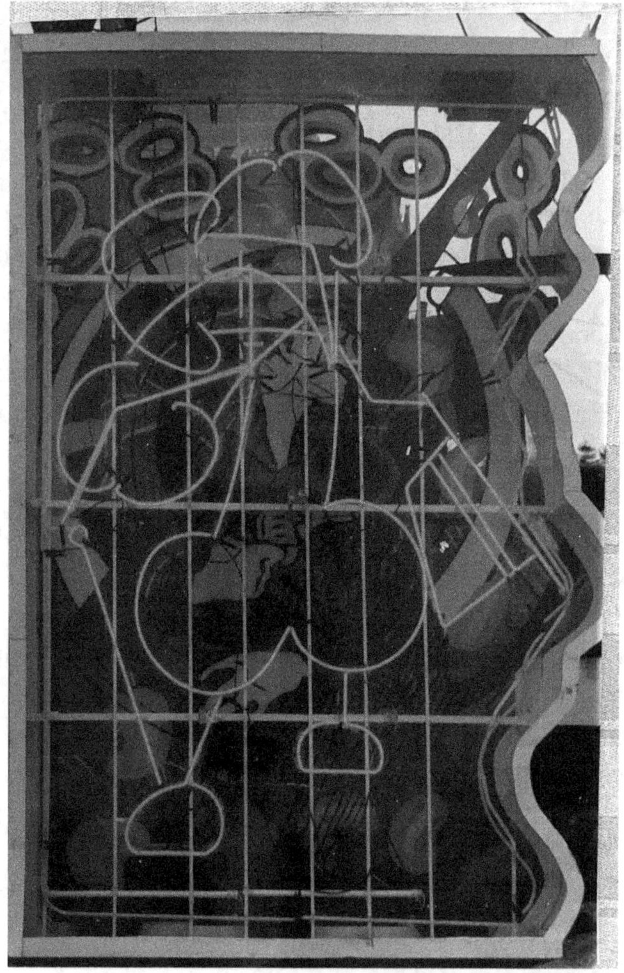

Panel 4 of "Green Lightning," the "Fleeing Bandi- to" and Mr. Peanut taking a bow. From November, 1984. Photo by Debra Kolodczak.

One point came up during the trial was that Billie had family trouble growing up. In an interview in the Cleveland *Plain Dealer* in 1989, he said there were tumultuous times at the family home growing up.[8]

Or, could it have been that the kid who didn't want to work a 9 to 5 job, be a lawyer like dear old dad, was outside the family norm and a rebellious kid? Mike Risman thought he remembered Billie's father showing up once one day for an hour during the entire trial and then left. But in 1997, Billie said his father never showed, but his mother came one day. Billie had mocked the system and possibly embarrassed his family.

When questioning continued, Dr. Wilson testified that "I believe Mr. Lawless would continue to experience depression, and I believe he'll continue to ruminate over the events of *Green Lightning*, that is, the post-traumatic symptomatology." He agreed that the "partial dismantling and destruction of *Green Lightning* were the primary contributing factors."[9]

When cross-examined by Dick Griffin, Wilson said he met with Svetlana Schreiber and Alan Rossman in Cleveland. He based his diagnosis on the information they provided and prior medical records of Lawless. Wilson acknowledged Lawless' childhood and experiences may have caused his symptoms. He also said that chronic lying could also contribute to depression. [10]

Billie had not seen a therapist until January 1986, and he had relationship problems with his girlfriend Pamela Mays. (They broke up that year.) "Billie has behaved very irresponsibly and perhaps abusively in his relationship," and "needs to work on becoming more responsible and considerate," a therapist wrote. One of those irresponsible acts was the unauthorized use of his girlfriend's credit card. The medical records from 1986 never mention *Green Lightning*, loss of sleep, or low self-esteem. [11]

By 1987, medical reports show he was concerned with the unwarranted censorship of *Green Lightning*, but he refused therapy. Again, there was nothing about depression, loss of sleep, or reliving the events of November 1984.

From November 1989 to March 1990, he attended therapy sessions with his girlfriend. There were references to family problems and to interpersonal problems between the two of them. They did not bring up embarrassing details in court. Attorneys said Billie had criminal trespass charges filed against him by his girlfriend Cindy. He also "had to deal with his ego and his egomania." Cindy helped him "challenge his egomania regarding his art." But Billie was sarcastic, and patronizing, calling her "pathetic." He said he hired Svetlana Schreiber to "fight" her. [12]

It was during this exchange between Griffin and Wilson that it came out that after March 1990, Svetlana Schreiber and Billie were living together.

Under redirect by Alan Rossman, Dr. Wilson said that he had diagnosed 8,000 people with PTSD. Not all suffered with it, but there was a way to test if Billie was lying, and Wilson said he believed Billie had answered all the questions honestly. He said that Billie's chronic lying or personal relationships could contribute to depression, but not to PTSD. Dr. Wilson said that it wasn't unusual for people who experience traumatic events to delay seeking mental help.

Regarding Billie being an egomaniac ("someone who thinks that they're God's gift to the world") Wilson said the events of *Green Lightning* had a devastating effect on Billie Lawless. "The specific reason that I see it as having an adverse impact on his ego is that Mr. Lawless' identity is that of an artist, and at this point in his — his life, career development as a professional artist, he was in a fairly early stage of that development, and then the events around *Green Lightning* and the stresses attendant thereto I think adversely affected how he saw himself professionally in terms of his identity as an artist and so that he began to have self-doubts." [13]

Wilson said that Lawless questioned whether he would continue to be an artist. "So at the core of it, it's an injury that's internal to the ego, it's an injury, in a sense, to his soul and identity as an artist, and I think that was a devastating blow." There was no question in Dr. Wilson's mind that Billie Lawless suffered from PTSD and depression as a result of the *Green Lightning* events. [14]

When looking back on it almost 40 years later, attorney Alan Rossman said, "If you're a satirist, if you're doing art, and it's controversial art... then you're anything but sort of status quo. We're real good at labeling people." He said that almost every artist he knows is somewhat of an egomaniac because they see the world differently and they're proud of their art. When it's attacked or when it becomes a source of controversy, the response is not to run away from it, it's to defend it. "You can make the argument art is so personal, right?" [15]

He said Billie genuinely felt outraged. "He took pride in his art. The size and the enormity of the undertaking was huge, and it's not like he had a crew." When they attack your art, you might defend it, but is that your ego? Rossman said "all great ideas are ...very personal and, anchored in terms of who you are." Everyone doesn't see the world the same way, so "it's like you're over the top, you're out of your mind, you're arrogant, and if you defend yourself then, how are you not arrogant? But it's by whose standards, in art, and there's so much great art, that is by nature controversial."[16]

· · · ● · · ● · ● · · ·

James Militello was called to testify. Under questioning by Dick Griffin, Militello read the termination letter sent to Billie Lawless, dated November 16, 1984.

"Would you tell the jury why you terminated in this instance?" Griffin asked.

"Well, what was built was not what we approved," Militello responded.

Militello said they approved a sculpture that they believed would have more of a daytime intent to it. "It's hard for me to describe art, but I'll tell you what we didn't approve. We did not approve the neon panels that were lit up that evening, that was not what we voted on." He said what Lawless created was devastating to Buffalo. "I mean, you have to understand, back in the late 70s, early 80's, you know, Buffalo was still the brunt of Johnny Carson's jokes." They were having trouble enticing investors and were trying to build an era of confidence. "We had created some very elaborate design controls. So this was very much against all that planning and against the effort we'd been trying to make and was pretty much insulting to the project and the City."[17]

When asked why they used Walt's Tree Service, Militello explained the city did a lot of work with Walt's. "They did a lot of basic construction work, assembly, put signs up; I mean, they were basically a contractor. It was kind of misleading to call them Walt's Tree Service."[18]

· · · · ● · ● · ● · · ·

Buffalo Mayor James Griffin arrived to take the stand and justify his decisions in November 1984, as everyone had been waiting for. Henry Wyman, known for suing the city, would question him. Griffin told Wyman that in his press release of November 19, 1984, it was the lighting component which caused the uproar in the City. He said as mayor he believed there would have been no uproar, "but in my personal opinion, it wasn't a structure that should have been in that area. To me, it would have caused accidents. I thought the structure itself was bad art. I'm not a connoisseur. I don't know the first thing about art, but I do know that the structure was an embarrassment to downtown Buffalo."[19]

He insisted he ordered nothing to happen to *Green Lightning*. "I let Jim Militello... and Greg Dudek handle the situation...and ordered Jim Militello to contract with someone to dismantle ... the structure."[20]

He said hiring Walt's was one of the temporary legal remedies he was pursuing. Griffin said he felt his order to dismantle it was legal because he was head of the Buffalo Urban Renewal Agency and the mayor. Like Jim Militello said, Griffin said that people were concerned that it would do damage to the image of the city, "and I agreed with them."[21]

Griffin said he received about 30 letters praising him for his decision to dismantle the sculpture. In one letter, he said,

> Dear Arnold,
>
> Thank you for your letter of support in the controversy concerning the so-called artwork located in the Elm-Oak development area in the City of Buffalo. It's just too bad that citizens of Western New York have had to be subjected to viewing this piece of work, which does not help our image. I'm not an art critic, don't propose to be one, but as an average citizen I believe the work is childish, it does not befit the City of Buffalo, the City of Good Neighbors. As you stated, bad art is still bad art. It was my duty as mayor of the City of Buffalo to have this work removed as — as soon as possible. And after reading the many letters such as yours which I've received, I'm sure I did the right thing.
>
> Sincerely, James D. Griffin[22]

He truly believed in his decision. Griffin, good or bad, as he may seem, was a man of conviction and didn't shy away from his beliefs.

Henry Wyman pressed Griffin about the supposed "public calamity" that he mentioned in his press release. "Did you then mean that public clamor and public calamity pretty much meant the same thing?"

Griffin said, "I'm not an English major. What I meant by calamity is going downtown and seeing this structure and having traffic jams and maybe accidents. Sure. I don't think I needed anybody to tell me about traffic jams."[23]

Did Griffin seriously think there would be traffic jams because of a neon sculpture? He said, "Yes." When asked if there were there any reports of traffic jams, he said, "Not after we — I think we sort of handled the situation as best we could, and that's the reason why there weren't any."

He admitted there weren't any traffic jams anytime the day after the unveiling, or any automobile accidents because the neon lights were off.[24]

When asked again about the supposed public clamor, Griffin said, "Well... I mentioned about the TV station that called the house and mentioned that their switchboard was lit with all the comments that they were receiving, the phone calls that we received at City Hall the next day and then the letters started coming in my office."

Wyman quipped, "Well, Mayor, TV station switchboards are lit up every time you're re-elected; does that indicate to you a public clamor?"

"It all depends on what TV station I guess," Griffin joked.[25]

Griffin also admitted that the number of calls that came into City Hall varied every single day, so there was no actual way to say that the calls that came into the switchboard had increased after the fifteen minute lighting ceremony.

· · · ● · ● · ● · · ●

Alan C. Birnholz, an associate art professor at University at Buffalo, teaching art history, was called to explain the meaning of a sculpture like *Green Lightning*. He explained you had to look at the sculpture on several levels. First was the literal meaning, including identification, a catalog of the objects in it, "including, quite clearly, the phallic figures that appeared when the work was lit, that would be a listing of what the sculpture contains."[26]

He said an art historian would then look beyond the immediate level of meaning and discuss the symbolic meaning, and try to interpret the work. In his conversations with Billie Lawless, he said that Lawless believed *Green Lightning* involved a manifestation of male dominance. "As an art historian who frequently has to rely on what our artists tell us, I would have no difficulty accepting that kind of interpretation based on my assessment of the literal meaning of the work." Finally, he said there was a sacrilegious and humorous aspect, "which have been a basic pair in the art of our times. We find this again and again throughout modern art. There's been a basic stance on the part of our artists to oppose authority, to challenge the way things are, to irritate those who are in positions of power, and so for a work to come along and do that would represent a continuation of what has been a basic theme in the art of our times."[27]

He didn't mean sacrilegious in relation to religion, and found nothing in *Green Lightning* opposed to any organized religion. "Much of modern art has involved that use of humor to reach an audience, to engage an audience, to try to convey the artist's viewpoint." Birnholz said that there was a lot he didn't understand and anyone engaged in art in the past or present has to accept that it takes time to understand a work. "So it may well be the meanings of this work, meanings of a work of art such as this would become known only after a considerable period of time, study and reflection." [28]

Birnholz said that art is meant "...to displease a good number of the people who do look at them, that's where the quality resides. Works of art are to engage, they're to irritate, they're to get us to think, to reflect, to get us to go beyond business as usual. So if we're going to start assessing works of art in terms of pleasing, then we're going to wind up with, qualitatively speaking, the poorest kinds of art."[29]

He related *Green Lightning* directly to the pop art of the 1960s.

Henry Wyman asked him if *Green Lightning* evoked serious thought and comment as a work of art. "My answer is that it would have done that, certainly, had the work been permitted to remain up. It has certainly evoked more than shock and dismay in me."

Dick Griffin, under cross exam, asked Birnholz if he said "there's a manifestation of male dominance as part of the theme?"

"I said that I agreed with the artist's viewpoint that that was a possible interpretation of the work, correct, I had no trouble accepting that, yes."[30]

• • • ● • ● • ● • • •

While the trial was taking place, Buffalo native Mark Russell, a celebrated political comedian, was inducted into the Entertainment Hall of Fame at Shea's Buffalo Theater in June 1992. When asked about his portrait, he said, "I am so grateful to the artist George Palmer for doing this portrait. Because I was worried. I was afraid the artist might be Billie Lawless."[31] Much like Johnny Carson did to Buffalo in the '70s, everyone was piling on Billie at this point.

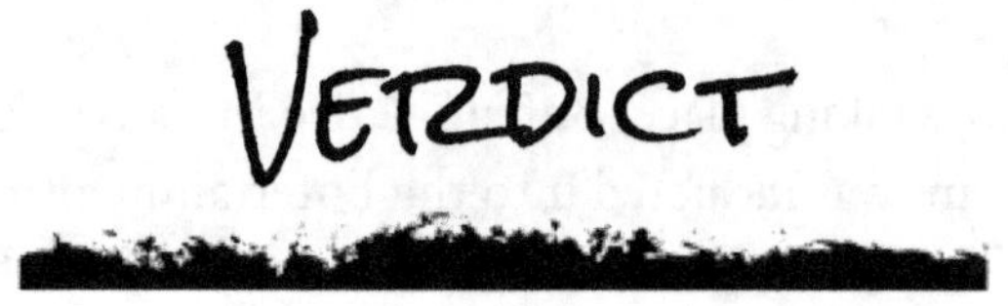VERDICT

"No, no, we were taken advantage of, we were
duped. Not just me, the entire board was duped."
Edmund Karnofsky

T HE LAWLESS LEGAL TEAM was confident they could win his case, so
they flew George Howell in from Los Angeles (where he lived since
January 1985) to sit for a deposition. They thought his testimony would
help to prove some of Billie's statements. When it was over, they decided
his testimony wasn't helpful and sent him home, never calling him as a
witness.

On the 22nd day of June 1992, Billie's attorneys rested at about 11:15
AM.

The defendant's City of Buffalo and B.U.R.A. presented their case by
calling just two witnesses, Edmund Karnofsky and Ronald J. Anthony.

Karnofsky was a founding member of the Buffalo Arts Commission and
an artist for over 50 years. He was the owner of the men's clothing store,
The Squire Shop, and in 1967 he created the Buffalo neck tie, which Jimmy
Griffin apparently wore every day.

In the deposition he gave in April 1992, he pulled no punches. He
said the model was crude and not detailed. "Furthermore, there was no
mention of neon, in any fashion, being a part of this sculpture," Karnofsky
said.

He testified that the sculpture was "very embarrassing" and no neon
penises were on the acetate.

Henry Wyman asked if Karnofsky was upset with the artwork. He said
as an artist, no, but as a member of the Buffalo Arts Commission, he

was. "No, no, we were taken advantage of, we were duped. Not just me, the entire board was duped," Karnofsky said. He said Lawless presented a model that was noncontroversial, "and then what was constructed was something entirely different from the model that was presented to us for approval."[1]

The other witness for Buffalo, Ronald J. Anthony, was one of Mayor Griffin's closest aides, with an office in City Hall, while apparently being employed full time by IBM.

Anthony was an active volunteer for the city, sitting as advisor on several of the mayor's committees and panels. "He's a tireless volunteer," Jim Militello said. "He helped structure public events, such as the jazz festival. He's just a fellow that has volunteered hours and hours of his time to help us in the revitalization of the City."[2]

Anthony supposedly had a lot of power in Griffin's office, including approving hires. He had a well-known reputation for being quite a "stickler" on items, so his testimony was crucial to the city.

When questioned, Anthony said he was "personally embarrassed" and promoted the line that Lawless duped them about the sculpture. He said the picture he saw on TV in November 1984 was "diametrically opposed" to the model he and other members of B.U.R.A. approved in October 1983. He said Lawless never mentioned his plans to include "male genitalia" or use "neon male penises" on the sculpture.[3]

David More had been prepping to take the stand for the City. Other than Billie, David was probably the person most involved, and with the most to lose. He had spent about 10 days in the gallery watching the trial.

But Dick Griffin and Mike Risman felt the trial was going their way, so they decided not to call him and the defense rested their case at 3:15 PM.

Lawless' attorneys were expecting More to take the stand and wanted to call him as a rebuttal witness. Since a New York subpoena was only good to the state border, if he wasn't in the state, he couldn't testify. David More headed to his friend's home in Canada for a couple of days.

"We don't know where he is," Mike Risman told Lawless' attorneys when asked. He said it's not their job to make arrangements for their witnesses. "We can't legally ethically help them out," he explained.[4]

Another person they had wanted to call was Councilperson James Pitts. But, like More, Pitts was unavailable, as he was supposedly home with pneumonia.

Mike Risman said the Koessler family of Greater Buffalo Press had donated to the sculpture and was mad that Billie had misrepresented it. They attended the trial for three or four days. He said they were on his side, so they were thinking about calling the elderly Mr. Koessler, but in the end decided not to. [5]

• • • • ● • ● • • • •

Attorneys for both sides sent Judge Dadd their opinion on how to have the jury decide the facts of the case, called a Request to Charge.

B.U.R.A. and the City filed a joint document that reiterated the points they made during the trial:

Billie had a permit agreement that said the sculpture must "fully resemble the model presented to B.U.R.A."

They said that if Billie was at fault, the jury should find for the defendants and not award him any compensation. They also said they weren't responsible for any damage Walt's Tree Service did.

And just because Jimmy Griffin was B.U.R.A. chairperson and also mayor of the City, does not, of itself, mean that he "acted for the City as opposed to B.U.R.A."

They also discounted Billie's assertion that it was a Constitutional right the City infringed on his freedom of expression. "In order for plaintiff to recover under this theory, he must establish by clear and convincing evidence that the City, as opposed to B.U.R.A., ordered the dismantling of the sculpture in order to suppress or curtail the plaintiff's expression of an idea."[6]

It seems like they were trying to point fingers at each other and confuse the jury, while saying they were not responsible for what happened.

Henry Wyman submitted a Request to Charge. The highlights were:

They said Ronald Anthony was an "interested witness," meaning he is "not necessarily less credible than a disinterested witness." But because he was interested in the case's outcome, the jury should question his testimony.

The City didn't call David More as a witness, and "have offered no reasonable explanation for failing to call such a witness." Because of that, "you may infer, if you deem it proper to do so, that the testimony of the uncalled person would not contradict the opposing evidence, or would not support the defendant's version of the case."

Because Edmund Karnofsky was a member of the Buffalo Arts Commission, and B.U.R.A. relied on their approval, could determine "whether his testimony is in any way influenced by his role in the events that form the basis of this action."

"In determining whether the model presented 'fully resembled' the finished sculpture, you must consider the model itself and its likeness and similarities to the final sculpture. 'Fully resemble' does not mean that the final sculpture must exactly replicate the model as presented, for there are inevitably thousands of differences between a model presented and a final full size sculpture. 'Fully resemble' means only that the final sculpture must fully be like or similar to the model in appearance or nature.' [Webster's Unabridged 2d Edition.]"

Wyman argued the First Amendment protected *Green Lightning*. Since the city provided a public forum and gave permission to Lawless to display *Green Lightning*, "the artist's right of expression may not be infringed by the denial of or the placing of conditions upon the benefit or privilege."[7]

Late on the afternoon of June 22, 1992, Judge Mark Dadd suggested they should charge the jury in two phases, called bifurcation. The first phase would be a "threshold" question of misrepresentation, then the second phase would be damages based on the first phase.

Richard Griffin responded to Judge Dadd on June 23 and Henry Wyman responded on June 24.

Wyman said the idea had merit, but if they had known this from the beginning, they might have tried the case differently. Billie Lawless had no burden to prove he misrepresented the sculpture. Even Dick Griffin wanted to remove the second threshold question from the jury and focus on the question of misrepresentation "providing the jury with what might be... an easy out and an early ride home."[8]

Just as the trial was concluding, Buffalo radio station, WUFX got in on the fun. They got a working model of *Green Lightning* and displayed it in their parking lot at 425 Franklin Street. The station encouraged listeners to stop by and vote on whether they should display the sculpture in Buffalo.[9]

On June 24, 1992, the attorneys met with Judge Dadd, where he delivered his final verdict sheets based on the information from all parties. Henry Wyman argued that David More probably would have been a hostile witness. "We had plans to impeach him based on some other things that he said. Our calling him as our witness would have put us at a disability in terms of impeachment." [10]

Regardless, Judge Dadd denied the missing witness charge.

The following morning, June 25, at 9:00 AM, the parties again met. The media circus continued and Judge Dadd said that WKBW Channel 7 had requested permission to televise and tape the entire proceeding. Neither party objected, but there was no one there from Channel 7.

Mike Risman said he was nervous about Channel 7 showing the summations live on T.V. at 10:30 AM. "I was a little nervous about it because I intended to use the 'P' word, because it was the theme of it. I didn't know how that might look on TV." He said they were preparing for it and then Channel 7 never showed up. [11]

They brought in the jury, and Judge Dadd prepared them for summations. "I remind you ...that the summations are not evidence themselves, they're simply the attorney's argument on the evidence, and the attorneys will tell you what they think the evidence was and what opinions — or, what conclusions, rather, you should draw from that evidence. Basically, you're going to have to rely on your own judgment as to what the facts are and which facts you believe and how much weight you give to those facts." [12]

Dick Griffin argued during his summation that Billie Lawless misrepresented *Green Lightning* to city decision-makers and the jury should not award him $500,000 in damages for its subsequent removal. Lawless committed "a disservice" to both the art world and the community by building "an avant-garde sculpture with male phallic symbols to irritate" people.

He testified that the model that was in the courtroom was "materially different" from the model Lawless showed the Urban Renewal Agency, the Common Council, and the Buffalo Arts Commission in 1983. The city's counterclaim would cover the costs the city paid in having the sculpture dismantled in November 1984. Griffin suggested they gave Lawless a permit to build the sculpture because he "came from a known family" of Buffalonians.

The final sculpture, he said, "was not what Lawless presented" to city officials to get the city contract. The case boiled down to Lawless' "arrogance" his artistic "egotism" and his desire for "publicity," Griffin told the jury. "We have no responsibility to Mr. Lawless." [13]

Billie's team reiterated their talking points, but could provide nothing new. His testimony was what they had to rely on.

After summations, Judge Dadd told the jury to take a one hour lunch and reconvene at 1:25 PM. "I remind you again," he stated, "you may not discuss the case amongst yourselves or with anyone else, or allow anyone to discuss the case in your presence. Do not go to the site of the sculpture. Do not conduct any independent research or investigation. Do not listen to, watch or read any media report of the trial." [14]

After lunch, Judge Dadd began giving the jury instructions.

"Members of the jury, we come now to that portion of the trial where you are instructed on the law applicable to the case and then you will retire for your final deliberations. You've heard the evidence introduced to you by all sides, and through the arguments of their attorneys, you have learned the conclusions that they wish you to draw from the evidence which has been presented to you."

Judge Dadd went through the rule of law and explained that each juror may or may not accept a witness's testimony. He explained not to take anything he said as for or against either party, as his opinion did not matter.

When Judge Dadd explained the verdict sheet, it appeared to be skewed toward the defense.

1. Did Lawless misrepresent material aspects of or fail to provide material information about Green Lightning to the defendant B.U.R.A.?

2. Did the material misrepresentation or failure to provide material information cause B.U.R.A. to grant a permit it would not have granted?

3. Did the sculpture, as completed and operated on November 15th, 1984, fully resemble the model as shown, explained and described by Lawless when presented to B.U.R.A. on October 13, 1983?

Judge Dadd told the jury they should not to be affected by sympathy for any of the parties, regardless of whether it would be popular or unpopular. He gave them direct and explicit instructions that they should consider only the evidence, the testimony, and exhibits. "Find the facts from what you consider to be the believable evidence and apply the law as I have given it to you. Your verdict will be determined by the conclusion thus reached, no matter who the verdict hurts or helps."[15]

The jury of four women and two men began deliberations at 1:52 PM, with Juror 1, Grunthaner, assigned foreperson. At 2:35 PM, 43 minutes later, the jury re-entered the courtroom.

The court clerk asked, "Will the foreman please rise? In the matter of William B. Lawless versus the City of Buffalo, the City of Buffalo Urban Renewal Agency and Walt's Tree Service, has the jury reached a verdict in accordance with verdict sheet number one?"

Foreperson Grunthaner responded, "Yes." It was a unanimous verdict.

The first question, "Did plaintiff Lawless misrepresent material aspects of or fail to provide material information about *Green Lightning* to defendant Buffalo Urban Renewal Agency, and your answer is?" Yes.

The second question, "Did the material misrepresentation or failure to provide material information cause B.U.R.A. to grant a permit it would not have granted, and your answer is?" Yes.

Judge Dadd then addressed the jury. He said, once they had shut the power to the sculpture off, the defendants owed a duty to Lawless not to act negligently in removing the sculpture. He reminded them that even though Griffin was mayor and chairperson of B.U.R.A. they needed to look at them as separate jobs.

"In reaching your verdict, you must consider carefully the capacity in which any person acted. Also, defendant Walt's Tree Service is an independent contractor. No other defendant can be held liable for any negligent act or omission of the independent contractor Walt's Tree Service, unless you find that defendant was negligent in its selection of Walt's Tree Service, in that, it knew or should have known that ...damage would be caused to the sculpture by reason of the contractor not having the skill or ability to handle the work and that such absence of skill or ability was the proximate cause of the damage."[16]

He said that to recover money damages they had to establish that the City of Buffalo made a decision which violated Lawless' constitutional rights and it executed it with deliberate indifference to his constitutional rights. "As a result of the violation of his constitutional rights by the city only, what amount of emotional injury, again only emotional injury, if any, was suffered by Mr. Lawless?"[17]

Judge Dadd explained every question the jury would answer, and the jury resumed deliberations at 2:57 PM.

At 3:38 PM, they returned to the courtroom to have the judge explain the constitutional due process.

The jury again left the courtroom to continue deliberations at 3:42 PM. They then sent a note wanting to know how Billie Lawless received the letter from Jim Militello on November 16, 1984, that he said he never received.

Alan Rossman said, "Well, just so it's clear, there was a line of questioning ...whether he had received any letter of notification. I don't know whether that exhibit was used or not, but his testimony was clearly in the negative."

Jim Militello's testimony was read to the jury, and they resumed deliberations at 4:13 PM. They had another question, then returned to deliberations at 4:35 PM, and at 4:53 PM, they returned with their verdict.

"Jury, all parties present, Your Honor," the clerk announced. "Will the foreperson please stand. In the matter of William B. Lawless versus the City of Buffalo, City of Buffalo Urban Renewal Agency and Walt's Tree Service, did the jury reach a verdict in accordance with verdict sheet 2-A?"

Foreperson Grunthaner replied, "Yes."

When asked if it was unanimous, the foreperson said, "Yes and no."

Judge Dadd said they would go question by question.

When asked if the Buffalo Urban Renewal Agency negligently caused damage to the Lawless sculpture, they unanimously said no.

Next, did the City of Buffalo negligently cause damage to the Lawless sculpture? No, to this question, but this was not unanimous. There was one dissenting juror.

Did Walt's Tree Service negligently cause damage to the Lawless sculpture? Unanimous no.

But the next question, did the City, not B.U.R.A. or Walt's, violate Lawless constitutional right to due process of law? Yes, but there was a dissenting juror.

The court clerk asked, "As a result of the violation of his constitutional right by the City only, what amount of emotional injury, if any, was suffered by Lawless?"

Foreperson Grunthaner, "None."

Did the defendant B.U.R.A. suffer damage as a result of Lawless' misrepresentation or his failure to construct a sculpture that fully resembled the model? That was a unanimous no.

Did the defendant City suffer damage as a result of Lawless' misrepresentation or his failure to construct a sculpture that fully resembled the model? Another unanimous no.

Judge Dadd said, "All right. Ladies and gentlemen of the jury, I want to thank you for your service. This has been a much longer trial than any that we had, and it's certainly been an unusual and interesting trial. I apologize for the many delays we had and short days and all the conferences we had out here while you were sitting in there reading the newspaper or talking or having that brunch that you usually brought with you. We're all very grateful for your service."

He told them they were free to discuss this case with anyone, to read news articles, to listen to the radio and TV, "because I'm sure you'll see something about that tonight. You are also free to discuss this with the litigants and their lawyers, if you wish, but you're, of course, under no obligation to talk with anybody about it if you'd just rather not. Again, the jury's discharged, and we thank you very much for your service."[18]

The jury found that Walt's Tree Service, Inc., and Buffalo Urban Renewal Agency were not negligent in damaging the structure. Billie Lawless would get no restitution and the City of Buffalo and B.U.R.A. would receive no monetary damages.

After the eight-year ordeal, the outcome understandably disappointed Billie Lawless. "I've had my day in court and will take it from here," he told reporters afterward. "That's what the (legal) process is all about, and you live with it."[19]

One member of the jury, Russ Albee, said the jurors believed the sculpture was obscene. "I think they had the right to tear down the sculpture."[20] Unfortunately for Billie Lawless, their task was not to decide that, although it appears it was a factor in the outcome.

The headline of a brief article in the *Akron (Ohio) Beacon Journal* on June 27 read: "Sculpture is a loser and so is its artist."[21]

The Buffalo *News'* editorial team weighed in on the verdict on June 29, 1992. "It's hard to dismiss the suspicion that Lawless was playing a sophomoric joke on his old home town," they wrote. "When the work was unveiled, it was obscene by most Buffalonians' standards. The episode raises the issue of what is appropriate for public art. Even without the phallic figures, it was of questionable artistic value. And it is perfectly reasonable for the public to expect that artwork standing on the public's own property is not going to be offensive to mainstream tastes. But there's no good reason to further the irritation with an award of taxpayer funds for the artist. That, in its own way, would have been obscene." [22]

Once again, we come to the question of what is the public's place in public art? The editorial was very demeaning to the artwork, which was lit for fifteen minutes in 1984. The *News* said it was of "questionable artistic value," even without the neon. Should the city have had any say since private money financed the artwork? What exactly was their definition of "mainstream tastes?"

A happy Mayor Jimmy Griffin issued a statement that same day stating the decision upheld the city's long-standing view and wasn't a negative ruling on public art. "From the beginning, (we) felt that a hoax had been perpetrated by Mr. Lawless," Griffin wrote. "In ruling that misrepresentation had occurred, the jury confirmed what we have been saying all along," and the verdict "completely vindicated" Griffin's order to dismantle the sculpture, which wasn't exactly true, as the verdict was not unanimous on that count. [23]

The Buffalo *News'* Jeff Simon decided to tackle the jury's verdict in a column on June 30, 1992. In it, Simon said that Lawless' attempt to be the next avante-garde artist ultimately failed.

> The jury took the common-sense view that most people took 10 years ago: The mayor acted peremptorily and repressively after the politically connected Lawless played a trick on local pols by not telling them in advance that he was going to grace the Elm-Oak arterial with dancing penises in neon.

> Obviously, the city overreacted. Just as obviously, Lawless was a sniggering, superannuated adolescent playing the kind of joke on the world of public sculpture that probably only the children of political families yearn to play. And all the while he no doubt thought he was in the great tradition of Marcel Duchamp's urinals, Man Ray's fur-covered teacups,

Christo's tarp-covered bridges and Andy Warhol's soup cans.

In a world where "The Today Show's" Katie Couric can interview a woman who demonstrates condom use on a banana, making a big deal out of *Green Lightning* seems more than a bit silly. But then, it always did. That's why the Buffalo-connected writers of "Hill Street Blues" got a wonderful episode of the show out of a fictionalization of the *Green Lightning* case.

That's why the sculpture didn't seem to bother the city of Chicago when it rested comfortably there right after Buffalo dismantled it.

The only time pols seem to care about the arts is when money is involved. The minute taxpayer dollars enter into it, they have their ticket to line up 20 deep for their turn to make speeches at the "Family Values" pavilion.

Any working critic -- especially one who has spent a long time in the trenches of pop music, TV and movies -- has no doubt watched in amazement as the "Family Values" banner has been un-furled and paraded up and down by the most unlikely people. Obviously, very few proponents of "family values" are renowned pederasts, substance abusers, drunken drivers and worm-hearted backstabbers whose professional ethics might embarrass Herman Goering.

Still, I never cease to be amazed at the distance between the homey values some people profess at the top of their lungs and the ones they display in their daily working and professional lives. We call that distance good old-fashioned hypocrisy, and it's one old-style "value" that seems to be very much to the fore in the '90s.

If your own particular "family values" are to raise kids who grow up to be intelligent, compassionate, honest, honorable, loyal, witty, decent and self-respecting, how are you helping them by tearing down a juvenile piece of public sculpture?

Most parents figure out early on that there is no surer way to give kids the wrong ideas about things than to hide them and refuse to discuss them. That's just asking for trouble.

That's what both Lawless and the mayor did. And they both got what they asked for.

Justice seems to have been served.[24]

• • • • • • • • • •

Billie's Buffalo-based trial attorney, Henry E. Wyman, found himself in hot water in 1992 after a two-month criminal probe. It was determined that he had embezzled at least $429,000 from client escrow accounts. In April 1993, he gave up his law license before they disbarred him. In early August 1993, he pleaded guilty to bilking over 20 clients dating back to early 1990. He never disclosed what he spent the money on, although it was for personal use.

Apparently, Wyman wore the same sports jacket and pants every day during Billie's trial, except for one. So when it came out that Wyman had embezzled from his clients, it was a shock. Mike Risman said, "Despite the large amount of stolen money involved, he did not live extravagantly. He was a marginal lawyer whose whole practice appeared to be appealing to people who were on the opposite side of the political fence from Mayor Griffin and suing the Griffin Adminstration."[25]

They ordered Wyman to repay five former clients, but prosecutors didn't know if he even had the funds. He may have served jail time.[26]

• • • • • • • • • •

Richard F. Griffin, the lead attorney who represented the Buffalo Urban Renewal Agency, penned a letter to the editor that was published July

9, 1992. In it he said that a headline in the Buffalo *News* "conveyed the impression that the city interfered with a right of free expression. The contrary is true." According to Griffin, Lawless misrepresented the facts to B.U.R.A. and his permit was null and void from day one. "The jury's verdict is not a setback for public art or sculpture, but it vindicates truth and integrity. The entire *Green Lightning* episode has been a disservice to responsible artists who may seek permission to exhibit their work in public. The issue here was not taste in art or whether anyone should support avante-garde sculpture. "What was at issue was the responsibility of an artist to truthfully describe what he intends to exhibit."[27]

It was early July. The jury had gone back to their private lives. Judge Mark Dadd had returned to sleepy Wyoming County. Billie and his legal team had returned to Cleveland, but the verdict was not what they wanted after the two and a half week trial. The jury was not supposed to decide if *Green Lightning* was obscene, but whether Lawless had misrepresented his work and whether the City jumped the gun with dismantling it.

Instead, they used their bias in the decision making, which may have been why attorney Alan Rossman said since Judge Dadd had not yet issued his final legal judgement, they would seek a judgment against the city for "negligent trespass. We think that, in spite of the verdict, there was evidence of trespass, and the sculpture was damaged, making the city negligent," Rossman said.

In his affidavit, Rossman stated that the testimony regarding Walt's Tree Service was uncontested, as was the testimony that the sculpture had been damaged. Last, "had any effort been made to examine the sculpture as an artwork or talk to the artist; that it was possible to remove the panels with a screwdriver and a wrench, and that torches were neither proper nor necessary."[28]

Dick Griffin said he and Mike Risman would contest the maneuver. "There is no basis for that motion," Griffin said. It was "a shotgun approach which attempts to invade the prerogatives of the Court and jury in this case and is not consistent with the complaint, the law or the facts, and misquotes the evidence and issues in several significant respects."[29]

In addition, Griffin said, "Mr. Wisenbaugh's testimony was most likely totally rejected by the jury in that it was not credible; he made no independent evaluation but merely attempted to endorse the improper analysis of Mr. Lawless, which was changed several times. He failed to bring any photographs or evidence of damage or any notes of any damage that he received. He was an arrogant witness whose testimony was not credible. The Court should deny the motion."[30]

John Hoffman, owner of The Buffalo Store, planned on cashing in on the renewed publicity of *Green Lightning* and designed a t-shirt based on the original *Green Lightning* shirt he printed for a Lawless fundraiser in 1985 (see photo elsewhere in the book). When asked if he would send Mayor Griffin a free t-shirt, he said, "Oh, that would be too funny, wouldn't it?"[31]

Attorneys for both sides met on Monday, July 21, 1992 in Judge Dadd's Wyoming County courtroom, over an hour southeast of Buffalo.

Alan Rossman argued that Billie Lawless was entitled to a judgment for "negligent trespass," citing trial testimony that damage totaling $100,000 to $225,000 was done to *Green Lightning*.

Richard Griffin countered, saying there was no basis for awarding damages to Lawless.[32]

On Monday August 3, 1992, Justice Dadd wrote, "The Court finds no ground for disturbing the verdict of the jury and no relief shall be granted from its terms. ORDERED that the Court shall grant a judgment in accordance with the jury verdict in this action and no costs shall be awarded; and it is further ORDERED that the motions are otherwise denied." The jury verdict stood, and they awarded no claims for either party.[33]

And that was that. Or so you would believe. But in this case, as in all of Billie Lawless's life, there would always be another chapter.

On September 3, 1992, Lawless appealed to the Appellate Division, Fourth Judicial Department, Rochester, New York, which allowed to stand the jury verdict in favor of the Defendants, dismissing the first five causes of action, and his Section 1983 claim for violation of his First Amendment rights.[34]

In September 1992, he filed a new unrelated lawsuit, this time against the estate of his former neighbor, Charles Daniels, on Highgate Avenue in Buffalo. According to Lawless, he had stored more than $80,000 worth of artwork in Daniels' garage in the summer of 1986 after he moved from Buffalo. He said he paid Daniels $150 up front and gave him a poster of artwork he called "The Politician: A Toy."

Lawless said he paid another $550 in storage fees over the years and also gave Daniels a $400 limited edition silk screen print called "Fleeing Bandits." After he moved to Cleveland, Lawless began removing artwork from the garage.

He said he returned in December 1990 to find that, seven months after Daniels died, artwork worth about $15,000 was missing. The "Gates of Fertility" sculpture was missing, as was "Reclining Nude Banquet" table, and a glass tabletop.

Lawless placed the value of "Gates of Fertility" at $10,000, "Reclining Nude Banquet" at $5,000 and the glass table at $1,000.

The Daniels family said they were going to sell the home and make Lawless an offer with the proceeds.[35]

In July 1993, the attorneys for Billie Lawless argued that the case against the city of Buffalo should be reversed for retrial, "with the exception of the verdict rendered in favor of the Plaintiff against the Defendant City for violation of his Constitutional rights." They said the verdict should stand, but damages should be reversed and retried.[36]

They said there was "uncontested evidence of damage to the sculpture... whether or not a jury believed the estimates of those damages to be inflated. To find absolutely no damage is clearly against the weight of the credible evidence." [37]

Laurence K. Rubin, Buffalo Corporation Counsel wrote, "The intent of the sculpture was to irritate those in positions of power. The function of the sculpture was to displease and irritate a good number of people." He said the Elm-Oak Arterial was a prime development area in which $22 million was invested, and 1,000 jobs created. Billie's contract was void under New York law, because he misrepresented his model. The jury decided that more notice should have been given before they began dismantling *Green Lightning*, but no damages resulted from that failure.[38]

They said they didn't warrant a new trial because Billie Lawless made a claim for lost income, although he had not filed income tax returns for over ten years. Also, they said that his "alleged" emotional injury was even more outlandish. He was "comparing the impact of seeing his property damaged to the experience of a Vietnam veteran or rape trauma victim. This outlandish attempt to build a damage claim where none existed was rejected by the jury."[39]

Richard Griffin tried to diminish Lawless and his work by saying he was in his late thirties, but had made no money. He said that Billie most likely did this for notoriety, his fifteen minutes of fame.

In January 1994, Buffalo ushered in a new era as they inaugurated Anthony Masiello, mayor of the city. David More received his walking papers one Friday, not long after and was told to leave City Hall after 17 years.

That same month, the five-member Appellate Division of State Supreme Court in Rochester heard the appeal from attorney Alan Rossman for a new trial. They issued their decision and rejected the demand in May 1994.

Mike Risman said the city was "very pleased with the result. The jury correctly ruled that Mr. Lawless misrepresented" his artwork to the Urban Renewal Agency "and he sustained no damages." [40]

Years later, Risman recalled that Billie Lawless used "male power over women." He assumed that Lawless was abusing his girlfriend, and that was part of his mental state, that he was trying to abuse her. [41]

Mike Risman said *Green Lightning* wasn't a sophisticated piece, and was meant to be controversial. The jury was disgusted. "I could just see the look on their face like they just had it. He was just lying about everything. The girlfriend, his mental health, lying to the city, lying about his drawing, lying about his damages, lying about his financial cost. You know, just everything's not truthful. I think the whole intent of it was to create a controversy to help promote himself, his artwork. But he couldn't control what happened afterwards." [42]

He said that it surprised him that at the unveiling, Billie looked like he hadn't shaved in three days. "He looks sort of disheveled, and he didn't look like someone that you expect promoting a legitimate piece of artwork. I think it was like, 'Haha, screw you Buffalo. I'm gonna go out on controversy.' He just never expected the city to respond in kind." [43]

Risman asked why Lawless looked disheveled at such an important piece of public art? If the public was taking it seriously, why wasn't he?

Many people that worked for Jimmy Griffin still praise him till this day. Mike Risman is no different. He said that although they portray Griffin in an unpleasant light; he was a good guy and was very decisive, often following the advice of his commissioners. [44]

Risman said Judge Dadd "was an excellent judge. Every time an ethics or an evidence question came up, you'd make your arguments. He'd go into his law library and research it himself." [45]

Risman praised his co-counsel, Dick Griffin. He said that Griffin was a distinguished lawyer and one of the lead lawyers in the school desegregation case for the plaintiffs in Buffalo in the 1970s.

"He had far more trial experience than me," Risman said, "so I brought him in. He was very proud to be involved in a city issue." Together, they prepped Mayor Griffin for the trial. Risman was young, "so it was an exciting thing for me."[46]

David More said they won hands down "except that there was one stupid little mistake I made," about sending the letter to Billie without return receipt. [47]

The eight-year lawsuit took a toll on Billie Lawless and his family. It led to an estrangement from his father that was never resolved. "My mother made a public appearance with me in the courtroom," Billie said. "My father did not." They were not friends after that and "that is a sadness in my life." His father died in 2007 at 84 years old. [48]

Jim Militello said that Lawless was a terrible witness, but he (Militello) was a better witness. He felt it was a straightforward case for the city to win, because Billie lied. "I was not very good for them because I studied (the model) intently because of my interest in model making. And I didn't see any dancing dog biscuits and nothing in the transcripts of the Urban Renewal Agency meeting. He never said there's gonna be penises, dancing little girls. It was a cute little Lawless joke." He said that Billie got his "international fame or whatever. I guess we didn't destroy it. So it did have a second life in some community. Somebody who liked dancing dog biscuits."[49]

But Billie didn't gain international fame from the incident. Instead, he became a fierce defender of freedom of expression.

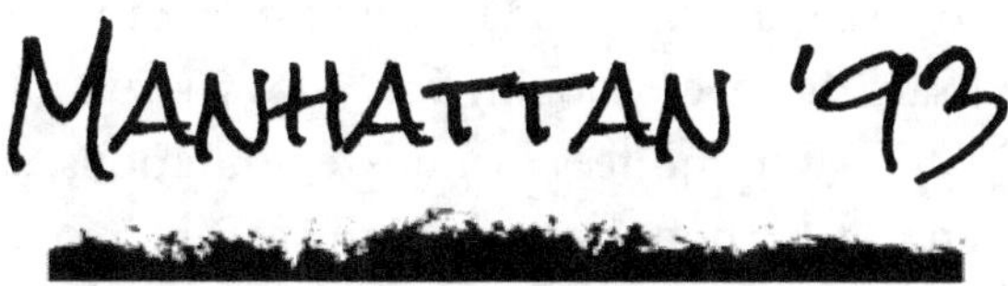 Manhattan '93

> "It is my further opinion, to a reasonable degree
> of medical certainty, that 'Green Lightning' is not
> sexually arousing and will not promote sexual vio-
> lence." Dr. Ladd Spiegel

AFTER *GREEN LIGHTNING* HAD been a hit in Chicago for four un-eventful years, it sat in storage in that city at Illinois Steel Service. They stored it for free because, according to Lawless, they liked the sculpture.

Billie Lawless subscribed to the periodical "Maquette," published by the International Sculpture Center. About February 15, 1993, he read an announcement that the Organization of Independent Artists (OIA) was reviewing slides for "Wards Island-Outdoor Sculpture '93" in New York City. After the controversy in Buffalo and the successful run in the larger metropolis of Chicago, Lawless thought the prospect of showing *Green Lightning* in New York City could be pivotal to his career. After all, New York City was the "center of the international art world," he said, and it would be "so invaluable to the center of an artist as to be priceless."[1]

Artists John Rosis and Glenn Reed conceived the show and would be curators. They approached OIA to be the umbrella sponsor for the exhibition. Talks between OIA, Manhattan Psychiatric Center (where the show would be held) and the curators took place in May 1992. One stipulation was that after the selection of work and proposed placement, the Center had the final say of the artwork and sites to assure they could be installed safely and not "potentially injurious in this psychiatric environment."[2]

Billie requested a prospectus and received one around February 28,

1993. The theme of the show said that "artists are encouraged to create work unrestricted by the definition of art. The emphasis should be on bringing in personal peculiarities and ignoring art's familiar conventions." The prospectus said they were looking for "all work suitable for outdoor installation."[3] There were no fees or no size limitations, so Billie had a specific piece in mind, his popular and controversial *Green Lightning*.

On March 3, 1993, he sent a submission packet with all the required information, photos, dimensions, including that it had neon lighting, meaning he would need electricity.

Outdoor Sculpture 1993
at Manhattan Psychiatric Center
Ward's Island, New York
Calls for Entries

THEME: Artists are encouraged to create work unrestricted by the definition of art. The emphasis should be on bringing in personal peculiarities and ignoring art's familiar conventions, exploring in a personal and artistic sense the relationship between that which is acceptable and that which is not.
MEDIA: All work suitable for outdoor installation for 6 - 12 months.
FEES: There are no fees to enter or be included in the exhibit.
SIZE RESTRICTIONS: There are no size restrictions.
ACCEPTED WORK: Accepted work will be based on slides showing the artist's ability to conceive of and execute work. After an artist's work has been accepted, a substitution cannot be made without the curators consent.
LIABILITY: Neither the curators nor Manhattan Psychiatric Center will be responsible for loss or damage to the accepted work. The exhibition s sponsors will provide public liabilty coverage for the artist. The artist is responsible for the expense of shipping or transport , insurance coverage and removal of work.
AGREEMENT: Submitting an entry to this show constitutes an agreement with all conditions of this show. The curators assume the right to photograph any accepted work for publicity or catalogue purposes.
SALES: Sales of work will be encouraged and there will be no commission requirement.
ENTRY INSTRUCTIONS: Curating is done by slides and completion of a proposal booklet Use the booklet to explain, through words, diagrams or both, what you plan to do. You may add larger pages or whatever, providing that the whole bundle functions as a book.
Artists may submit up to 12 35mm color slides. Slides must be clearly marked with artists name, media, dimensions (hxlxw). For entry; mail slides/proposal booklet, resume, and a SASE for return of slides to OUTDOOR SCULPTURE 1993, 518 East Eleventh Street, Box 4A, New York, N.Y. 10009. Deadline for entry is ~~February 1st~~ MARCH 15 1993. Materials without an SASE will not be returned.
CURATORS: Glenn Reed, artist, John Rosis, artist.
SPONSOR: Organiation of Independent Artists (OIA).

The call for entries for "Outdoor Sculpture 1993" at Manhattan Psychiatric Center. Lawless vs. Manhattan Psychiatric Center.

The Manhattan Psychiatric Center held a meeting with curators Rosis and Reed on March 24, 1993. They reiterated the curators would select the works and sites, but the Center would have a final review of the sculptures and their placement. The Center also would not provide electrical power, something that was not communicated to the artists and would be critical to *Green Lightning*. The contract between the artist and the Center was not available until after the selection, which would also be problematic.

Billie received a postcard in the mail on April 8: "Dear Artist; Your work has been selected for OUTDOOR SCULPTURE '93 at Manhattan Psychiatric Center at Ward's Island, New York, N.Y. You will be contacted about installation and opening dates." The only contact information was an address in New York.[4] Unknown to Billie, OIA and Manhattan Psychiatric Center did not approve of this.

He sent a letter to the OIA office in New York and on April 23, curator John Rosis called him. He told Billie that his proposal "was really great" and he admired Billie's work. Billie explained *Green Lightning* was in storage in Chicago and it would require a great deal of work, time, and money to move it.[5] Rosis asked Billie to send a photo and written description of *Green Lightning,* which he did.

Less than a week later, Rosis again phoned Lawless, which Billie recorded since he didn't trust people. Rosis said he knew Billie was up to something and told him he needed to contact several people regarding his artwork. Billie asked if his work was being removed from the exhibition. Rosis said no, that he would present it to the hospital administration, but he also "expressed vague concerns about the safety of the sculpture." [6]

Billie penned another letter to Rosis dated April 29, 1993 in which he stated, "you do not have the right to summarily break this agreement unless I have in some way refused to comply with 'conditions of the show.'"[7] He also admonished him for suggesting that he would have to contact others.

On May 1, Billie "drove from Cleveland, Ohio to Wards Island, New York" and attended the meeting of artists where he selected a site for *Green Lightning*. John Rosis informed Bille that there would be a safety meeting that was closed to the artists. Two days later, Billie faxed Helen Thomas, the director of public information, requesting to attend the meeting on May 5th. She faxed back that he was welcome to attend.

At that meeting Billie presented a letter from a renowned structural engineer "verifying the safety of the sculpture" to Walter Camargo, head of grounds, who said it satisfied his concerns. Camargo also said that providing power would not be a problem. He would later say, "I answered Mr. Lawless's question regarding electrical power as a hypothetical question. I never meant that his sculpture should be installed."[8]

Billie explained that the sculpture had previously stood with no incidents in both Buffalo and Chicago. Rosis then distributed a written description of *Green Lightning* and a photocopy of the maquette. Camargo "remarked that some of the figures... appeared phallic in nature." [9]

Billie admitted they were phallic symbols. Helen Thomas then asked to see the photo and said, "I have a problem with this," and said she would have to speak to Dr. Michael H. Ford, the executive director of the hospital. Lawless left the meeting for about twenty minutes when a thought occurred to him, so he returned and asked if he could "observe the proceedings as the other sculptures were discussed."[10]

About 90 minutes later, Rosis realized Billie had been taking notes and asked him why. "I informed all present that only the content of my sculpture had been discussed and that I feared my constitutional rights to freedom of expression was in the process of being violated."[11] Understanding a potential problem was at hand, Helen Thomas asked Billie to leave the meeting.

Joseph Stasko from OIA said he never signed agreements with anyone related to the exhibition, nor was he involved in the planning or selection of any artwork. But he "became aware of Billie Lawless and his work" in early May when John Rosis "mentioned to me that (Billie) was unhappy with the curators' suggestions to make his work safer."[12]

```
Dear Artist;
     Your work has been selected for OUTDOOR SCULPTURE
'93 at Manhattan Psychiatric Center at Ward's Island
New York, N.Y. This exhibition is sponsored by the
Organization of Independent Artists. You will be con-
tacted about installation and opening dates. You will
be assigned a site location. Tentative installation
dates begin in May. Please do not contact the Center
or OIA for information, write to address below.
     Congratulations, let's get busy!
Sculpture Show '93 518 E. 11th St #4A, NY NY 10009
```

Postcard that Billie Lawless received, saying they chose him to exhibit at Manhattan Psychiatric Center in 1993. Lawless vs. Manhattan Psychiatric Center.

On May 15 Billie called Stasko and asked him when he "could begin installation of *Green Lightning* at the Manhattan Psychiatric Center." Stasko explained that two days earlier, on May 13, Helen Thomas informed him that *Green Lightning* had been removed from the exhibition. Billie tried contacting everyone involved and received no response. In a letter to Stasko on May 24, 1993, he said, "your failure to communicate to me in any way whatsoever demonstrates total disregard of professional courtesy."[13]

Billie said he had already spent "230 hours and $7,300.00 in expenses in preparing *Green Lightning* for exhibition," and "the failure to exhibit will cause great embarrassment, loss of credibility and harm to my reputation."[14]

On May 18, 1993, Billie's attorney negotiated with the New York Attorney General's office and they offered a second site for *Green Lightning*. They said this would balance "the well-being of the patients on Ward's Island with plaintiff's right of expression. Relocation... away from the main road ...is also compelling because of the danger that patients and family members may view the prominence of the sexually explicit sculpture as an endorsement by the facilities of any substantive messages contained in the work."[15]

Billie tentatively approved that site from his home in Cleveland. He then had an associate of his attorney view the site. It turned out they were actually offering a different, even smaller site, not large enough for *Green Lightning* to fit. He said it would be like entering a ten by ten painting into an exhibition and being given a spot that was three by three to display it.[16]

Another of the Center's objections was the use of electricity, to which Billie said he clearly wrote "neon," in his proposal booklet. "The removal of any component from *Green Lightning* would destroy the sculpture. At that point, it would cease to exist as a work of art that I created." [17]

The Center limited the sculpture show to 10:00 AM to sundown because they only allowed patients on the grounds during daylight. Therefore, no one would see *Green Lightning* at night, so lighting it would be futile.

On June 1, 1993, The Center's director, Michael Ford, informed Billie's attorney Svetlana Schreiber that they never actually selected *Green Lightning*.

Because time was of the essence, Lawless finally resorted to having his attorney fax Michael Ford to request arrangements for the erection of the sculpture. "The violation of 1st Amendment Freedom of Expression is taken seriously by the New York courts."[18]

The biggest fact that came to light was actually the same thing that prevented *Green Lightning* from staying lit in Buffalo and almost caused the destruction of the sculpture: the dancing dog bones. Neither Michael Ford, nor anyone associated with the hospital, wanted children that were in their care to see neon penises. "More than 75% of the children in MCPC (Manhattan Children's Psychiatric Center) have been repeated victims of abuse. MCPC limits the sexual images offered to patients. The children are not allowed to 'see movies rated higher than 'G'; slow dancing, hugging and explicit sexual contact are not allowed.'"[19]

Lawless said the doctor and lawyers were just "throwing around a lot of Freudian gobbledy-gook."[20]

In order to placate Billie, in late May or early June, the curators telephoned Billie and asked him to submit a substitute piece, which he declined to do. It was *Green Lightning* or nothing. This was no longer just about the artwork; it was about principle and freedom of speech.

Was a dancing neon penis with a top hat and cane really sexually explicit? According to psychiatrist Dr. Ladd Spiegel, "the phallic displayed in Mr. Lawless's artwork is displayed in a humorous and not a violent manner. It is my further opinion, to a reasonable degree of medical certainty, that *Green Lightning* is not sexually arousing and will not promote sexual violence in adult or adolescent patients at Manhattan Psychiatric Center, if viewed."[21]

Psychiatrist Robert T. Latimer said, "I know of no research study that has proven that a sculpture such as *Green Lightning* could validate, reinforce and even provoke the sexual feelings and behaviour that comprise a focus of these patients' treatment. It is my opinion that Dr. Ford's suggestion is without support legally, medically or of any study."[22]

In the legal complaint dated June 8, 1993, Billie sought compensatory damages in the amount of $2,000,000, plus an order compelling Manhattan Psychiatric Center to display *Green Lightning*.

In a letter to John Stasko from OIA on June 9, Billie recounted exactly what Stasko said, as he had recorded the call. "When I pointed out to you… that I felt my Constitutional rights had been violated, you stated… can't agree with you on that, Billie."[23]

Lawless then said, "I would expect an organization, such as 'OIA,' … to be opposed to censorship in any form." Billie said his piece was selected, then rejected solely because of its content. "The honorable approach would be to support the selection of *Green Lightning*. It is a shame you cannot do so."[24]

Once again, the artistic community let Billie Lawless down by not coming to his defense. No one from the Organization of Independent Artists, or any other New York-based artists' organizations, said anything. He was on his own to fight the system of censorship and oppression. When Billie defends his Freedom of Expression as an artist, he doesn't care how big the opposition is. In Buffalo, he tangled with a conservative mayor in City Hall. Here, he was going after the state of New York and Attorney General Robert Abrams.

Maybe being a loner and not an eager member of the arts community had its downfalls.

The attorney that represented Billie in Manhattan was Steven Goldman of Goldman & Goldman. They filed an Order to Show Cause to force Manhattan Psychiatric Center to either allow Billie to exhibit, or compensate him. The suit claimed that his First and Fourteenth Amendments were being violated. Michael Ford and Manhattan Psychiatric Center intruded on the curatorial process, and the curators and OIA were unreasonable and discriminatory. But Billie and his legal team did not know that Dr. Ford had ultimate decision making over the artwork selection and placement.

On June 24, 1993, the judge denied the lawsuit for a preliminary injunction, and every other part of the order. The following day, June 25, 1993, attorney Steven Goldman filed an appeal because the Court erred in failing to grant the injunction "despite the fact that plaintiff met the three-part test under CPLR Section 63-01." Judge Joseph P. Sullivan denied the application for relief. [25]

Much to Billie's frustration, the exhibition opened on June 26, 1993, without *Green Lightning*.

On August 3, 1993, Judge Ira Gammerman ruled for the Manhattan Psychiatric Center and the other defendants, and dismissed the complaint. Judge Gammerman said the Center had to exhibit *Green Lightning*, but not at the site he chose. Billie said the final site was too small, so he opted not to exhibit.

Lawless considered pursuing a claim against the state in the Court of Claims. It would drag on for several years, but Billie did not receive the outcome he had hoped for.

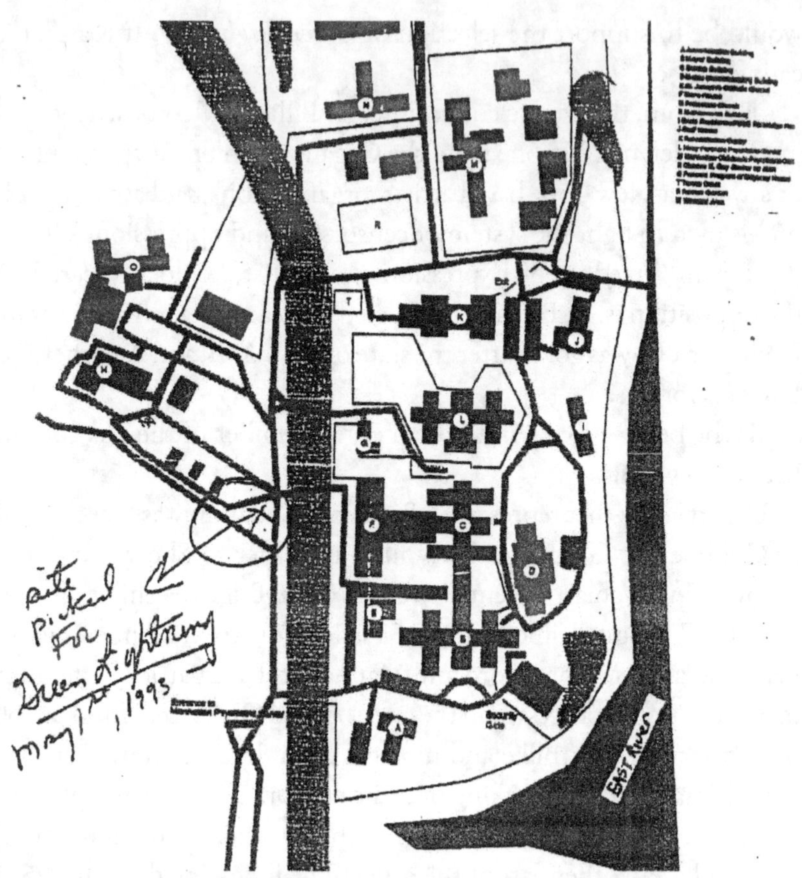

Map of area that Lawless chose for installing "Green Lightning." Lawless vs. Manhattan Psychiatric Center.

A Toy

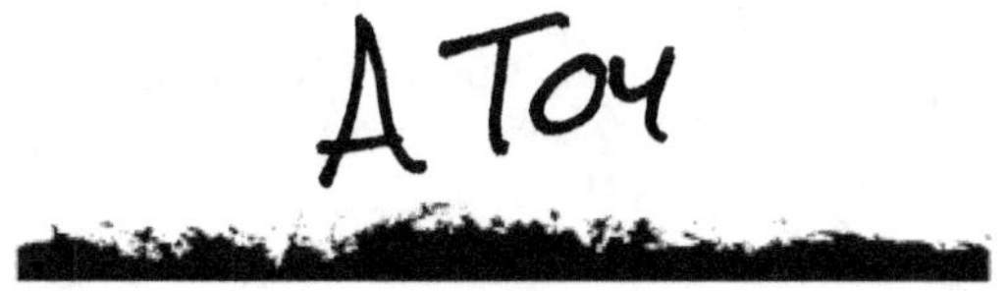

"I'm not a great judge of art, but I'm very impressed
with it as a piece of engineering." Joseph Prahl

IN 1994, BILLIE LAWLESS married his Cleveland attorney Svetlana Schreiber, originally from Sighetu Marmaţiei, Romania. She had been a counsel in his 1992 trial in Buffalo with her partner Alan Rossman. She has two sons, Mickey and Orin.

"Oh, he's very litigious," Schreiber said of Billie's various legal battles. "We welcome his cases. He's fighting for real issues, the First Amendment, civil rights."[1]

In 1994, Lawless admitted, "I just spend so much time doing my work that I'm not really part of the art community, I guess you would say. I'm not a real social person in terms of going to openings - just don't care for 'em. I have a family and have that life. I'm not interested in being part of a scene."[2]

His workshop was in the former Tyler Manufacturing complex in downtown Cleveland. The 6,000-square-foot studio contained his green lightning bolts, 1,800-pound steel-support superstructures, boxes, stacks of wood and steel. Inside the warehouse, he said that he saves everything. "This whole place is filled with stuff that could conceivably be put into a piece. It's like my palette." He talked about the books of photos he saved early in his career that he would use for ideas. "Everything starts out as a cartoon."[3]

In the 1990s, Cleveland, Ohio, was trying to brush off its rust belt image. The city had won out as the future location of the Rock -n- Roll Hall of Fame, which would open in 1995. In 1993, Midtown Corridor Inc. took on the task of placing public art in a commercial and gray zone in the city.

Billie, now a resident of Cleveland, knew there was a sculpture that he wanted to build. On July 23, 1992, he sent a letter to the board of directors at SPACES Gallery in Cleveland asking for their assistance.

> I would like to ask you to consider acting as an umbrella for a project I am about to begin in Cleveland for Cleveland.
>
> I have a sculpture from some years back that I would like to enlarge to monumental proportions and install in the mid-town corridor for a three-year period.
>
> The sculpture is entitled *The Politician: A Toy* and would stand approximately 26' high. It would be composed of steel plate, fibers, wood and a little neon. It would be kinetic with an electric motor operating the wheels and axels along with a working mouth. I have a maquette of the piece if you should seriously consider this proposal.
>
> I will raise all of the materials, services and whatever else might be necessary from local and national businesses. The use of the land will be also be obtained through some form of donation. I might add that the land will be privately owned.
>
> Obviously, if SPACES were to act as an umbrella, it would allow donors to make the donations to SPACES and (if they still exist) take a tax deduction as allowed by law. It would, at the same time, provide SPACES a different kind of visibility throughout the Cleveland area.
>
> I have no way of telling exactly what that might mean (though I would hope that it be positive) and put forward that you may want to address that issue among yourselves.
>
> I enclose a copy of the budget for the sculpture along with a few slides which show the piece.

Thank you.[4]

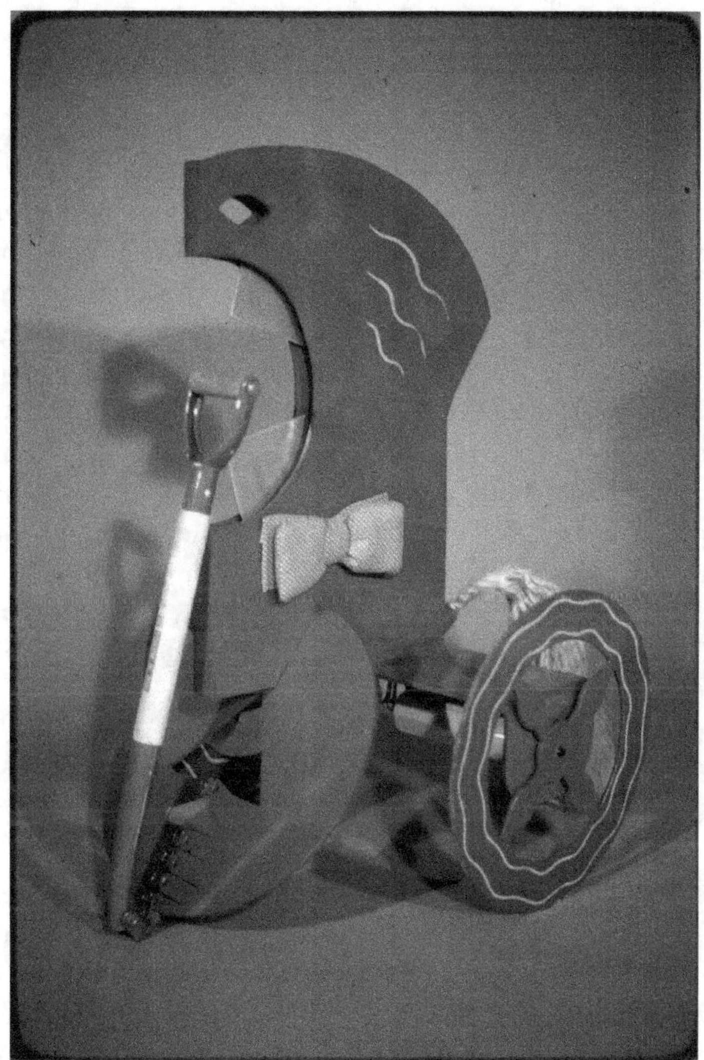

The model for "The Politician." Courtesy SPACES Archive
Collection, Kelvin Smith Library Special Collections.

Lawless wanted to submit *The Politician: A Toy,* an idea dating back to 1976. He said inspiration came from his father, who "was a politician. I grew up around politicians, so a lot of it was like self evident. I guess I was always being exposed to that." He said it took him less than 30 minutes to come-up with the basic concept for the sculpture.[5] It went from a crude, hand-sized cardboard model to a 36 inch version, and eventually, to the full-sized piece. He copyrighted the piece on January 2, 1986.

According to Billie, another inspiration for the sculpture he attributed to Aristotle. "It's really about us all and how we all try to influence each other with our speech - subtly or not so subtly."[6]

Midtown signed a contract with Lawless in March 1993 that gave him permission to install his sculpture at Chester Avenue and E. 57th Street. He agreed to raise $155,000 to build it. Cleveland City Planning Director Hunter Morrison reviewed the location, and objected, saying the land was for redevelopment, not public art, much like the Elm-Oak Arterial in Buffalo. The Cleveland Public Theatre agreed to sponsor the project.

So Billie, determined to install this new piece, found another location, mere blocks away, in an open field at E. 66th Street and Chester Avenue, where the owners of Atlas Packaging Inc. said he could install the sculpture. Lawless spent months trying to get the city of Cleveland to sign off on the project and provide him with the permits. He said city officials were trying to block his proposal because Cleveland Mayor Michael R. White objected to the sculpture. The mayor said, "I have seen (the sculpture), I don't like it and I'm not trying to block it. On the scheme of the things in my agenda, it's not even in the top 25."[7]

But then City Planning Director Hunter Morrison again raised questions, this time about the safety of the mechanical sculpture. Morrison did not return his calls for three months, which angered Lawless.

Billie finally met the planning commission on February 18, 1994. Before the meeting, he announced he would sue the mayor, Morrison, and members of the City Planning Commission on First Amendment grounds if they didn't approve his plans. When asked about the threat, Mayor White said for the artist "to suggest I have somehow harmed his effort to place his sculpture there (along Chester Ave.) is not only inappropriate but wholly inaccurate."[8]

Cleveland's Planning Commission voted to approve the sculpture, and granted a "certificate of appropriateness," but required Billie to provide a $1 million liability insurance policy, build a five-foot fence around *The Politician: A Toy,* and install an electrical kill switch. They didn't want kids climbing on it and getting maimed, which seemed reasonable.

Cleveland building inspectors refused to issue a building permit on

February 24. Billie told the *Village Voice* he believed there was a last-minute change of mind because someone from Buffalo contacted them about his *Green Lightning* lawsuit.[9]

"I'm going to make money off this thing," Lawless said, jokingly. "You can pay to kill *The Politician*."[10]

"To be perfectly frank," Hunter Morrison said, "Billie Lawless had an in-your-face attitude toward public officials, and he got the sort of reaction from the mayor that I think he expected. At the same time, the mayor instructed us to treat this very professionally and to address the real issues, not the content issues."[11]

The *Village Voice* said, "There are several more chapters of these Kafkaesque tales to be written, but you get the point: Billie Lawless is our pop Christo of the courtroom."[12]

The Politician: A Toy is a forty-foot tall kinetic sculpture with an operating mouth and wheels, which rotate eighteen hours a day, "composed of ten tons of steel, epoxy paints, two tons of polypropylene rope, steel armature structure, fiberglass, cedar, LEXAN, drives belts/chains, televisions and other electrical components."[13]

The finished sculpture looked like a gigantic child's pull toy, which Buffalo *News* reporter Margaret Sullivan saw as a model in Billie's Buffalo home in 1984. Cleveland journalist David Barnett said, "It sports a couple of slowly spinning wheels that never go anywhere... two eye sockets filled with flickering TV sets and a mouth in constant motion that never says anything." The axles look like large number two pencils. [14]

As with all of his large-scale projects, this one needed help from many people. Isaac Lewin and Associates of Cleveland performed engineering. Gedion, Fredericks and Company did electrical design. Initial lighting design was by the Centerior Energy Corporation.

Graduate students at the school of Mechanical and Aerospace Engineering at Case Western Reserve University in Cleveland, under the direction of Professor Joseph Prahl, designed the mechanical aspects of the sculpture. Rich Kucinski, a student of Prahl's, did the design for the mouth. Originally, the design took into consideration the weight of the mouthpieces, which were to be steel plate.

Ultimately, this design did not work as the connecting plates of the mouth pieces developed a slight flex, which caused the wheels of the mouth mechanism to bind up. The solution was to use a material called

Alucobond for the mouthpieces. A lightweight aluminum over-plastic material, this was applied to a skeleton of steel, cutting the weight of each mouth section from over 800 pounds to 80 pounds.[15]

"I'm not a great judge of art," Professor Prahl said, "but I'm very impressed with it as a piece of engineering."[16]

The sculpture is modular and bolted together in sections. He made the handle from a sixteen foot cedar beam, and he made the top of the handle of three pieces of cedar glued together. The bow ties were built by using a electrical conduit overlaid with fiberglass. They are two sections bolted together, then bolted to the side of the sculpture. They weigh individually about 800 pounds and are finished with an industrial automotive finish. He applied the white polka dots by hand using a sandblasters mask and white spray paint.[17]

He made the tail of approximately two tons of polypropylene rope. It is the same rope manufactured for barge boats on the Mississippi River. A heavy steel armature supports the rope and stands on its own foundation, attached to the back of the sculpture with heavy bolts.[18]

The Cleveland *Plain Dealer* said, "The notion of the politician as the producer of meaningless rhetoric is a pretty obvious and timeworn theme. In general, though, satirists don't traffic in novel themes so much as new representations of old ones. Their self-prescribed role, from the days of Juvenal and Horace, has been to ridicule. This sculpture does just that, by reducing the politician to a Picassoesque caricature in steel, fiber-glass, wood and polypropylene rope."[19]

Construction of the sculpture was exhausting to where "it seemed unproductive to pursue funding at the time," Lawless said. "It was more important to get the next bearing or the next motor. The hardest thing to get is cash," but a few passersby offered him donations while he was constructing it.[20]

The installation took a long time. In late September 1995, Lawless was installing the sculpture at its location on East 66th and Chester Avenue. They dedicated it in a private ceremony in November 1996. "Three-dimensional objects tend to excite people," Billie said. "Particularly when you call them art."[21]

Cleveland *Plain Dealer* art critic Steve Litt didn't like the artwork, though. He said that when Midtown Corridor Inc. was ready to add a second piece of public art; they did the correct thing and sought advice from the Committee for Public Art. "Entrepreneurial public artists, like Lawless, shouldn't be discouraged from seeking opportunities anywhere land is available in the city." He said that patrons should select the best locations for outdoor art, "not simply the most expedient."[22]

To be fair, Litt had consistently been condescending to Cleveland artists.[23]

"Any person who's a grown, rational, reasonable human being can see the humor in it and laugh at it," Lawless told journalist David Barnett. "And if you're a politician, you can't, and perhaps you should be in another field. I've never grown up, some part of me," Lawless laughed, "or some part doesn't want to grow up. But the part that matters, has, unfortunately."[24]

The neighbors called the sculpture "The Angry Chicken," or "The Funky Rooster."[25]

The Politician: A Toy remained at that location until 2008, when Billie learned the lot the artwork stood on was going to be sold. It was a popular site but not easily accessible, so a non-profit group headed by Cleveland attorney Douglas Whipple offered the intention of finding a more pedestrian friendly site to move it to.

Cleveland State University came to the rescue and offered a plot of land on CSU's campus on the south side of the Nance School of Business at Chester Avenue and 18th Street. They offered a set of hands-off clauses in their contract with Lawless, committing to reimbursement for upkeep, a small monthly stipend, and a promise to leave the sculpture unaltered and unedited.[26]

On the fence surrounding the sculpture, Lawless would install comical phrases poking fun at politicians. He altered them over the years with no complaints.

Former Cleveland planning director Hunter Morrison changed his tune by 2007, "It's a neat piece. The public officials that took umbrage at the time have moved on to other things, so life goes on."[27]

But that didn't last too long. In the fall of 2012, the University had agreed to let a student group install a community garden around the sculpture. When Lawless got wind, he and his wife Svetlana Schreiber raised a stink.

The lease with Lawless was about to expire and CSU spokesperson Joe Mosbrook announced they were going to remove the sculpture. However, officials changed their stance when they raised concerns about the maintenance of the garden.

Graduate student Peter Bode, who was behind the garden, felt that officials caved because they feared a lawsuit from Lawless. "The sad reality is his wife is a lawyer, and the school didn't want to deal with the legal battle," Bode said.[28]

"If it would have enhanced it," Lawless offered, "I would have thought about it in the first place."[29]

"I was the garden organizer and designer and they had told me nothing," Bode said. When he talked to the university, "they said the artist and his wife were threatening a lawsuit and they didn't want to deal with it, so they deconstructed the work." He tried to work out a deal with Lawless, but his wife "said the garden was compromising the art. The college loved it, the president approved and everybody was on board. Except for that guy."[30]

"I've never provoked intentionally," Lawless said. "Although people probably wouldn't believe that."[31]

Tell that to Peter Bode.

At War with CSU

"Due to the controversial nature of my work, I have experienced censorship throughout my career as an artist." Billie Lawless

BILLIE CONTINUED TO CARE for *The Politician: A Toy* over the years, updating it, repairing it, and adding new phrases on the fence surrounding it.

Douglas Max Utter wrote in *CAN Journal*, "In the twenty-three years since it first appeared, hallucination-like, along Chester Ave., Billy (sic) Lawless' over-sized, playful sculpture *The Politician: A Toy* has become one of Cleveland's most important pieces of public art. You can't miss it, and you really can't ignore it. *The Politician: A Toy* is one of those public art civic features that people either love, or hate, or love to hate. Certainly it doesn't inspire indifference, which for any work of art is a rare and desirable achievement."[1]

Cleveland State University's contract with Lawless, which was extended to 2020, said it would pay him $120 a year and reimburse him for maintenance and repair. It stated that the University had no right to "modify, disassemble or demolish" the sculpture or to change the area within the five-foot fence surrounding it. He added the phrase "Obama Scare" to the fence in February 2012, and the University did nothing about it between its installation and removal in June 2013. Former President Bush's 1988 campaign phrase about "A Thousand Points of Light" had been part of the fence-text from early on, lampooned as "A Thousand Points of Slight." The University said nothing about that phrase.

"On or about March 18, 2018, I updated the sculpture," Lawless said, "adding a textural element which read, 'Build a Wall of Pussie,'" (sic) a reference to then-President Donald Trump's claim to build a wall along the southern border of the United States, and his infamous phrase 'Grab them by the pussy' on *Access Hollywood* in 2005. The phrase stayed there until about April 1, when he removed it while doing some repairs. Billie then reinstalled the sign on October 15, 2018. [2]

Apparently, that was when Lawless crossed the line with CSU. They directed workers from the University to cover up the phrase, which they did by taping an old vinyl homecoming banner over it.

Two days later, on October 17, 2018, James Gross, director of facilities at Cleveland State University, sent Billie an email.

> Dear Billie:
>
> It has come to our attention that you added a phrase to the fence surrounding The Politician, which is under lease to the University. Because this was not part of the original agreement, we ask that you remove it immediately, no later than close of business tomorrow, Thursday, October 18, 2018. Thank you for your prompt attention to this matter.
>
> Very truly yours,
>
> Jim Gross[3]

Douglas Max Utter in the *CAN Journal* said, if Cleveland "were a curated exhibition (rather than a random mess of two centuries worth of projects and relics), you could say *The Politician* was an appropriate inclusion in the show, since so many of Cleveland's public sculptures are peculiar, politically pessimistic, and often controversial–which is actually something we can be proud of. Lawless's work, for instance, has recently provoked an incident of outright censorship, as well as a lawsuit in defense of the artist's First Amendment rights."[4]

The National Coalition Against Censorship issued a statement that urged "Cleveland State University to remove the cover the University used to block from view a political text featured on a sculpture displayed on campus. The University's action is not only an affront to artistic freedom, it is also an example of viewpoint discrimination and therefore likely to be in violation of the First Amendment."[5]

Billie's lawyer on this case, Terry H. Gilbert, sent a response to CSU the following day. Gilbert said that he saw nothing which prevented Lawless from modifying the sculpture. He wrote that "CSU shall have no right or power to alter, modify or demolish the sculpture... without the prior approval of the artist." He said the agreement allowed Lawless "to modify the sculpture or the area surrounding it, as the artist sees fit."[6]

"By CSU altering or removing the new phrase, it is not only a violation of the agreement, but most importantly a violation of the First Amendment, as Cleveland State is a public institution bound by this most important constitutional protection." Gilbert added that the phrase "Build a Wall of Pussie" is clearly protected speech and is consistent with the political messaging the sculpture is designed to promote."[7]

CSU was having none of it and on November 9, their general counsel, Sonali B. Wilson, responded with an unexpected offer. The University enacted the Third Amendment to the agreement that "mutually terminates the Agreement between Cleveland State University and your client regarding the referenced sculpture." To expedite the process, they offered the average cost of its maintenance over the last two years towards removal.[8]

On November 20, Terry Gilbert responded. Apparently, the two sides had met and afterward he declined the offer, stating it was still a First Amendment violation "by engaging in censorship of political art on public property."

"While I understand your position that the contract defines the terms of the relationship, and that you believe the contract prohibits the changing of the text, the contract clearly states that only CSU is prohibited from altering or changing the structure. In fact, over the years, my client has made alterations without objection from the university, thereby setting a factual precedent. It is clear that the only logical reason your client is opposed to the recent change is the content of the text, which cannot pass constitutional muster."[9]

The back and forth continued, with Ms. Wilson emailing on November 28. She asserted the University did not violate the contract by covering language outside of the fence. She said "the sculpture is art leased by a public entity and placed on its property with the public entity's permission," meaning the Expressive Activity policy did not apply.

"The University is not willing to permit any further changes to the fence surrounding the sculpture and it will remain covered until the sculpture is removed. My client has accepted your client's offer to terminate the contract. Accordingly, he has six months from such acceptance, the date of our meeting, October 24, 2018, to remove the sculpture at his cost, which is on or before April 24, 2019.[10]

It was apparent that CSU was not backing down. Billie weighed his options and retained attorney Andrew Geronimo of the Pattakos Law Firm in Fairlawn, Ohio. They met with Sonali Wilson on January 17, 2019. CSU was not interested in removing the banner and simply wanted to terminate the contract.

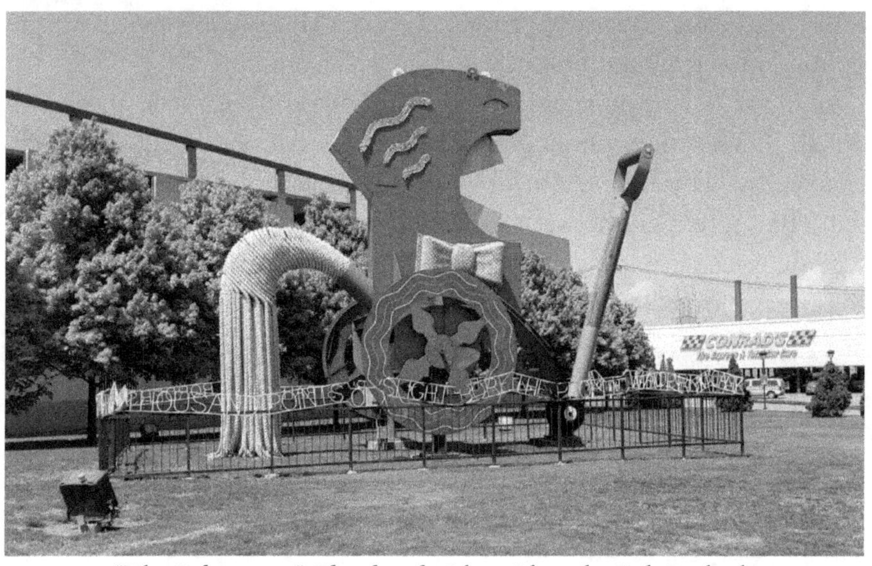

"The Politician," Cleveland, Ohio. Photo by Bob Perkoski

So, Geronimo sued on January 24, 2019, in Federal court in the Northern District of Ohio seeking a Temporary Restraining Order stopping the University from censoring the sculpture. The filing said that Lawless was "a visual artist, a sculptor of large, social political installations that are ongoing commentaries on political situations throughout the world and times. Political commentary is the essential aspect of my work, and the foundation of each of my pieces. Due to the controversial nature of my work, I have experienced censorship throughout my career as an artist, and

I have endeavored to fight censorship at every turn."[11]

His attorneys lambasted CSU for infringing on his Free Speech and argued that he did not create the sculpture as it was being displayed. They argued it was "offensive to his artistic vision" and by altering the sculpture, it damaged "Lawless's reputation as an artist who addresses censorship and other political topics." [12]

They said that every moment the banner remained, someone might believe that Lawless "acceded to CSU controlling his political message" and people might conclude that he was not willing to fight as hard as he did in Buffalo or Columbus, for *Green Lightning* and *Didy Wah Didy*, respectively.

They said CSU had no problem when there were references to President Obama and other politicians, but when he added a statement from President Trump, that was when they had an issue.

"...CSU is censoring 'BUILD A WALL OF PUSSIE' while, as of the date of this filing, the federal government has been largely shutdown because President Trump insists that a government-funding bill include appropriations for a wall along the border between the United States and Mexico. CSU's censorship of a reference to a Republican President on a sculpture generally critical of politicians is clear evidence of content- and viewpoint-based discrimination; this is especially true when CSU did not censor *The Politician: A Toy* when it referenced President Obama and numerous other U.S. politicians."[13]

The suit said of CSU's censorship: "any potential viewer would harm that Billie's reputation, on any given day, while walking by *The Politician: A Toy*, will see it in its modified and censored state. Mr. Lawless is an artist who carefully guards the reputation of his works. Members of the public who view *The Politician: A Toy* see an altered version of the sculpture."[14]

US District Judge Dan Polster encouraged out of court negotiations between the parties, and after some negotiations, CSU took the banner down.

"It was a pleasant surprise," Lawless said. "They saw everything there. Things began to change (in CSU's attitude toward the piece) about a year ago, but they did renew my contract last year. So the installation will remain in place until 2020, at which point they could choose to renew again."

On May 2, 2019, Lawless and CSU reached an agreement. After 11 years on the CSU campus, *The Politician: A Toy* would be no more. Cleveland State University agreed to settle the free-speech lawsuit and paid Lawless $50,000. He agreed to take the sculpture down as part of the settlement. They issued a joint statement where CSU thanked Billie Lawless for their 10-year relationship and said they attributed any phrases on the sculpture to the artist.[15]

The Cleveland *Plain Dealer* editorial board was unhappy with the outcome. "JEERS ...to Cleveland State University for a weakly worded contract that left it vulnerable when multimedia artist Billie Lawless added vulgar political commentary to his campus sculpture, *The Politician: A Toy*, and refused to remove it."[16] This certainly sounds like another conservative response to Lawless' artwork.

So, Lawless removed the sculpture and installed it outside his studio at E. 45th Street and Payne Avenue, in Cleveland.

Billie told journalist David Barnett, "This goes back to the beginning of time, right? People project on pieces what they want to project. So, how they interpret the piece or what they see, I just try to stay out of it. It is about how we, everybody tries to affect everyone politically. We want everyone to see the world exactly as we see it. That's kind of what the piece is about."[17]

"And, whether it's, you know, 'what movie you want to go to?' or ...'who sleeps in this bedroom' or ...'what do I get for breakfast?' and 'can't Timmy have the same thing?' And so we're all trying to influence one another. So that's kind of what the piece is about. But of course, politics, the bigger politics is always very overwhelming and people do tend to lay that kind of veneer on, the piece. So, so be it."[18]

In a 1997 interview with the Cleveland *Plain Dealer*, they asked Billie if he could make a living as an artist. "Look at me," Billie said. "Do I look like I'm living? I got clothes on me. My goldfish are getting fed. I don't need a lot. I don't have the 'want' disease."[19]

He was offering his pieces for sale. You could buy *Green Lightning* for $100,000, *Didy Wah Didy* for $95,000 and *The Politician: A Toy* for $300,000. With inflation, at 2023 prices, that would be $182,339, $173,222, and $547,018, respectively.

Not everyone appreciated the multiple page article on Lawless in the *Plain Dealer*.

Mary Chorney of Espyville, Pennsylvania said, "What a pity that talent is wasted by Lawless. He's the Howard Stern of the art world. He seems to need to provoke in order to make his art known. This shows a degree of immaturity. I hope he outgrows this vulgarity to let his true talent (if he has any) shine through." [20]

And to some, that may be how Billie looks, just a troublemaker artist who never grew up. And while his privilege allowed him to pursue a career in art, to him, it was always about the freedom to create what he wanted. For someone that has gone against the establishment so many times in his life, you probably wouldn't expect him to be a homebody. But he prefers a good book to a party. "I like to be anonymous," he said. [21]

"I'm by nature a shy person," Lawless said. "I'm not interested in all that. *Green Lightning* wrecked my life. That's why I didn't want to get involved with this again. You become a figure. You lose your sense of privacy."[22]

AFTERWORD

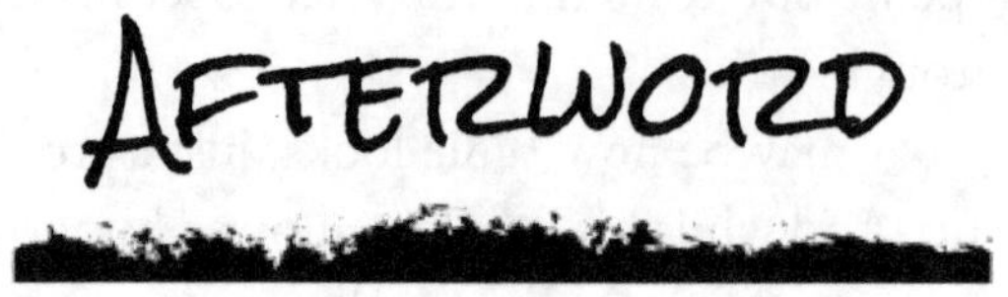

"He's the Yoko Ono of Buffalo." Joanne Posluzsny
Hoffsten

IN A 2014 INTERVIEW with the Buffalo *News*, Billie Lawless was asked if he would ever consider bringing *Green Lightning* back to Buffalo. The years and age had softened the sculptor up a bit. "If they want to bring it back? Any time," Lawless said. "And if they want to pay for it, that's not a problem."[1]

Newell Nussbaumber is a Buffalo native. Since the 1990s, he has been upselling Buffalo, and people listen. But when Billie Lawless unveiled *Green Lightning* that cold, rainy November night in 1984, it was a different place.

According to Nussbaumer's friend Lesley Horowitz (a photographer who lives in Buffalo and NYC), "everything appeared to be bleak." There were no jobs and her friends had all moved away.[2]

The dismantling of *Green Lightning* took place after she had also left town. Another artist, who moved to Buffalo in 2002, said "It seems like it was a horrible time to be an artist in Buffalo."

What was happening in Buffalo in 1984? Hot-headed, conservative Mayor Jimmy Griffin was at the end of his second term in office. He had endured political storms and actual storms and was still standing. One of his biggest positives, and simultaneously a negative, was his unwavering support for friends, like Robert Delano. Crime in 1984, though, was not as bad as the previous several years. Murder was down 40.3 percent from 1980 highs. Robbery, burglary, and stolen vehicles were also down double digits.[3]

Griffin was a polarizing politician that you either loved or hated. You could laugh at his beer drinking jokes, but you could also cringe at this nastiness towards members of the media who had the audacity to question his decisions.

He appealed to an audience not much different from the one that Donald Trump tied his coattails to: white, non-college educated. Nearly every Democratic primary, a strong Black candidate challenged him. Sometimes the party had had enough and endorsed another candidate.

Because of these challenges, Griffin didn't always win the Democratic primary, but running on minor party lines (Conservative, Right-to-Life) was usually enough to garner the needed votes to put him in office.

In Buffalo, the decades leading up to 1984 saw almost every mayoral election go to the Democrat. The last Republican to be elected was Joseph Mruk in 1950. The city was clearly in the "D" column, but the 1970s were a turbulent time, and things were changing. From the energy crisis to major plant closings, citizens were continually looking to their leaders for guidance.

In the 1980 and 1984 presidential races, Republican Ronald Reagan easily won New York state. Only four counties outside of New York City went Democrat in 1980, and three in 1984, and Erie County was one of them both times.

So when did Buffalo and western New York start down the spiral of conservatism that engulfed *Green Lightning*? It could be part of the fallout from the rebellious 1960s. But Buffalo was also a Catholic city and very blue collar.

Anna Blatto wrote in "A City Divided: A Brief History of Segregation in Buffalo: Semantic Scholar" that "Buffalo's contemporary segregation can be traced back to World War I. As a major steel city, Buffalo's factories suddenly needed to produce an abundance of war-related goods and weaponry. Throughout the Great Migration (1916-1970), many African Americans moved from the South in search of jobs such as these."[4]

"Throughout the 1950s and 60s, Buffalo Municipal Housing Authority," created "segregated public housing developments," some "over 90% Black occupied – which played a key role in maintaining segregated neighborhood compositions."[5]

The 1950s G.I. Bill caused city residents to move to new housing developments in the suburbs. This continued into the 1970s as white people left typical ethnic neighborhoods like Buffalo's Polish East Side neighborhood. The East Side would become overwhelmingly Black. Businesses left with the white residents, leaving few jobs for those still living there. This caused some white citizens to complain about black citizens taking over the neighborhood and pitting Blacks against whites. It was a vicious circle.

Deputy New York State Assembly Speaker Arthur Eve ran in the 1977 mayoral primary against Jimmy Griffin. Eve (a Black man that was a Civil Rights leader and had helped negotiate for the prisoners at the Attica Prison uprising in 1971) rallied Black voters. Almost 80 percent of the Black community voted, the highest turnout ever in the Northeast.[6] But racism and threats to Eve and his family plagued the campaign. Racists burned a cross on his front lawn. The only logical explanation is the white population trying to hold on to the power they held in Buffalo since its incorporation in 1832.

These people, often religious, often Roman Catholic like Jimmy Griffin, were usually conservative in their social and fiscal ideals. So by the time two-term mayor Jimmy Griffin encountered *Green Lightning* and its neon dancing dog bones, he and the public were already siding with conservative ideals. Public art was not something conservatives wanted to spend public dollars on, or in this case, temporarily borrowed land.

In the journal "The Public Discourse" the authors of the article "Conservatism and Culture," write "Some conservatives take issue with the rarefied notion of 'fine art' itself, pointing to the neglected beauty of common craft. Other conservatives distrust the arts on religious grounds. Finally, there is artistic radicalism that, conservatives rightfully perceive, remains a dominant cultural paradigm."[7]

Lance T. Izumi writes in 1997, "If you look at the Right's position on arts and individual artists, it basically consists of two lines of thinking. On one hand, the Right has a position based on economic arguments drawn from free-market theory. The other position has more to do with artistic judgment and the influence of government bureaucracy and ideology.

"In the economic area, the Right's position is mainly based on their general view that government's role in society must be limited. ...You could have the most outrageous art, yet someone on the Right probably wouldn't squawk very much as long as it was purely privately funded. It is only when you have government funding that the Right begins to take an interest."[8]

And this is where Buffalo found itself in 1984 with *Green Lightning*.

Billie Lawless created a work of art that was privately funded. It was something that, regardless of your political leaning, would be hard (pun intended) to argue that the dancing orange neon penises with top hat and cane were realistic, and therefore pornographic.

As an author, I can't see it and I can't believe that anyone could seriously argue the point. As someone who has written books knowing that my First Amendment freedoms could be obstructed, I side with the artist. Whether it was a wonderful sculpture that should have been installed on public land is a completely different question.

Lawless took no public funds and didn't ask to install it on public land. To know that land owned by a conservative real estate developer and attorney Carl Paladino was where he originally planned to install *Green Lightning,* makes the outcome even more interesting. Paladino wasn't always a Republican, which could explain why he was open to installing the sculpture on his land when Billie made his presentation in 1983.

In 2018, Buffalo *News* art critic Colin Dabkowski wrote a piece called "9 of Buffalo's most controversial public art projects" after a controversy over a planned neon sign of Buffalo native, musician Rick James, was announced.

In the article, Dabkowski named, among others, The Martin Luther King Jr. bust in Martin Luther King Jr. Park; Larry Griffis' sculpture *Spirit of Womanhood*; and *Green Lightning*, calling it the most controversial piece of public art in Buffalo history. The article rehashed the same comments from years past on all the works of art, not bringing anything new to the table.[9]

David More maintained that the public should have some input over public art. "Influence a little. But actual control over the approval process, NONE at all. The approval process should be largely limited to knowledgeable, educated people with a well-developed aesthetic sensibility. Art is not democratic, never was and never will be."[10]

But, public art is never a straightforward decision. There was a call to artists in 2017 to create a memorial to Martin Luther King Jr. and his wife Coretta Scott King, who met in Boston. They eventually chose Hank Willis Thomas, a renowned Brooklyn-based artist.

They unveiled the 22 foot tall sculpture, *The Embrace*, on Friday, January 13, 2023 in Boston Common, the nation's oldest public park. From the moment the public saw it, they made their dislike well known. The same disdain some people had for the MLK statue in Buffalo in 1983 or *Green Lightning* in 1984, the citizens of Boston had for this artwork.

People heckled and jeered the ten million dollar sculpture, online and in the press. Thomas said, "I hope people who experience *The Embrace* understand or overstand the power of connection for the enhancement of our lives."[11]

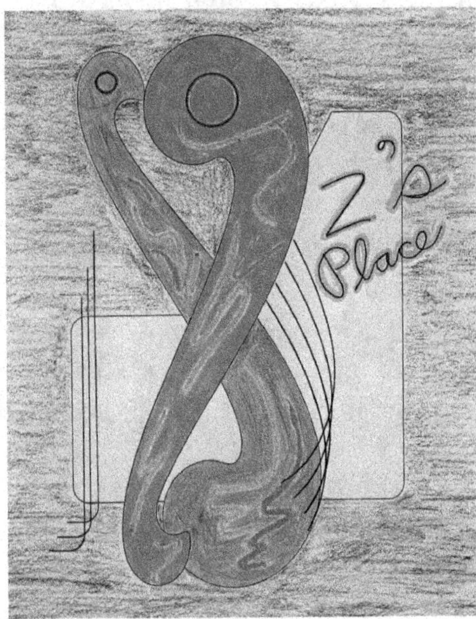

©Copyright, 1982, Buscaglia-Castellani Art Gallery
Niagara University, Niagara Falls, New York

Cover of Billie Lawless New Works catalogue, 1982. Courtesy of Castellani Art Museum.

In "Arresting Images," Steven C. Dubin explains when he believes public art controversies are likely to occur— "at times when there is a high degree of communal fragmentation and polarization, and widespread civic malaise and low communal morale. What becomes controversial are generally those works which address volatile, unsettled issues. And where this takes place is most typically at strategic public locations. While any of these conditions is likely to spark trouble, their combination virtually assures conflagration."[12]

Public art has always and will always make someone happy and make another angry. Billie Lawless has done that over and over in his career. Whether he intended *Green Lightning* to be that literal lightning rod or not, it was. In the end, it didn't stifle public art in Buffalo, but David More and his successor David Granville of the Buffalo Arts Commission were much more careful about approving future projects.

It would be hard to deny that *Green Lightning* changed Billie Lawless' trajectory. If there had not been the fallout in Buffalo, maybe he would not have left for Cleveland. *The Politician: A Toy* was conceived in the '70s in Buffalo, but ended up in Cleveland. Would that have been in Buffalo if he didn't leave? The notoriety some say he sought with the incident in 1984 didn't seem to boost his stock value. It did seem to send him on a journey fighting censorship for the rest of his career.

The incident also nearly cost David More his job as executive director of the Buffalo Arts Commission. He fell on his sword and handed Jimmy Griffin his resignation. If he had caught Griffin on a bad day, maybe he would have accepted it. Instead, he said that More was also a victim.

Lawless became the scapegoat when the city couldn't explain how they allowed *Green Lightning* to be installed on public land. In the end, no one lost their jobs over the event. Not Militello, More, Dudek, Risman, Anthony. But Billie Lawless fled Buffalo and started anew in Cleveland. It doesn't appear that he gained international fame and notoriety over the incident, if that's what he was really trying to achieve.

Eight years after the unveiling, it was hard for the jury in the *Green Lightning* trial to judge what happened with a critical eye. When it took place, Billie Lawless might have "perpetrated a hoax" on the city. But, regardless, it's highly doubtful that he and his co-creator Kathie Simonds would have spent the better part of two years working on the massive sculpture, expecting the city to tear it down in the dark. When he began his lawsuit, he probably hadn't expected the City of Chicago to pay for most of the repairs.

If he had dropped the case, the city would have claimed victory. Because the jury believed Billie did not suffer financially from the incident, they voted with their "family values" hats on and not necessarily with an unbiased eye.

There are still some people happy that Lawless left Buffalo. Mayor Jimmy Griffin won another term, and in the end, Buffalo lost a talented artist, and Cleveland gained one. But, as artist Joanne Posluszny Hoffsten said, he was the Yoko Ono of Buffalo.

ACKNOWLEDGMENTS

After not writing for four years, it felt amazing to sit down and start researching, then writing this book. I find the research aspect one of the most rewarding aspects of writing. Digging through newspaper articles, court files, photos, and, for the first time, interviewing people involved, I was able to recreate the story of *Green Lightning* and artist Billie Lawless.

While researching, I read that there was a storyline on the TV show "Hill Street Blues" that Buffalo native David Milch was involved in, that sounded very similar to the *Green Lightning* saga. I couldn't find it, so I asked on a "Hill Street Blues" Facebook page. The next day I got the answer, Season 6, Episode 6, "Oh, my kid." The art story was a minor one in the episode, but there were many similarities, except in the episode the city actually knocks the sculpture down. According to Billie Lawless, the writer was a friend. "Some friend," he commented in a story in the Cleveland *Plain Dealer* in 1989.[1]

There are many people that helped to make this work possible. My family, as always, has been supportive and a great sounding board for everything from story, layout, to cover.

Thank you to former Buffalo Corporation Counsel Mike Risman, who was one of the first people I spoke with. He quickly opened up about his feelings on the subject nearly 40 years later. Jim Militello, former vice-chair of the Buffalo Urban Renewal Agency, was also open to speak to me about the topic.

David Granville, Executive Director of the Buffalo Arts Commission, was so helpful and quick to answer emails and pull files from the archives, even on the day of a blizzard!

I spoke with David More, the former Executive Director of the Buffalo Arts Commission, multiple times. He gratefully opened his personal archives and sent me original photos and documents that were invaluable and unavailable anywhere else.

Artists Mark Griffis and George Palmer, and Steve Wisenbaugh, George Howell, and Mitch Flynn all spoke with me and recounted their stories.

In late December 2022, I spoke with the late Al Price. He recounted many stories about the formation of the Buffalo Arts Commission and his role in it.

The law library staff at the law firm Hodgson Russ in Buffalo was instrumental in helping to track down the original court appeal. The staff at courts in Rochester, Manhattan, Cleveland, and Cincinnati were also helpful.

Thank you to Billie's lead trial attorney, Alan Rossman, (now a federal public defender) for taking time out of his busy schedule to speak with me.

Artist Joanne Polsluszny-Hoffsten graciously answered questions and called me from overseas to recall the story.

I'd like to thank artist and *Green Lightning* collaborator Kathie Simonds. She originally spoke with me, but even 40 years isn't enough time to fix the fear and pain of the events of 1984. Thank you for your contribution to the artwork, and I hope this book does not bring you any pain.

Thanks to Lore Levin, daughter of Harold Cohen, for keeping his legacy alive and your contributions.

Thank you to former co-worker and friend Tammy Raasch-Shurtleff for trekking to county hall to get copies of files and photos.

Others who were invaluable in providing information, documents and more: Michael McKee, WTTW-TV, Chicago; Sam Magavern III; Mary Jane Jacob; Kellen Boice, Executive Director, Sioux Falls Arts Council; Nila Griffis Lampman, Executive Director, Ashford Hollow Foundation; Rochelle Steiner, Global Curator, Artpark; Mark Mahoney; Marsha Moss, Public Art Curator & Consultant; Lehigh University Libraries Archives; Christine Liebson, Archivist, Special Collections, Kelvin Smith Library, Case Western Reserve University.

Mark Fox-Morgan, Cleveland Public Library, who enlightened me about inter-library loans. Thank you to the inter-library loan people from Sno-Isle Libraries for helping to get documents from across the country!

Isaac, Grosvenor Room, Buffalo & Erie County Public Library; Ed Cardoni; Nicole, Local History & Genealogy, Columbus Metropolitan Library; Caryn, The Plain Dealer and Cleveland.com; Mary Helen Miskuly, Castellani Art Museum; Pauline Wolstencroft, Senior Librarian, Balch Art Research Library; Joshua Sulser, Cleveland Museum of Art; James Maynard, PhD Curator, The Poetry Collection Coordinator, Rare & Special Books Collection University at Buffalo; Special Collections at Chicago Public Library; Beth Piwkowski, Special Collections, Michael Schwartz Library, Cleveland State University.

And to the dozens of people that responded but didn't have anything to add, or answered quick questions, thank you as well.

Thank you to everyone that contributed photos.

Thank you to Billie Lawless for creating *Green Lightning* and pushing the boundaries of public art. Unfortunately, he didn't return requests for an interview.

Lastly, there were dozens of people who didn't even respond. If I missed anyone, I truly apologize! I accidentally deleted ALL my email and tried to recall everyone I interacted with.

ALSO BY MICHAEL F. RIZZO

Novels
Bloody Valentine
Double Rush
Screaming in the Night

Non-fiction
Washington Beer
Buffalo Beer
The Glory Days of Buffalo Shopping (Nine Nine Eight updated)
Gangsters and Organized Crime in Buffalo
Buffalo's Legacy of Power and Might
They Call Me Korney
Nine Nine Eight: The Glory Days of Buffalo Shopping
Through The Mayors' Eyes

About Michael F. Rizzo

Michael F. Rizzo is an acclaimed author and researcher, focusing on the city of Buffalo. Through his meticulous investigations and profound understanding of the subject, Rizzo has become a leading authority on his topics, unearthing hidden stories in Buffalo's intriguing history.

Driven by a deep passion for history and a relentless curiosity, Rizzo embarked on a quest to uncover the secrets of his city.

Rizzo's tireless efforts in research and documentation have yielded remarkable insights. His ability to dig beyond the surface and present historical narratives with a keen eye for detail has earned him widespread acclaim and respect.

With a writing style that seamlessly blends historical accuracy with riveting storytelling, Rizzo has captivated readers worldwide.

He continues to devote himself to uncovering hidden truths, shedding light on forgotten stories, and preserving the legacy of the past.

Mike lives with his family in the Seattle area where he is either writing a new book or working on his old house.

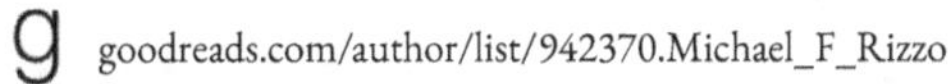 goodreads.com/author/list/942370.Michael_F_Rizzo

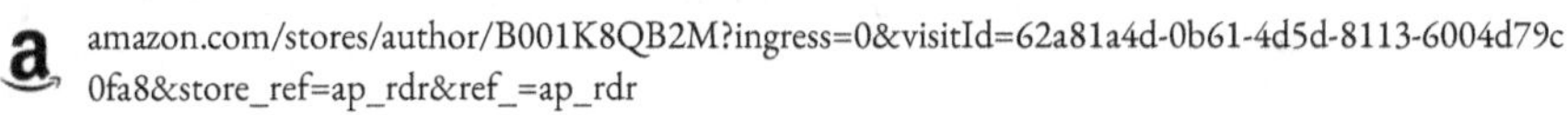 amazon.com/stores/author/B001K8QB2M?ingress=0&visitId=62a81a4d-0b61-4d5d-8113-6004d79c0fa8&store_ref=ap_rdr&ref_=ap_rdr

ENDNOTES

Early Years

1. Matt Gryta. "Confrontation over Lawless Sculpture Recalled." Buffalo News. June 10, 1992. p.

2. Charlotte Johnson. "Heavy metal sculptor enjoys his art, his life." Courier-Express. November 7, 1980. p.9.

3. "Billie Lawless." Wikipedia. Wikimedia Foundation, August 30, 2022. https://en.wikipedia.org/wiki/Billie_Lawless.

4. Mark Griffis. Email with the author. October 12, 2022.

5. Johnson. "Heavy metal sculptor enjoys his art, his life."

6. Jim McAvey. "Litigation Over Attica Goes Back to 1965." Courier-Express. January 1, 1972. p.9.

7. Rebecca Freligh. "It's been a real roller coaster." Plain Dealer (Cleveland), February 1989. p.1-H, 8.

8. Freligh. "It's been a real roller coaster."

9. David More. Lawless deposition. More private collection.

10. "Induction ban is requested." Buffalo Courier-Express. December 1, 1971. p. 4.

11. "Induction ban is requested."

12. "Board Cancels Induction for Lawless." Courier-Express. December 21, 1971. p.4.

13. City of Buffalo, 4-94-89, H-67943

14. Id.

15. Mike McKeating, "Art is winning corporate patrons here," Buffalo News, October 14, 1979:B-4.

16. City of Buffalo, 4-94-89, H-67943

17. Margaret Sullivan, "Naiveté shapes sculpture dispute," Buffalo News, November 25, 1984, p.1.

18. Charlotte Johnson. "Painted jackets prized as art." Courier-Express. May 29, 1980. p.9.

19. City of Buffalo, 4-94-89, H-67943

20. City of Buffalo, 4-94-89, H-67943

21. Niagara University. Billie Lawless New Works March 5 - April 19, 1982.

22. "Duayne Hatchett." Duayne Hatchett Art. Accessed March 20, 2023. http://www.duaynehatchett.com/.

23. "Gatekeepers to the art market part II: Artists's views." Gowanda News and Observer. June 1980. p.4.

24. Anthony Bannon. "An Artists Place." The Buffalo News. January 29, 1982. Gusto p.3, 12.

25. Charles Clough. Email with the author. April 10, 2023.

26. Richard Chon. "Sculpture at the Artist's Gallery." Buffalo News. August 30, 1981. p.67.

27. Chon. August 30, 1981.

28. Chon. August 30, 1981.

Buffalo Arts Commission

1. Alfred Price (retired assistant dean of the University of Buffalo School of Architecture), Phone interview with author, December 29, 2022.

2. Price, December 29, 2022.

3. Price, December 29, 2022.

4. Price, December 29, 2022.

5. Price, December 29, 2022.

6. Price, December 29, 2022.

7. Price, December 29, 2022.

8. Price, December 29, 2022.

9. Price, December 29, 2022.

10. Price, December 29, 2022.

11. Price, December 29, 2022.

12. Price, December 29, 2022.

13. Price, December 29, 2022.

14. Price, December 29, 2022.

15. Price, December 29, 2022.

16. Price, December 29, 2022.

17. David More. Interview with the author. October 18, 2023.

18. Price, December 29, 2022.

19. Price, December 29, 2022.

20. More. October 18, 2023.

21. Dan MacDonald. "Griffin warms to art lovers." Buffalo News. July 22, 1978. p.1.

22. Price, December 29, 2022.

23. James Militello (former Vice Chair Community Development). Phone call with author. October 7, 2022.

24. Militello. October 7, 2022.

25. MacDonald. "Griffin warms to art."

26. "Maxine Newman Brandenburg." prabook.com. Accessed March 20, 2023. https://prabook.com/web/maxine_newman.brandenbur g/1360158.

27. "Walter A. Prochownik." Walter A. Prochownik - Burchfield Penney Art Center. Accessed March 20, 2023. https://burchfieldpenney.org/art-and-artists/people/profile: walter-a-prochownik/#walter-a-prochownik.

28. Price. December 29, 2022.

29. City of Buffalo, 4-94-89, H-67943

30. David More. Private collection.

31. Militello, October 7, 2022.

32. Anthony Bannon. "Selecting Statues." Buffalo News. March 30, 1984. Gusto, p.2.

33. Militello. October 7, 2022.

34. "Artists want theater district input." Buffalo Courier-Express. June 2, 1980. p.3.

35. "Artists want theater district input." Buffalo Courier-Express. June 2, 1980. p.3.

36. Gary Spencer. "Suspension of safety law urged to keep firm alive." Courier-Express. July 15, 1980. p.3.

37. Price. December 29, 2022.

38. Richard Huntington. "Arts Commission's role explained by chairman." Courier-Express. September 7,1980. p.E-1.

39. Bannon. "Selecting Statues," p.3.

40. Huntington. "Arts Commission's role explained by chairman."

41. More. October 18, 2023.

42. Bannon. "Selecting statues," p.16.

43. Bannon, "Selecting statues," p.16.

44. Bannon, "Selecting statues," p.16.

Before the Lightning

1. "Calendar." Buffalo News. August 10, 1979. Gusto, p.50.

2. City of Buffalo, 4-94-89, H-67943

3. City of Buffalo, 4-94-89, H-67943

4. "Nichols school has one Lament." Buffalo News. October 18, 1980. p.32.

5. City of Buffalo, 4-94-89, H-67943

6. City of Buffalo, 4-94-89, H-67943

7. "7-ton steel sculpture to rise at Buffalo State." Buffalo News. October 31, 1981. p.16.

8. Richard Huntington. "Exhibit delights, confuses." Buffalo Courier-Express. September 13, 1981. p.E-1,5.

9. Anthony Bannon. "Science, art at Aquarium." Buffalo News, April 26, 1981. p.71.

10. Bannon. "Science, art at Aquarium."

11. Mike Billington. "Falls Aquarium branches out to sculpture." Courier-Express. March 15, 1981. p.B-15.

12. "Aquarium schedules Mother's day events." Buffalo Courier Express. April 22, 1981. p.22-D.

13. City of Buffalo, 4-94-89, H-67943

14. Niagara University. Billie Lawless New Works March 5 - April 19, 1982.

15. City of Buffalo, 4-94-89, H-67943

16. Erik Brady. "Obscenity: Whose standards apply?" Courier Express. March 22, 1981. p.B-1.

17. Brady. "Obscenity: Whose standards apply?" Courier Express. March 22, 1981. p.B-1.

18. Richard Huntington. "ECC-Censored sculpture withdrawn art gets showing." Courier-Express. February 6, 1982. p.A-4.

19. Huntington. "ECC-Censored sculpture withdrawn art gets showing."

20. Erik Brady. "Obscenity: Whose standards apply?" Courier Express. March 22, 1981. p.B-1.

21. Brady. "Obscenity: Whose standards apply?" Courier Express. March 22, 1981. p.B-1.

22. Richard Huntington. "ECC-Censored sculpture withdrawn art gets showing." Courier-Express. February 6, 1982. p.A-4.

23. Huntington. "ECC-Censored sculpture withdrawn art gets showing."

24. Buffalo Arts Commission. April 1, 1982. Meeting Minutes.

25. Howell, George. "The Public Ordeal of Billie Lawless." Buffalo Arts Review, 1984, Winter edition.

26. *Billie Lawless New Works March 5 - April 19, 1982*. Niagara Falls, NY: Buscaglia-Castellani Art Gallery, Niagara University, 1982.

27. Niagara University. Billie Lawless New Works March 5 - April 19, 1982.

28. Howell, "The Public Ordeal of Billie Lawless."

29. Howell, "The Public Ordeal of Billie Lawless."

30. Howell, "The Public Ordeal of Billie Lawless."

31. Howell, "The Public Ordeal of Billie Lawless."

32. Niagara University. Billie Lawless New Works March 5 - April 19, 1982.

33. Niagara University. Billie Lawless New Works March 5 - April 19, 1982.

34. Niagara University. Billie Lawless New Works March 5 - April 19, 1982.

35. Niagara University. Billie Lawless New Works March 5 - April 19, 1982.

36. Niagara University. Billie Lawless New Works March 5 - April 19, 1982.

37. Niagara University. Billie Lawless New Works March 5 - April 19, 1982.

38. Niagara University. Billie Lawless New Works March 5 - April 19, 1982.

39. "Butt-Fugly Public Art: Life Savers by Billie Lawless." Philaphilia. Accessed March 20, 2023. http://philaphilia.blogspot.com/2015/07/butt-fugly-public-art-life-savers-by.html.

40. "ALLENTOWN COUPLE GIVE SCULPTURE TO VET SCHOOL." Philadelphia, PA: University of Pennsylvania, 1983. University of Pennsylvania.

41. "ALLENTOWN COUPLE GIVE SCULPTURE TO VET SCHOOL." Philadelphia, PA: University of Pennsylvania, 1983. University of Pennsylvania.

42. "Butt-Fugly Public Art: Life Savers by Billie Lawless."

43. "ALLENTOWN COUPLE GIVE SCULPTURE TO VET SCHOOL." Philadelphia, PA: University of Pennsylvania, 1983. University of Pennsylvania.

44. "Butt-Fugly Public Art: Life Savers by Billie Lawless."

45. "Art notes." Buffalo News. March 16, 1983. p.31.

Mr. Peanut

1. City of Buffalo, 4-94-89, H-67943

2. Id.

3. Id.

4. Id.

5. "About Us: Western New York's Premier Destination for Music, Theatre, Family Fun." Artpark. Accessed March 20, 2023. https://www.artpark.net/about-artpark.

6. Lawless vs. Manhattan Psychiatric Center, 114643/93 (NY 1993).

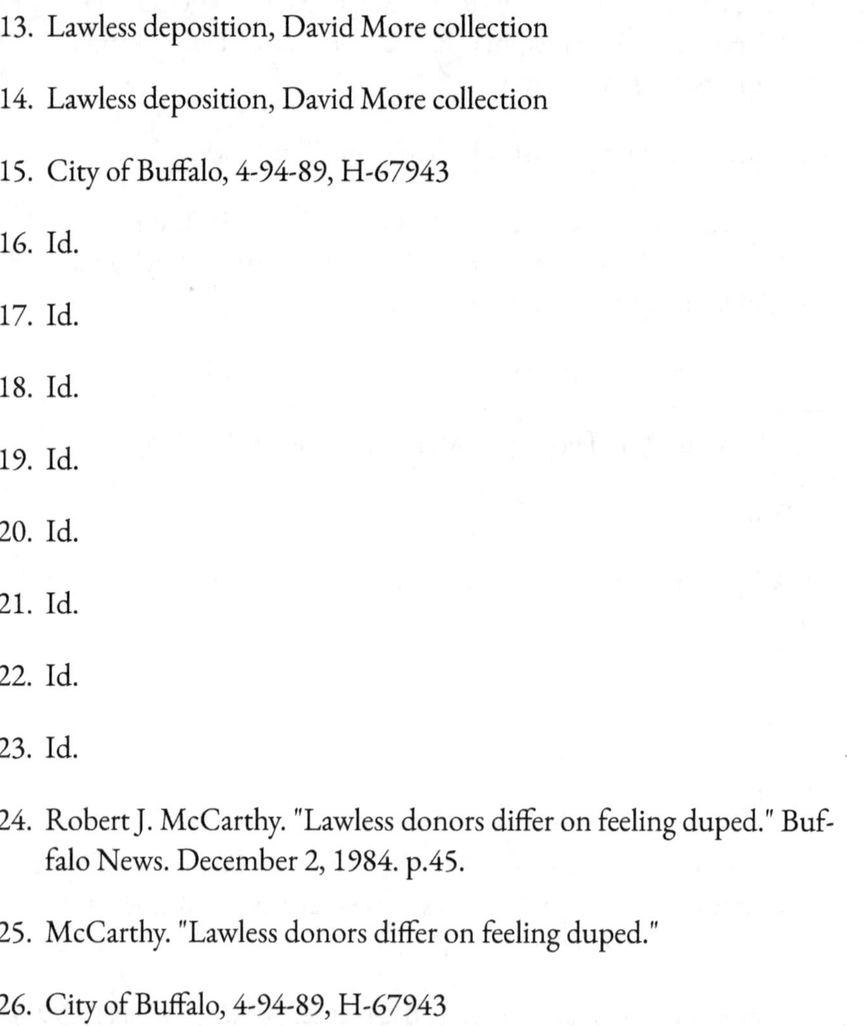

7. City of Buffalo, 4-94-89, H-67943

8. Id.

9. Id.

10. Id.

11. Id.

12. City of Buffalo, 4-94-89, H-67943

13. Lawless deposition, David More collection

14. Lawless deposition, David More collection

15. City of Buffalo, 4-94-89, H-67943

16. Id.

17. Id.

18. Id.

19. Id.

20. Id.

21. Id.

22. Id.

23. Id.

24. Robert J. McCarthy. "Lawless donors differ on feeling duped." Buffalo News. December 2, 1984. p.45.

25. McCarthy. "Lawless donors differ on feeling duped."

26. City of Buffalo, 4-94-89, H-67943

27. Id.

28. Howell. "The Public Ordeal of Billie Lawless."

29. Lawless deposition, David More collection

30. Lawless deposition, David More collection

31. Lawless deposition, David More collection

32. Lawless deposition, David More collection

33. City of Buffalo, 4-94-89, H-67943

City Hall

1. Id.

2. Tonawanda News, 5-14-1983.

3. City of Buffalo, 4-94-89, H-67943

4. Id.

5. Howell, "The Public Ordeal of Billie Lawless."

6. Lawless deposition, David More collection

7. City of Buffalo, 4-94-89, H-67943

8. Howell, "The Public Ordeal of Billie Lawless."

9. Howell, "The Public Ordeal of Billie Lawless."

10. City of Buffalo, 4-94-89, H-67943

11. Id.

12. Id.

13. Howell, "The Public Ordeal of Billie Lawless."

14. Joanne Posluszny-Hoffsten. Phone interview with the author. April 2, 2023.

15. City of Buffalo, 4-94-89, H-67943

16. Id.

17. Id.

18. Howell, "The Public Ordeal of Billie Lawless."

19. Buffalo Arts Commission, Meeting Minutes, August 22, 1983

20. Price, December 29, 2022.

21. Price, December 29, 2022.

22. Price, December 29, 2022.

23. City of Buffalo, 4-94-89, H-67943

24. McCarthy, "Lawless donors differ on feeling duped."

25. Lawless deposition, David More collection

26. McCarthy, "Lawless donors differ on feeling duped."

27. Buffalo News, November 22, 1984, page 2

28. Price, December 29, 2022.

29. Price, December 29, 2022.

30. Lawless deposition, David More collection

31. Buffalo Urban Renewal Agency, Meeting Minutes, October 13, 1983

32. Militello, October 7, 2022.

33. Howell, "The Public Ordeal of Billie Lawless."

34. Buffalo Urban Renewal Agency, Meeting Minutes, October 13, 1983

35. Lawless deposition, David More collection

36. Buffalo Urban Renewal Agency, Meeting Minutes, October 13, 1983

37. Howell, "The Public Ordeal of Billie Lawless."

38. Buffalo Urban Renewal Agency, Meeting Minutes, October 13, 1983

39. Militello, October 7, 2022.

40. Militello, October 7, 2022.

41. City of Buffalo, 4-94-89, H-67943

42. Id.

43. Id.

44. Buffalo Arts Commission, letter dated, November 1, 1983

45. City of Buffalo, 4-94-89, H-67943

46. Id.

47. Id.

48. Buffalo Arts Commission original files

49. City of Buffalo, 4-94-89, H-67943

50. Buffalo Arts Commission, letter dated November 15, 1983

51. Buffalo Arts Commission, Letter dated November 23, 1983

52. City of Buffalo, 4-94-89, H-67943

53. Buffalo Arts Commission, Letter dated November 30, 1983

54. City of Buffalo, 4-94-89, H-67943

55. Buffalo Arts Commission, Letter date January 7, 1984

56. Buffalo Arts Commission, Meeting Minutes, January 26, 1984

57. City of Buffalo, 4-94-89, H-67943

58. Id.

59. Buffalo Arts Commission, Meeting Minutes, April 9, 1984

60. City of Buffalo, 4-94-89, H-67943

61. Id.

Permit Me To Introduce Myself

1. Mark Griffis, phone call with author, October 12, 2022.

2. Griffis, October 12, 2022.

3. Griffis, October 12, 2022.

4. City of Buffalo, 4-94-89, H-67943

5. Manhattan Psychiatric Center, 114643/93

6. Id.

7. Marsha Moss. Email with author. December 18, 2022.

8. Howell, George. "What happened." Buffalo Arts Review, 1984, Winter edition.

9. Howell. "What happened."

10. Howell. "What happened."

11. Howell. "What happened."

12. Howell. "What happened."

13. City of Buffalo, 4-94-89, H-67943

14. Id.

15. Lawless vs. City of Buffalo, 4-94-89, H-67943, NY4d (1993)

16. Buffalo Arts Commission, July 1, 1984, Meeting Minutes

17. Nels Nelson. Philadelphia Daily News, August 3, 1984, p.64.

18. City of Buffalo, 4-94-89, H-67943

19. Howell. "The Public ordeal of Billie Lawless."

20. City of Buffalo, 4-94-89, H-67943

21. City of Buffalo, 4-94-89, H-67943

22. Buffalo Arts Commission, Meeting Minutes, October 22, 1984

23. Manhattan Psychiatric Center, 114643/93

24. Howell. "The Public ordeal of Billie Lawless"

25. City of Buffalo, 4-94-89, H-67943

26. City of Buffalo, 4-94-89, H-67943

27. Id.

28. Howell. "The public ordeal of Billie Lawless."

29. Howell. "The public ordeal of Billie Lawless."

30. Howell. "The public ordeal of Billie Lawless."

31. Howell. "The public ordeal of Billie Lawless."

32. Howell. "The public ordeal of Billie Lawless."

33. David More collection

1980s and Collaborating

1. "Art of the 1980s." Artsy. Accessed March 16, 2023. https://www.artsy.net/gene/1980s.

2. Morgan, Tiernan. "The Decade That Changed the Art World: Money, Media, and Brands in the 1980s." Hyperallergic, May 10, 2018. https://hyperallergic.com/439334/the-decade-that-changed-the-art-world-money-media-and-brands-in-the-1980s/.

3. Otten, Liam. "American Art of the 1980s - the Source - Washington University in St. Louis." The Source, November 6, 2020. https://source.wustl.edu/2003/12/american-art-of-the-1980s/.

4. Courier-Express (Buffalo). April 14, 1982. p.B-6.

5. Diane Bertolo. "It's the idea behind the show not the art in the show that confronts the viewers of the Artists' Gallery's Directives." Buffalo News. October 10, 1980. p.82.

6. Jack Foran. "UB artists reawaken the old Psych Center." Buffalo News. May 29, 1981. p.58.

7. George Howell. "Sculpture '83 a thought-provoking show." Buffalo News. September 20, 1983. p.36.

8. Richard Huntington. "What's so funny?" Buffalo News. October 18, 1987. p.148.

9. Huntington. "What's so funny?"

10. Kathie Simonds. Text with author. December 27, 2022.

11. Niagara University. Billie Lawless New Works March 5 - April 19, 1982.

Unveiling

1. City of Buffalo, 4-94-89, H-67943

2. Id.

3. More, October 13, 2022.

4. Unveiling Transcript, David More collection

5. Unveiling Transcript, David More collection

6. "Interview with former President D. Bruce Johnstone, 1979-1988" (1994). SUNY Buffalo State Oral Histories, 1975-1995. Archives & Special Collections Department, E. H. Butler Library, SUNY Buffalo State.
https://digitalcommons.buffalostate.edu/bsc_oral_history/36

7. billielawless.com and David More collection

8. David More collection

9. More, October 13, 2022.

10. More, October 13, 2022.

11. Griffis, October 12, 2022.

12. Dedication transcript, David More collection

13. Dedication transcript, David More collection

14. Dedication transcript, David More collection

15. Dedication transcript, David More collection

16. Joanne Posluszny-Hoffsten. April 2, 2023.

17. More. October 18, 2023.

18. More, October 13, 2022.

19. More. October 18, 2023.

20. Howell, "What happened."

21. Howell, "What happened."

22. City of Buffalo, 4-94-89, H-67943

23. City of Buffalo, 4-94-89, H-67943

24. City of Buffalo, 4-94-89, H-67943

25. Howell, "What happened."

26. David More collection

27. Gryta, "Confrontation over Lawless sculpture recalled."

28. More, October 13, 2022.

29. City of Buffalo, 4-94-89, H-67943

30. Alan Pergament, "So Lightning never strikes twice?" Buffalo News, December 7, 1984.

31. Pergament, "So Lightning never strikes twice?"

32. More, October 13, 2022.

33. David More. Interview with the author. October 18, 2023.

34. Pergament, "So Lightning never strikes twice?"

35. Pergament, "So Lightning never strikes twice?"

36. Robert J. McCarthy, "Green lightning sculptor pursuing legal recourse." Buffalo News, November 21, 1984, p.2.

37. Dan Herbeck. phone interview with author, October 21, 2022.

38. Price, December 29, 2022.

39. George Palmer, phone interview with author, October 11, 2022.

40. Palmer, October 11, 2022.

41. Griffis, October 12, 2022.

42. Buffalo News, "Torn-Down Tuesday: 'Green Lightning' sculpture – an amplified hoax?" Jun 21, 2016.

43. Pergament, "So Lightning never strikes twice?"

Aftermath

1. "Artists go to court to restore sculpture in Buffalo." NY Times, December 2, 1984.

2. Militello, October 7, 2022.

3. Militello, October 7, 2022.

4. Militello, October 7, 2022.

5. City of Buffalo, 4-94-89, H-67943

6. Id.

7. Robert J. McCarthy, "Artist takes stand on Sculpture but agrees to pull plug on neon," Buffalo News, November 17, 1984, p.1.

8. "Artist puts more than his name in lights." UPI Archives, November 16, 1984.

9. David More. Interview with the author. October 18, 2023.

10. David More, October 10, 2022.

11. Gryta, "Confrontation over Lawless sculpture recalled."

12. Mark J. Mahoney, email with author, November 7, 2022.

13. City of Buffalo, 4-94-89, H-67943

14. Id.

15. Gryta, "Confrontation over Lawless sculpture recalled."

16. City of Buffalo, 4-94-89, H-67943

17. Id.

18. John Pauly. "Hearings set in complaints filed against 6 policemen." Courier-Express. February 8, 1978. p.2.

19. City of Buffalo, 4-94-89, H-67943

20. Id.

21. Id.

22. Id.

23. McCarthy, "Artist takes stand on Sculpture but agrees to pull plug on neon."

24. Id.

25. City of Buffalo, 4-94-89, H-67943

26. Gryta, "Confrontation over Lawless sculpture recalled."

27. McCarthy, "Artist takes stand on Sculpture but agrees to pull plug on neon."

28. McCarthy, "Artist takes stand on Sculpture but agrees to pull plug on neon."

29. City of Buffalo, 4-94-89, H-67943

30. "Lightning editorial erred." Buffalo News, June 21, 1985.

31. City of Buffalo, 4-94-89, H-67943

32. Id.

33. McCarthy. "Green Lightning sculptor pursuing."

34. McCarthy. "Green Lightning sculptor pursuing."

35. David More collection

36. City of Buffalo, 4-94-89, H-67943

37. Id.

In The Dark of Night

1. City of Buffalo, 4-94-89, H-67943

2. Id.

3. Id.

4. Id.

5. Id.

6. Id.

7. Id.

8. Id.

9. Id.

10. Id.

11. Id.

12. Id.

13. Id.

14. Id.

15. Id.

16. Id.

17. Id.

18. McCarthy. "'Green Lightning' Sculptor Pursuing Legal Recourse." November 21, 1984. p.1.

19. McCarthy. "'Green Lightning' Sculptor Pursuing Legal Recourse." p.1.

20. McCarthy. "'Green Lightning' Sculptor Pursuing Legal Recourse." p.2.

21. "Lightning editorial erred."

22. City of Buffalo, 4-94-89, H-67943

23. City of Buffalo, 4-94-89, H-67943

24. McCarthy. "'Green Lightning' Sculptor Pursuing Legal Recourse." p.2.

25. Howell. "What happened."

26. Howell. "What happened."

27. Id.

28. BURA meeting minutes, David More collection

29. BURA minutes, David More collection

30. McCarthy. "'Green Lightning' Sculptor Pursuing Legal Recourse." p.2.

31. City of Buffalo, 4-94-89, H-67943

32. BURA minutes, David More collection

33. McCarthy. "'Green Lightning' Sculptor Pursuing Legal Recourse." p.2.

34. Matt Gryta. "Judge rips Griffin, bars sculpture razing." Buffalo News, November 22, 1984. p.1.

35. Tonawanda News, November 22, 1984

36. Tonawanda News, November 22, 1984

37. Gryta. "Judge rips Griffin, bars sculpture razing." p.1.

38. Manhattan Psychiatric Center, 114643/93

39. Billie Lawless. "Lightning editorial erred." Buffalo News. June 21, 1985. p.C-2.

40. Militello, October 7, 2022.

41. "Straight Talk." Buffalo News, November 30, 1984.

42. Sullivan, "Naivete shapes sculpture dispute." p.1.

43. Sullivan, "Naivete shapes sculpture dispute." p.1.

44. Sullivan, "Naivete shapes sculpture dispute." p.2.

45. Hallwalls, Inc, Tentative Press Release, July 1, 1983

46. Sullivan, "Naivete shapes sculpture dispute." p.2.

47. Sullivan, "Naivete shapes sculpture dispute." p.2.

48. Howell. "What happened."

49. Jane Kwiatkowski. "Making a case for the art scene." Buffalo News, March 24, 1985. p.155.

50. More. October 18, 2023.

51. Howell. "What happened."

52. City of Buffalo, 4-94-89, H-67943

53. "George Segal Sculptures, Bio, Ideas." The Art Story. Accessed April 17, 2023. https://www.theartstory.org/artist/segal-george/.

54. Howell. "What happened."

55. Buffalo Arts Commission, Meeting Minutes, November 29, 1984

56. Murray Light. "Editorial inaccurate, disturbing." Buffalo News, December 11, 1984.

57. Light. "Editorial inaccurate, disturbing."

58. Robert J. McCarthy. "Murray light, former News editor dies." Buffalo News, October 16, 2011. p.1.

59. Chicago Tribune, May 18, 1985, Page 11

60. "Torn-Down Tuesday: 'Green Lightning' sculpture – an amplified hoax?" Buffalo News, Jun 21, 2016.

61. Helen Cullinan. "Spaces is taking the wraps off an adult-rated art show." The Plain Dealer (Cleveland). November 1, 1987. p.6-H.

62. Robert J. McCarthy. "Lightning sculptor threatens lawsuit." Buffalo News, December 1, 1984.

63. McCarthy. "Lightning sculptor threatens lawsuit."

64. Ray Herman. "Sun Political Columnist Offers Yule Gift List for Politician." The Sun. December 5, 1985. p.4.

65. Ray Herman. "Ten Years Of Griffin." Front Page (Blasdell). June 10, 1987. p.4.

Under the Magnifying Glass

1. Michael Beebe. "Lightning strikes a familiar note." Buffalo News, Nov 23, 1984. p.39.

2. Beebe. "Lightning strikes a familiar note."

3. Beebe. "Lightning strikes a familiar note."

4. Michael Beebe, Dave Condren. "Local sign makers wouldn't bend for Lightning sculptor." Buffalo News, November 22, 1984. p.1-2.

5. Beebe, Condren. "Local sign makers wouldn't bend for Lightning sculptor." p.2.

6. Beebe, Condren. "Local sign makers wouldn't bend for Lightning sculptor." p.1.

7. Beebe, Condren. "Local sign makers wouldn't bend for Lightning sculptor." p.1.

8. Beebe, Condren. "Local sign makers wouldn't bend for Lightning sculptor." p.2.

9. "Lawless donors differ.." Buffalo News, December 2, 1984. p.45.

10. "Lawless donors differ.." Buffalo News, December 2, 1984. p.45.

11. "Lawless donors differ.." Buffalo News, December 2, 1984. p.45.

12. "Lawless donors differ.." Buffalo News, December 2, 1984. p.45.

13. "Lawless donors differ.." Buffalo News, December 2, 1984. p.45.

14. "Lawless donors differ.." Buffalo News. December 2, 1984. p.45.

15. Buffalo News. December 2, 1984. page 45

16. "Lawless donors differ.." Buffalo News. December 2, 1984. p.45.

17. Anthony Bannon. "Green Lightning - A posthumous review." Buffalo News, December 16, 1984. p.86.

18. Bannon. "Green Lightning - A posthumous review."

19. Bannon. "Green Lightning - A posthumous review."

20. Bannon. "Green Lightning - A posthumous review."

21. Lawless, Billie, and Kathie Simonds. "'Green Lightning' Is The Victim of Cultural Myopia." *Buffalo News*. December 5, 1984.

22. Brown, Taylor Whitten. "Why Is Work by Female Artists Still Valued Less than Work by Male Artists?" Artsy, March 8, 2019. https://www.artsy.net/article/artsy-editorial-work-female-artists-valued-work-male-artists.

23. Flynn, Mitch. "How Green (and Obscene) Was My Sculpture." Buffalo News. May 19, 1985, May/June 1985 edition, sec. Buffalo Magazine.

Blizzard

1. "Straight Talk." Buffalo News. February 8, 1985. p.40.

2. City of Buffalo, 4-94-89, H-67943

3. City of Buffalo, 4-94-89, H-67943

4. Lawless vs. Cleveland State University, 1:19-cv-00178-DAP (2019).

5. Matt Gryta. "City countersues sculptor, seeks jury trial." Buffalo News, February 12, 1985. p.27.

6. Gryta. "City countersues sculptor, seeks jury trial."

7. Matt Gryta. " Lawyer says police threatened Lawless." Buffalo News. June 11, 1992. p.23.

8. City of Buffalo, 4-94-89, H-67943

9. City of Buffalo, 4-94-89, H-67943

10. Id.

11. Id.

12. Id.

13. Id.

14. McCarthy. "City doesn't offer enough green to end Lawless' Lightning suit."

15. Kwiatkowski. "One man's fight against City Hall."

16. Kwiatkowski. "One man's fight against City Hall."

17. Kwiatkowski. "One man's fight against City Hall."

18. Robert J. McCarthy. "City doesn't offer enough green to end Lawless' Lightning suit." Buffalo News. May 15, 1985. p.B1.

19. McCarthy. "City doesn't offer enough green to end Lawless' Lightning suit."

20. "Arts news." Buffalo News. May 13, 1985. p.39.

21. City of Buffalo, 4-94-89, H-67943

22. Id.

23. Id.

24. City of Buffalo, 4-94-89, H-67943

25. Id.

26. Id.

27. Wisenbaugh. October 6, 2022.

28. City of Buffalo, 4-94-89, H-67943

29. Id.

30. Wisenbaugh. October 6, 2022.

Sculpture Chicago '85

1. Susan Schulman. "Bolt of Lightning goes astray." Buffalo News. May 1, 1985. p.B-4.

2. Lauerman, Text by Connie, and a SUNDAY staff writer. "Sculpture Chicago Brings Monumental Art and the Process of Creating It to the Public." Chicago Tribune, August 8, 2021. https://www.chica gotribune.com/news/ct-xpm-1989-05-07-8904100447-story.html.

3. Alan G. Artner. "10 picked for Sculpture '85." Chicago Tribune. June 6, 1985. p.90.

4. Anthony Bannon. "Green Lightning invited to Chicago for Sculpture fest." Buffalo News. May 28, 1985. p.1.

5. City of Buffalo, 4-94-89, H-67943

6. "Sculpture Chicago, 1985 May 21 (Page 1)." Digital Collections. Accessed March 15, 2023. https://cdm16818.contentdm.oclc.org/ digital/collection/HWashington/id/3429/rec/1.

7. David McCracken. "Sculpture Chicago bridges gap between artists, public." Chicago Tribune, August 30, 1985. p.100.

8. Bannon. "Green Lightning invited to Chicago for Sculpture fest."

9. Bannon. "Green Lightning invited to Chicago for Sculpture fest." p.1-2.

10. Lawless deposition, David More collection.

11. Lawless deposition, David More collection.

12. Cleveland State University, 1:19-cv-00178-DAP

13. "Artist Billy Lawless Has Vowed to Re-light His Controversial..." *UPI Archives*, June 8, 1985. https://www.upi.com/Archives/1985/06/08/Artist-Billy-Lawless-has-vowed-to-relight-his-controversial/1179487051200/.

14. "'Green Lightning' to Leave Buffalo." *UPI Archives*, June 14, 1985. https://www.upi.com/Archives/1985/06/14/Green-Lightning-to-leave-Buffalo/1133487569600/.

15. "Green Lightning fiasco doesn't deserve sequel." Buffalo News. June 12, 1985. p.B-2.

16. "'Green Lightning' to Leave Buffalo." *UPI Archives*, June 14, 1985.

17. "Green Lightning fiasco doesn't deserve sequel."

18. "Green Lightning fiasco doesn't deserve sequel."

19. Lawless deposition, David More collection.

20. Bannon. "Green Lightning invited to Chicago for Sculpture fest." p.2.

21. Lawless. "Lightning editorial erred."

22. Richard Huntington. "Green Lightning strikes Chicago as unobjectionable." Buffalo News. November 10, 1985. p.E-5.

23. "I don't know if it's art, but.." Chicago Tribune, June 25, 1985. p.14.

24. City of Buffalo, 4-94-89, H-67943

25. Wendy Conlin. "Lawless readies Green Lightning for its truck trip to Chicago." Buffalo News. July 31, 1985. p.B-1.

26. Conlin. "Lawless readies Green Lightning for its truck trip to Chicago."

27. McCracken. "Sculpture Chicago bridges gap between artists, public."

28. McCracken. "Sculpture Chicago bridges gap between artists, public."

29. McCracken. "Sculpture Chicago bridges gap between artists, public."

30. Conlin. "Lawless readies Green Lightning for its truck trip to Chicago."

31. Tom Bohling. Phone interview with author. October 11, 2022.

32. Bohling. October 11, 2022.

33. Bohling. October 11, 2022.

34. "Art Facts: Billie Lawless and his dancing electric organs." Chicago Reader. January 7, 1988.

35. Calloway, John. Episode. Chicago Tonight Season 2. Chicago, IL: PBS, September 17, 1985.

36. Calloway. Chicago Tonight Season 2.

37. Calloway. Chicago Tonight Season 2.

38. Mary Jane Jacobs. Email with the author. October 7, 2022.

39. Huntington. "Green Lightning strikes Chicago as unobjectionable."

40. Huntington. "Green Lightning strikes Chicago as unobjectionable."

41. "Art Facts: Billie Lawless and his dancing electric organs."

42. City of Buffalo, 4-94-89, H-67943

43. Id.

44. Christine Ingraham. Message via Linkedin with author. October 28, 2022.

45. "Inside Straight." Buffalo News. May 16, 1986. Gusto. p.2.

46. "Art Facts: Billie Lawless and his dancing electric organs."

47. "Art Facts: Billie Lawless and his dancing electric organs."

48. City of Buffalo, 4-94-89, H-67943

49. "Inside Straight."

50. Lawless, Billie. "Laying down the Lawless." Chicago Reader, August 20, 2021. https://chicagoreader.com/news-politics/laying-down-the-lawless/. February 4, 1988.

I Know It When I See It

1. Lawless deposition, 1989

2. City of Buffalo, 4-94-89, H-67943

3. City of Buffalo, 4-94-89, H-67943

4. Id.

5. Id.

6. Id.

7. Lynn, Christopher. "Spaces at 40 Years." Temporary Art Review, June 5, 2018. https://temporaryartreview.com/spaces-at-40-years/.

8. Kelvin Smith Library Special Collections, Case Western Reserve University, Series 5, Box 49, Folder 19

9. Kelvin Smith Library Special Collections, Case Western Reserve University, SPACES Archive, Series 5, Box 49, Folder 19

10. Niagara University. Billie Lawless Lightworks January 6 - February 18, 1989. Niagara Falls,, NY: Buscaglia-Castellani Art Gallery, 1982.

11. Manhattan Psychiatric Center, 114643/93

12. Id.

13. The Plain Dealer. (Cleveland) December 1, 1987.

14. Flynn, Mitch. "How Green (and Obscene) Was My Sculpture." Buffalo News. May 19, 1985, May/June 1985 edition, sec. Buffalo Magazine.

15. Christopher Evans. "Is Billie Lawless? A look at the artist behind the mask." The Plain Dealer (Cleveland). July 06, 1997. p.23.

16. Plain Dealer (Cleveland). November 12, 1987. p.85.

Highway to Hell

1. Michael Levy. "Green Lightning artist leaves hard feelings, lawsuit in Buffalo." Buffalo News. February 27, 1988. p.1.

2. Levy. "Green Lightning artist leaves hard feelings, lawsuit in Buffalo."

3. Levy. "Green Lightning artist leaves hard feelings, lawsuit in Buffalo."

4. Heritage Village. 88CV-10-7001.

5. "Martin Greenberg Obituary (2011) - Columbus, OH - This Week Community Newspapers." Legacy.com. Accessed March 15, 2023. https://www.legacy.com/us/obituaries/thisweeknews/name/martin-greenberg-obituary?id=25423206.

6. "Billie Lawless: Lightworks."

7. Jacqueline Hall. "Heritage show big on 'think about it' art." Columbus Dispatch. June 12, 1988. p.76.

8. Heritage Village. 88CV-10-7001.

9. Schreiber, Svetlana. "Didy_wah." didy_wah. Accessed March 15, 2023. http://www.didywahdidy.com/.

10. Robert Albrecht. "That's art, dear traveler." Columbus Dispatch. August 31, 1988. p.3.

11. Schreiber, Svetlana. "Didy_wah." didy_wah. Accessed March 15, 2023. http://www.didywahdidy.com/.

12. Heritage Village. 88CV-10-7001.

13. Schreiber, Svetlana. "Didy_wah." didy_wah. Accessed March 15, 2023. http://www.didywahdidy.com/.

14. Schreiber, Svetlana. "The ARTS, The Cleveland Edition, September 22, 1988." Didy. Accessed March 15, 2023. http://www.didywahdidy.com/cleve_edition_2.html.

15. http://www.didywahdidy.com/cleve_edition_2.html.

16. http://www.didywahdidy.com/new_art.html.

17. Schreiber, Svetlana. "Didy_wah." didy_wah. Accessed March 15, 2023. http://www.didywahdidy.com/.

18. http://www.didywahdidy.com/new_art.html.

19. http://www.didywahdidy.com/cleve_edition_2.html.

20. http://www.didywahdidy.com/cleve_edition_2.html.

21. Lawless, Billie, 1989, 4, Box: 38, Folder: 49. SPACES Archive collection, Spec-Coll-00052. Kelvin Smith Library Special Collections.

22. Phyllis Redshaw. "So-called piece of art looks more like an advertisement." Columbus Dispatch. November 30, 1988. p.10.

23. Matt Gryta. "Ohio ruling expected on Lawless sculpture." Buffalo News. December 12, 1988. p.1.

24. Matt Gryta. "It's goodbye Columbus for Lawless as Ohio court says no to neon sculpture." Buffalo News. March 28, 1989. p.C-8.

25. Nancy Gilson. "Sculpture show goes on two-year hiatus." Columbus Dispatch. February 18, 1989. p.17.

26. "Neon art will stay on display." Plain Dealer (Cleveland). March 06, 1989. p.17.

27. "Neon art will stay on display."

28. Evans. "Is Billie Lawless? A look at the artist behind the mask." p.31.

29. Plain Dealer (Cleveland). April 25, 1999.

Spearfish

1. Pitta, Matt. "The Kings of Cape Cod: Remembering the Legendary Cape Cod Happy Hour." CapeCod.com, September 29, 2017. https://www.capecod.com/newscenter/the-kings-of-cape-cod-remembering-the-legendary-cape-cod-happy-hour/.

2. "Spearfish City Council Minutes." Spearfish City Council. February 03, 1986, Spearfish, South Dakota.

3. Evans. "Is Billie Lawless? A look at the artist behind the mask.". p.25.

4. The ARTS, The Cleveland Edition. September 22, 1988.

5. David Townsend. "Tastes in art collide over planned public sculpture." Spearfish Daily Queen City Mail, July 19, 1988. p.1.

6. The ARTS, The Cleveland Edition, September 22, 1988

7. Townsend. "Tastes in art collide over planned public sculpture."

8. Townsend. "Tastes in art collide over planned public sculpture."

9. Townsend. "Tastes in art collide over planned public sculpture."

10. David Townsend. "There's room here for imagination." Spearfish Daily Queen City Mail. August 6, 1988. p.4.

11. Townsend. "There's room here for imagination."

12. "Spearfish City Council Minutes." Spearfish City Council. August 15, 1988, Spearfish, South Dakota.

13. "Spearfish City Council Minutes." Spearfish City Council. March 06, 1989, Spearfish, South Dakota.

14. Dale Lamphere. Email with the author. December 28, 2022.

15. Evans. "Is Billie Lawless? A look at the artist behind the mask." p.25.

16. Search of Spearfish, SD Council records.

Cleveland

1. Alan Rossman. Phone interview with the author. March 30, 2023.

2. Alan Rossman. March 30, 2023.

3. Freligh. "It's been a real roller coaster."

4. "Opening tonight." Plain Dealer (Cleveland). January 06, 1989. p.60.

5. Niagara University. Billie Lawless Lightworks January 6 - February 18, 1989.

6. Niagara University. Billie Lawless Lightworks January 6 - February 18, 1989.

7. Helen Cullinan. "Modern Society in ruin and decay." The Plain Dealer (Cleveland). March 4, 1989. p.1

8. Cullinan. "Modern Society in ruin and decay." p.1

9. Cullinan. "Modern Society in ruin and decay."

10. Cullinan. "Modern Society in ruin and decay."

11. Cullinan. "Modern Society in ruin and decay."

12. Evans. "Is Billie Lawless? A look at the artist behind the mask." p.17.

13. Evans. "Is Billie Lawless? A look at the artist behind the mask." p.17.

Pre-Trial

1. Billie Lawless deposition. David More private collection.

2. Kevin Collison. "City will spend $43,129 in legal fees in battle over dismantling of sculpture." Buffalo News. April 13, 1990. p.

3. Lawless v. City of Buffalo. 202AD2d1074 (NY).

4. Lawless v. City of Buffalo. 202AD2d1074 (NY).

5. Alan Rossman. March 30, 2023.

6. Alan Rossman. March 30, 2023.

7. "Court ruling clears the way for 'Green Lightning' Trial." Buffalo News. November 19, 1991. p.B-5.

8. Lawless v. City of Buffalo. 202AD2d1074 (NY).

9. "City claims in art suit dismissed." Buffalo News. May 14, 1992. p.C-4.

10. Matt Gryta. "Sculptor to subpoena Griffin in art dispute suit." Buffalo News. May 24, 1992. p.C-5.

11. Lawless v. City of Buffalo. 202AD2d1074 (NY).

12. Militello. October 7, 2022.

13. Gryta. "Sculptor to subpoena Griffin in art dispute suit."

14. Gryta. "Sculptor to subpoena Griffin in art dispute suit."

15. Matt Gryta. "Judge threatens to fine the city for 'Green Lightning' documents." June 2, 1992. p.B-1.

Opening Statements

1. Mark Mahoney. Email with the author. November 7, 2022.

2. Alan Rossman. April 2, 2023.

3. Matt Gryta. "City officials 'Vandalized' Lawless sculpture, jury told." Buffalo News. Jun 8, 1992. p.B-4.

4. Lawless v. City of Buffalo. 202AD2d1074 (NY).

5. Lawless v. City of Buffalo. 202AD2d1074 (NY).

6. Lawless v. City of Buffalo. 202AD2d1074 (NY).

7. Matt Gryta. "Lawless details cost of sculpture repairs." Buffalo News. June 11, 1992. p.D-7.

8. Lawless v. City of Buffalo. 202AD2d1074 (NY).

9. Lawless v. City of Buffalo. 202AD2d1074 (NY).

10. Lawless v. City of Buffalo. 202AD2d1074 (NY).

11. Lawless v. City of Buffalo. 202AD2d1074 (NY).

12. Lawless v. City of Buffalo. 202AD2d1074 (NY).

13. Lawless v. City of Buffalo. 202AD2d1074 (NY).

14. Lawless v. City of Buffalo. 202AD2d1074 (NY).

15. Lawless v. City of Buffalo. 202AD2d1074 (NY).

16. Lawless v. City of Buffalo. 202AD2d1074 (NY).

17. Lawless v. City of Buffalo. 202AD2d1074 (NY).

18. Lawless v. City of Buffalo. 202AD2d1074 (NY).

19. Lawless v. City of Buffalo. 202AD2d1074 (NY).

20. Lawless v. City of Buffalo. 202AD2d1074 (NY).

21. Lawless v. City of Buffalo. 202AD2d1074 (NY).

22. Lawless v. City of Buffalo. 202AD2d1074 (NY).

23. Lawless v. City of Buffalo. 202AD2d1074 (NY).

24. Lawless v. City of Buffalo. 202AD2d1074 (NY).

25. Lawless v. City of Buffalo. 202AD2d1074 (NY).

26. Risman. October 10, 2022.

27. Lawless v. City of Buffalo. 202AD2d1074 (NY).

28. Lawless v. City of Buffalo. 202AD2d1074 (NY).

29. Lawless v. City of Buffalo. 202AD2d1074 (NY).

30. Matt Gryta. "Sculpture repairs put at $225,000 by expert." Buffalo News. June 19, 1992. p.C-4.

31. Richard Huntington. "Observations from the trial hot seat in 'Green Lightning.'" Buffalo News. July 3, 1992. p.C-7.

32. Huntington. "Observations from the trial hot seat in 'Green Lightn ing.'"

33. Huntington. "Observations from the trial hot seat in 'Green Lightn ing.'"

34. Huntington. "Observations from the trial hot seat in 'Green Lightn ing.'"

35. Huntington. "Observations from the trial hot seat in 'Green Lightn
ing.'"

36. Huntington. "Observations from the trial hot seat in 'Green Lightn
ing.'"

Testimony

1. Lawless v. City of Buffalo. 202AD2d1074 (NY).

2. Lawless v. City of Buffalo. 202AD2d1074 (NY).

3. Lawless v. City of Buffalo. 202AD2d1074 (NY).

4. Lawless v. City of Buffalo. 202AD2d1074 (NY).

5. Lawless v. City of Buffalo. 202AD2d1074 (NY).

6. Michael Risman. Phone interview with the author. October 10,
2022.

7. Risman. October 10, 2022.

8. Freligh. "It's been a real roller coaster."

9. Lawless v. City of Buffalo. 202AD2d1074 (NY).

10. Lawless v. City of Buffalo. 202AD2d1074 (NY).

11. Lawless v. City of Buffalo. 202AD2d1074 (NY).

12. Lawless v. City of Buffalo. 202AD2d1074 (NY).

13. Lawless v. City of Buffalo. 202AD2d1074 (NY).

14. Lawless v. City of Buffalo. 202AD2d1074 (NY).

15. Rossman. April 2, 2023.

16. Rossman. April 2, 2023.

17. Lawless v. City of Buffalo. 202AD2d1074 (NY).

18. Lawless v. City of Buffalo. 202AD2d1074 (NY).

19. Lawless v. City of Buffalo. 202AD2d1074 (NY).

20. Lawless v. City of Buffalo. 202AD2d1074 (NY).

21. Matt Gryta. "Griffin testifies he ordered 'Green Lightning' taken down." Buffalo News. June 18, 1992. p.B-1.

22. Lawless vs. City of Buffalo.

23. Lawless v. City of Buffalo. 202AD2d1074 (NY).

24. Lawless v. City of Buffalo. 202AD2d1074 (NY).

25. Lawless v. City of Buffalo. 202AD2d1074 (NY).

26. Lawless v. City of Buffalo. 202AD2d1074 (NY).

27. Lawless v. City of Buffalo. 202AD2d1074 (NY).

28. Lawless v. City of Buffalo. 202AD2d1074 (NY).

29. Lawless v. City of Buffalo. 202AD2d1074 (NY).

30. Lawless v. City of Buffalo. 202AD2d1074 (NY).

31. Leah Rae. "Russell inducted into Shea's shrine." Buffalo News. June 19, 1992. p.1.

Verdict

1. Lawless v. City of Buffalo. 202AD2d1074 (NY).

2. Lawless v. City of Buffalo. 202AD2d1074 (NY).

3. Matt Gryta. "Jury to begin deliberations in Lawless suit." Buffalo News. June 23, 1992. p.B-4.

4. Michael Risman. Phone interview with the author. July 7, 2022.

5. Risman. October 10, 2022.

6. Lawless v. City of Buffalo. 202AD2d1074 (NY).

7. Lawless v. City of Buffalo. 202AD2d1074 (NY).

8. Lawless v. City of Buffalo. 202AD2d1074 (NY).

9. Buffalo News. June 24, 1992.

10. Lawless v. City of Buffalo. 202AD2d1074 (NY).

11. Risman. October 10, 2022.

12. Lawless v. City of Buffalo. 202AD2d1074 (NY).

13. Matt Gryta. "Lawless misrepresented art, city lawyer says." Buffalo News. June 25, 1992. p.B-5.

14. Lawless v. City of Buffalo. 202AD2d1074 (NY).

15. Lawless v. City of Buffalo. 202AD2d1074 (NY).

16. Lawless v. City of Buffalo. 202AD2d1074 (NY).

17. Lawless v. City of Buffalo. 202AD2d1074 (NY).

18. Lawless v. City of Buffalo. 202AD2d1074 (NY).

19. Matt Gryta. "Jury denies Lawless' claim for monetary damages." Buffalo News. June 26, 1992. p.1.

20. Gryta. "Jury denies Lawless' claim for monetary damages."

21. "Sculpture Is a Loser and so Is Its Artist." Akron Beacon Journal, June 27, 1992.

22. Editorial. "'Green Lightning' -- Snuffed." Buffalo News. June 29, 1992. p.B-2.

23. Matt Gryta. "Lawless edict vindicated dismantling, Griffin says." Buffalo News. June 29, 1992. p.B-1.

24. Jeff Simon. "There's a lesson for both parents and kids in 'Green Lightning'." Buffalo News. June 30, 1992. p.C-1.

25. Michael Risman. Email with author October 16, 2022.

26. Matt Gryta. "Wyman pleads guilty in theft of client funds." Buffalo News. August 3, 1993. p.B-1.

27. Editorial. "Sculpture verdict was about truth, not art." Buffalo News. July 9, 1992. p.C-2.

28. Lawless vs. City of Buffalo, Appeal, 1992

29. Buffalo News. "Sculptor Still Pressing City For Damages Hearing Set On Lawless' Post-Trial Motion In 'Green Lightning' Case." July 11, 1992.

30. Lawless v. City of Buffalo. 202AD2d1074 (NY).

31. Lauri Githens. "Dancing bones return." Buffalo News. July 2, 1992. p.C-1.

32. Tom Buckham. "Ruling reserved on Lawless' bid to collect money." Buffalo News. July 22, 1992. p.B-5.

33. Lawless v. City of Buffalo. 202AD2d1074 (NY).

34. Lawless v. City of Buffalo. 202AD2d1074 (NY).

35. Matt Gryta. "Lawless files legal action against neighbor's estate." Buffalo News. September 13, 1992. p.B-4.

36. Lawless v. City of Buffalo. 202AD2d1074 (NY).

37. Lawless v. City of Buffalo. 202AD2d1074 (NY).

38. Lawless v. City of Buffalo. 202AD2d1074 (NY).

39. Lawless v. City of Buffalo. 202AD2d1074 (NY).

40. Matt Gryta. "Appellate court rejects Lawless' bid for a new trial on 'Green Lightning.'" Buffalo News. March 13, 1994. p.C-9.

41. Risman. October 10, 2022.

42. Risman. October 10, 2022.

43. Risman. October 10, 2022.

44. Risman. October 10, 2022.

45. Risman. October 10, 2022.

46. Risman. October 10, 2022.

47. More. October 13, 2022.

48. Evans. "Is Billie Lawless? A look at the artist behind the mask."

49. Militello. October 7, 2022.

Manhattan '93

1. Lawless vs. Manhattan Psychiatric Center, 114643/93 (NY 1993).

2. Lawless vs. Manhattan Psychiatric Center, 114643/93 (NY 1993).

3. Lawless vs. Manhattan Psychiatric Center, 114643/93 (NY 1993).

4. Lawless vs. Manhattan Psychiatric Center, 114643/93 (NY 1993).

5. Lawless vs. Manhattan Psychiatric Center, 114643/93 (NY 1993).

6. Lawless vs. Manhattan Psychiatric Center, 114643/93 (NY 1993).

7. Lawless vs. Manhattan Psychiatric Center, 114643/93 (NY 1993).

8. Lawless vs. Manhattan Psychiatric Center, 114643/93 (NY 1993).

9. Lawless vs. Manhattan Psychiatric Center, 114643/93 (NY 1993).

10. Lawless vs. Manhattan Psychiatric Center, 114643/93 (NY 1993).

11. Lawless vs. Manhattan Psychiatric Center, 114643/93 (NY 1993).

12. Lawless vs. Manhattan Psychiatric Center, 114643/93 (NY 1993).

13. Lawless vs. Manhattan Psychiatric Center, 114643/93 (NY 1993).

14. Lawless vs. Manhattan Psychiatric Center, 114643/93 (NY 1993).

15. Lawless vs. Manhattan Psychiatric Center, 114643/93 (NY 1993).

16. Lawless vs. Manhattan Psychiatric Center, 114643/93 (NY 1993).

17. Lawless vs. Manhattan Psychiatric Center, 114643/93 (NY 1993).

18. Lawless vs. Manhattan Psychiatric Center, 114643/93 (NY 1993).

19. Lawless vs. Manhattan Psychiatric Center, 114643/93 (NY 1993).

20. David Kocieniewski. "All dressed up with nowhere to go." Newsday. June 24, 1993. p.3.

21. Lawless vs. Manhattan Psychiatric Center, 114643/93 (NY 1993).

22. Lawless vs. Manhattan Psychiatric Center, 114643/93 (NY 1993).

23. Lawless vs. Manhattan Psychiatric Center, 114643/93 (NY 1993).

24. Lawless vs. Manhattan Psychiatric Center, 114643/93 (NY 1993).

25. Lawless vs. Manhattan Psychiatric Center, 114643/93 (NY 1993).

A Toy

1. Evans. "Is Billie Lawless? A look at the artist behind the mask." p.17.

2. Cleveland Magazine, 1994

3. Evans. "Is Billie Lawless? A look at the artist behind the mask." p.17.

4. Programming, The Politician by Billie Lawless, 1992, 1, Box: 11, Folder: 57. SPACES Archive collection, Spec-Coll-00052. Kelvin Smith Library Special Collections.

5. Barnett, David C. "Moving 'the Politician.'" Ideastream Public Media. Ideastream Public Media, December 1, 2022. https://www.ide astream.org/news/moving-the-politician.

6. A Greater Clevelander, Cleveland Magazine, 1996

7. Steven Litt. "'The Politician' gets a three-year seat at Midtown." The Plain Dealer. February 19, 1994. p.29.

8. Litt. "'The Politician' gets a three-year seat at Midtown."

9. The Village Voice, Scene & Heard, Controversy, March 22, 1994

10. Litt. "'The Politician' gets a three-year seat at Midtown."

11. Barnett. "Moving 'the Politician.'"

12. "SCENE AND HEARD." Village Voice. March 22, 1994.

13. Heritage Village. 88CV-10-7001

14. Barnett. "Moving 'the Politician.'"

15. "Billie Lawless." Billie Lawless Multimedia Artist. Accessed March 24, 2023. http://billielawless.com/.

16. Evans. "Is Billie Lawless? A look at the artist behind the mask." p.24.

17. https://billielawless.com

18. https://billielawless.com

19. Cleveland Plain Dealer, July 26, 1995

20. A Greater Cleveland, Cleveland Magazine, 1996

21. Evans. "Is Billie Lawless? A look at the artist behind the mask." p.24.

22. Steven Litt. "Midtown's step into public art a little wobbly." Plain Dealer. February 5, 1994. p.F-1, 4.

23. "Pathetic Plain Dealer Article." Pathetic Plain Dealer Article | WOLFS Fine Paintings and Sculpture. Accessed August 29, 2023. https://wolfsgallery.com/news-events/controversial-article-from-the-plain-dealer.

24. Barnett. "Moving 'the Politician.'"

25. Evans. "Is Billie Lawless? A look at the artist behind the mask." p.23.

26. http://canjournal.org/2019/04/billie-lawless-and-the-politician-a-toy/

27. Barnett. "Moving 'the Politician.'"

28. Karen Farkas. "Garden goes but sculpture stays." Plain Dealer. June 21, 2013. p.69.

29. Farkas. "Garden goes but sculpture stays."

30. Farkas. "Garden goes but sculpture stays."

31. Evans. "Is Billie Lawless? A look at the artist behind the mask." p.23.

At War With CSU

1. Gill, Michael. "Billie Lawless and the Politician: A Toy." Collective Arts Network - CAN Journal, April 3, 2019. http://canjournal.org/2019/04/billie-lawless-and-the-politician-a-toy/.

2. Lawless vs. Cleveland State University, 1:19-cv-00178-DAP (2019).

3. Lawless vs. Cleveland State University, 1:19-cv-00178-DAP (2019).

4. Gill, Michael. "Billie Lawless and the Politician: A Toy." Collective Arts Network - CAN Journal, April 3, 2019. http://canjournal.org /2019/04/billie-lawless-and-the-politician-a-toy/.

5. Ncac. "NCAC Protests Political Censorship at Cleveland State University." National Coalition Against Censorship, November 20, 2018. https://ncac.org/news/ncac-protests-political-censorship -at-cleveland-state-university.

6. Lawless vs. Cleveland State University, 1:19-cv-00178-DAP (2019).

7. Lawless vs. Cleveland State University, 1:19-cv-00178-DAP (2019).

8. Lawless vs. Cleveland State University, 1:19-cv-00178-DAP (2019).

9. Lawless vs. Cleveland State University, 1:19-cv-00178-DAP (2019).

10. Lawless vs. Cleveland State University, 1:19-cv-00178-DAP (2019).

11. Lawless vs. Cleveland State University, 1:19-cv-00178-DAP (2019).

12. Lawless vs. Cleveland State University, 1:19-cv-00178-DAP (2019).

13. Lawless vs. Cleveland State University, 1:19-cv-00178-DAP (2019).

14. Lawless vs. Cleveland State University, 1:19-cv-00178-DAP (2019).

15. "Sculptor Billie Lawless and Cleveland State University Reach Settlement in Lawsuit over Censorship of Criticism of President Trump." Pattakos Law Firm LLC, May 3, 2019. https://pattakoslaw.com/sculptor-billie-lawless-cleveland-state-univ ersity-reach-settlement-lawsuit-censorship-criticism-president-trum p/.

16. Editorial Board. "Jeers Tears Cheers." Cleveland.com and The Plain Dealer. May 10, 2019.

17. Barnett, David C. "Controversial Cleveland Sculpture Moves Again after Lawsuit." Ideastream Public Media. Ideastream Public Media, December 1, 2022. https://www.ideastream.org/news/controversial-cleveland-sculpture-moves-again-after-lawsuit.

18. Barnett. "Controversial Cleveland Sculpture Moves Again after Lawsuit."

19. Evans. "Is Billie Lawless? A look at the artist behind the mask."

20. Mary Chorney. "Billie Lawless." Plain Dealer (Cleveland). August 03, 1997. p.15.

21. Evans. "Is Billie Lawless? A look at the artist behind the mask." p.17.

22. Freligh. "It's been a real roller coaster."

Afterword

1. Dabkowski, Colin. "Where Are They Now? Looking up Billie Lawless, Jim Lorentz, Semyon Bychkov and More." *Buffalo News*. March 23, 2014, sec. Lifestyles.

2. Queenseyes. "Does Buffalo Miss Green Lightning?" Buffalo Rising, September 2, 2014. https://www.buffalorising.com/2014/09/does-buffalo-miss-green-lightning/.

3. 1984 Report Buffalo Police Department https://www.ojp.gov/pdffiles1/Digitization/107686NCJRS.pdf

4. Blatto, Anna. "[PDF] a City Divided: A Brief History of Segregation in Buffalo: Semantic Scholar." [PDF] A City Divided: A Brief History of Segregation in Buffalo | Semantic Scholar, January 1, 1970. https://www.semanticscholar.org/paper/A-City-Divided%3A-A-Brief-History-of-Segregation-in-Blatto/1902eb0f60c4b2cade27d9feab6a0708ef4dd800.

5. A City Divided: A Brief History of Segregation in Buffalo, Partnership for Public Good, 2018
https://ppgbuffalo.org/files/documents/data-demographics-history/a_city_divided__a_brief_history_of_segregation_in_the_city_of_buffalo.pdf

6. https://en.wikipedia.org/wiki/1977_Buffalo_mayoral_election

7. Milliner, Matthew J., Matthew J. Milliner, James E. Hartley, James E. Hartley, Samuel Gregg and Kelly Hanlon, Samuel Gregg, Kelly Hanlon, et al. "Conservatism and Culture." Public Discourse, June 17, 2019. https://www.thepublicdiscourse.com/2009/09/856/.

8. How the Political Right Views Arts Funding, Lance T. Izumi, 1997
https://www.giarts.org/article/how-political-right-views-arts-funding

9. Colin Dabkowski. "Nine of Buffalo's most controversial public art projects." Buffalo News. March 25, 2018. p.D.1.

10. More. October 18, 2023.

11. Andrews, Travis M. "Martin Luther King Jr. Statue in Boston Draws Online Mockery, Disdain." The Washington Post. WP Company, January 16, 2023. https://www.washingtonpost.com/lifestyle/2023/01/15/mlk-statue-boston-backlash/.

12. Dubin, Steven C. "The Bachelor Stripped Bare." Essay. In *Arresting Images: Impolitic Art and Uncivil Actions*, 38–38. London: Routledge, 1994.

Acknowledgments

1. Freligh. "It's been a real roller coaster."

www.ingramcontent.com/pod-product-compliance
Lightning Source LLC
Chambersburg PA
CBHW050318160726
48002CB00001B/77